R. Gupta's®

Dictionary of Science

by
RPH Editorial Board

 **RAMESH PUBLISHING HOUSE,** New Delhi

Published by
O.P. Gupta *for* Ramesh Publishing House

Admin. Office
12-H, New Daryaganj Road, Opp. Officers' Mess,
New Delhi-110002 ℐ 23261567, 23275224, 23275124

E-mail: info@rameshpublishinghouse.com
Website: www.rameshpublishinghouse.com

Showroom
- Balaji Market, Nai Sarak, Delhi-6 ℐ 23253720, 23282525
- 4457, Nai Sarak, Delhi-6, ℐ 23918938

© *Reserved with the Publisher*

No Part of this book may be reproduced or transmitted in any form or by any means, electronic or mechanical including photocopying, recording or by any transformation storage and retrieval system without written permission from the Publisher.

Indemnification Clause: This book is being sold/distributed subject to the exclusive condition that neither the author nor the publishers, individually or collectively, shall be responsible to indemnify the buyer/user/possessor of this book beyond the selling price of this book for any reason under any circumstances. If you do not agree to it, please do not buy/accept/use/possess this book.

Book Code: R-917

ISBN: 978-93-5012-605-9

15th Edition: 1912

HSN Code: 49011010

Preface

In preparing this dictionary of Science, we have constantly held before ourselves the grand purpose of serving the greatest possible number of people who are interested in Science. This may include not only professionals and students, but also the layman who has frequent need for information about terms used in Science. The terms defined in this book is taken from all fields of Science such as Physics, Chemistry, Botany and Zoology. All sub-fields are covered in detail. Latest developments, research and new emerging fields are taken into consideration.

Various latest technological developments in the fields such as Nanotechnology, Biotechnology, Genetics, Bioinformatics, Computer Science, Information Technology and much more are dealt in detail. Different laws, relationships, equations, basic principles and concepts are covered comprehensively and wherever possible explained with illustrations. In short, the terms both of pure science and of its applications are covered. Further to make easy the use of this book for reference purposes, cross-referencing has also been used. It is the hope of all who have worked on this book that it may contribute in some measure toward a widening of interest in the field of Science and toward an extension of the range of its applications.

Users of this Dictionary will find it easy to understand the various terms as they are explained in a very lucid manner. It will benefit not only the general public concerned with Science, but also professionals, parents, students at all levels, researchers, and scholars. We owe a great debt to all those scholars and authors in this field whose work we have consulted and who have influenced our understanding of the field. We have not included a bibliography of works consulted for this dictionary because it could not be completed but we express our appreciation. We can only hope that those who consult this book will find it useful. Any suggestions for additional improvement of this book will be greatly valued.

—**Publisher**

Dictionary of Science

***AB* toxins** The structure and activity of many exotoxins are based on the *AB* model. In this model, the *B* portion of the toxin is responsible for toxin binding to a cell but does not directly harm it. The *A* portion enters the cell and disrupts its function.

Absolute humidity The maximum amount of water vapour, which could be present in 1 m³ of the air at any given temperature, is called absolute humidity.

Absolute magnitude A classification scheme, which compensates for the distance, differences to stars. It calculates the brightness that stars would appear to have if they were all at a defined, standard distance of 10 parsec.

Absolute scale Temperature scale set so that zero is at the theoretical lowest temperature possible. This would occur when all random motion of molecules has ceased.

Absolute zero Theoretically attainable lowest temperature. This is zero of thermodynamically temperatures (0 Kelvin). At this temperature kinetic energy of atoms and molecules is minimum. It value is equivalent to $-273.15\,°C$ or $-459.67\,°F$

Absorbance Absorbance (A) is defined as $-\log(1-\alpha) = \log(1/\tau)$, where α is the absorptance and τ the transmittance of a medium through which a light beam passes.

Absorbed dose For any ionising radiation, absorbed dose (D) is the mean energy imparted to an element of irradiated matter divided by the mass of that element.

Absorptance Absorptance (α) is ratio of the radiant or luminous flux in a given spectral interval absorbed in a medium to that of the incident radiation. Also called absorption factor.

Absorption What happens when wave passes through a medium and gives up some of its energy.

Absorption coefficient, molar Molar absorption coefficient (ε) is absorption coefficient divided by amount-of-substance concentration of the absorbing material in the sample solution ($\varepsilon = a/c$). The SI unit is $m^2 mol^{-1}$. Also called extinction coefficient, but usually in units of $dm^3 cm^{-1} mol^{-1}$.

Acceleration due to gravity The acceleration produced in a body due to the earth's attraction is called acceleration due to gravity. It is denoted by the letter g. Its SI unit is m/s^2. On the surface of the earth, its average value is 9.8m/s². The value of g on the surface of the earth increases in going towards the poles from the equator. The acceleration due to gravity of the earth decreases with altitude and with depth inside the earth. The value of g at the center of the earth is zero.

Acceleration The rate of change of velocity of a moving object is called its acceleration. The SI units of acceleration are m/s². By definition, this change in velocity can result from a change in speed, a change in direction, or a combination of changes in speed and direction.

Accelerator A machine used to accelerate particles to high speeds (and thus high energy compared to their rest-mass energy).

Acceptor An atom which is likely to take on one or more electrons when placed in a crystal.

Accessory pigments Photosynthetic pigments such as carotenoids and phycobiliproteins that aid chlorophyll in trapping light energy.

Acetate Acetate ion. 1. An ion formed by removing the acidic hydrogen of acetic acid.
2. A compound derived by replacing the acidic hydrogen in acetic acid.
3. A fiber made of cellulose acetate.

Acetic acid (CH_3COOH, $HC_2H_3O_2$) Ethanoic acid; vinegar acid; methanecarboxylic acid.

A simple organic acid that gives vinegar its characteristic odour and flavour. Glacial acetic acid is pure acetic acid.

Acetyl Chemical group derived from acetic acid. Acetyl groups are important in metabolism and often added as a covalent modification of proteins.

Acetyl CoA Small water-soluble molecule that carries acetyl groups in cells. Comprises an acetyl group linked to coenzyme A (CoA) by an easily hydrolyzable thioester bond.

Acetyl coenzyme A (acetyl-coA) A combination of acetic acid and coenzyme A that is energy rich; it is produced by many catabolic pathways and is the substrate for the tricarboxylic acid cycle, fatty acid biosynthesis, and other pathways.

Acetylcholine Neurotransmitter that functions at cholinergic chemical synapses, found both in the brain and in the peripheral nervous system. It is the neurotransmitter at vertebrate neuromuscular junctions.

Acetylcholine receptor Lone channel that opens in response to acetylcholine binding, thereby converting a chemical signal into an electrical one. Best understood example of a ligand-gated channel. Sometimes called the nicotinic acetylcholine receptor to distinguish it from a muscarinic receptor, which is a G-protein-linked cell-surface receptor.

Acid Acid is a type of compound that contains hydrogen and dissociates in water to produce positive hydrogen ions. The reaction, for an acid HA is commonly written:

$$HA \rightleftharpoons H^+ + A^-$$

In fact, the hydrogen ion (the proton) is solvated, and the complete reaction is:

$$HA + H_2O \rightleftharpoons H_3O^+ + A^-$$

This definition of acids comes from the Arrhenius theory. Such acids tend to be corrosive substances with a sharp taste, which turn litmus red and give colour changes with other indicators. They are referred to as protonic acids and are classified into strong acids, which are almost completely dissociated in water, and weak acids, which are only partially dissociated. The strength of an acid depends on the extent to which it dissociates, and is measured by its dissociation constant.

In the Lowry-Bronsted theory of acids and bases (1923), the definition was extended to one in which an acid is a proton donor, and a base is a proton acceptor. An important feature of the Lowry-Bronsted concept is that when an acid gives up a proton, a conjugate base is formed that is capable of accepting a proton.

$$Acid \rightleftharpoons base + H^+$$

Similarly, every base produces its conjugate acid as a result of accepting a proton.

$$Base + H^+ \rightleftharpoons acid$$

For example, acetate ion is the conjugate base of acetic acid, and ammonium ion is the conjugate acid of ammonia.

As the acid of a conjugate acid/base pair becomes weaker, its conjugate base becomes stronger and vice versa.

A further extension of the idea of acids and bases was made in the Lewis theory. In this, a G. N. Lewis acid is a compound or atom that can accept a pair of electrons and a Lewis base is one that can donate an electron pair. This definition encompasses "traditional" acid-base reactions, but it also includes reactions that do not involve ions, e.g.

$$H_3N: bCl_3 \longrightarrow H_3NbCl_3$$

In which NH_3 is the base (donor) and bCl_3 the acid (acceptor).

Acid dissociation constant Acid dissociation constant (K_a) is the equilibrium constant for the dissociation of an acid HA through the reaction

$$HA + H_2O \rightleftharpoons A^- + H_3O^+$$

The quantity $pk_a = -\log K_a$ is often used to express the acid dissociation constant.

$$Pk_a = -\log K_a$$

Acid dyes Dyes that are anionic or have negatively charged groups such as carboxyls.

Acid fast Refers to bacteria like the mycobacteria that cannot be easily decolorized with acid alcohol after being stained with dyes such as basic fuchsin.

Acid-fast staining A staining procedure that differentiates between bacteria based on their ability to retain a dye when washed with an acid alcohol solution.

Acidophile A microorganism that has its growth optimum between about pH 0 and 5.5.

Acoustic barrier Solid walls or partitions, solid fences, earth mounds, earth berms, buildings, etc used to reduce noise, without eliminating it.

Acquired enamel pellicle A membranous layer on the tooth enamel surface formed by selectively adsorbing glycoproteins from saliva. This pellicle confers a net negative charge to the tooth surface.

Acquired immune deficiency syndrome (AIDS) An infectious and usually fatal human disease syndrome caused by the human immunodeficiency virus and is characterized by the loss of a normal immune response, followed by increased susceptibility to opportunistic infections and an increased risk of some cancers.

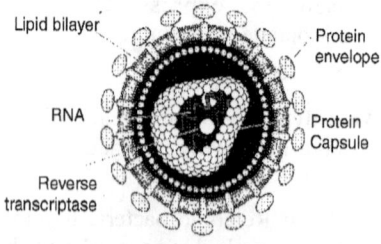

Figure HIV Virus

Acquired immune tolerance The ability to produce antibodies against nonself antigens while "tolerating" self-antigens.

Acquired immunity Refers to the type of specific immunity that develops after exposure to a suitable antigen or is produced after antibodies are transferred from one individual to another.

Acrosomal process Long, thin, actin-containing spike produced from the head of certain sperm when they make contact with the egg. Seen in sea urchins and other marine invertebrates whose eggs are surrounded by a thick gelatinous coat.

Acrosome Region at the head end of a sperm cell that contains a sac of hydrolytic enzymes used to digest the protective coating of the egg.

Actin Abundant protein that forms actin filaments in all eucaryotic cells. The monomeric form is sometimes called globular or G-actin; the polymeric form is filamentous or F-actin.

Actin filament Helical protein filament formed by the polymerization of globular actin molecules. A major constituent of the cytoskeleton of all eucaryotic cells and part of the contractile apparatus of skeletal muscle.

Actin-binding protein Protein that associates with either actin monomers or actin filaments in cells and modifies their properties. Examples include myosin, and profilin.

Actinide The actinides are the fourteen elements from thorium to lawrencium inclusive, which follow actinium in the periodic table. The position of actinium is somewhat equivocal and, although not itself an actinide, it is often included with them for comparative purpose. The series includes the following elements: thorium (Th), protactinium (Pa), uranium (U), neptunium (Np), plutonium (Pu), amercium (Am), curium (Cm), berkelium (Bk), californium (Cf), einsteinium (Es), fermium (Fm), mendelevium (Md), nobelium (No) and lawrencium (Lr). Every known isotope of the actinide elements is radioactive. Traces of Pa, Np and Pu are consequently found, but only Th and U occur naturally to any useful extent.

Actinobacteria A group of gram-positive bacteria containing the actinomycetes and their high G 1 C relatives.

Actinomycete An aerobic, gram-positive bacterium that forms branching filaments and asexual spores.

Actinorhizae Associations between actinomycetes and plant roots.

Action potential A spontaneous self-propagating change in membrane potential that travels as a 'wave' along electrically excitable cell membranes found in neurons and muscle cells. Action potentials are triggered when the cell's membrane potential depolarizes beyond a threshold value of usually -40mV. Voltage sensitive ion channels open and close in fast succession causing first in influx of sodium ions followed by potassium efflux. The potassium efflux brings the membrane potential below the threshold and thus to rest. A new action potential can only be triggered with a new stimulus which comes from neurotransmitter activated ion channels at locations of synaptic interaction between neurons or neurons and muscle cells.

Activated sludge Solid matter or sediment composed of actively growing microorganisms that participate in the aerobic portion of a biological sewage treatment process. The microbes readily use dissolved organic substrates and transform them into additional microbial cells and carbon dioxide.

Activation energy In general, activation energy is the energy that must be added to a system in order for a process to occur, even though the process may already be thermodynamically possible. In chemical kinetics, the activation energy is the height of the potential barrier separating the products and reactants. It determines the temperature dependence of the reaction rate.

Activation product A radioactive isotope of an element which has been created by neutron bombardment.

Active carrier An individual who has an overt clinical case of a disease and who can transmit the infection to others.

Active immunization The induction of active immunity by natural exposure to a pathogen or by vaccination.

Active site The part of an enzyme that binds the substrate to form an enzyme-substrate complex and catalyze the reaction. Also called the catalytic site.

Active transport The transport of solute molecules across a membrane against an electro-chemical gradient; it requires a carrier protein and the input of energy.

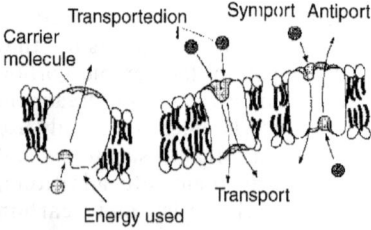

Figure Active transport process

Activity Activity (a) is a thermodynamic function used in place of concentration in equilibrium constants for reactions involving nonideal gases and solutions. For the species i activity is defined as

$$a_i = f_i \times c_i$$

Where a_i is the activity of the species i, c_i is its molar concentration, and f_i is a dimensionless quantity called the activity coefficient.

Activity coefficient Activity coefficient (γ or f) is a fractional number which when multiplied by the molar concentration of a substance in solution yields the chemical activity. This term gives an idea of how much interaction exists between molecules at higher concentration.

In solutions of very low ionic strength, when m is less than 0.01, the Debye-Henckel limiting law can be used to calculate approximate activity coefficients

$$\log \gamma_i = -0.5 . z_i^2 . \sqrt{\mu}$$

Where γ_i = activity coefficient of the species i, z_i = charge on the species i and μ = ionic strength of the solution.

Acute infections Virus infections with a fairly rapid onset that last for a relatively short time.

Acute viral gastroenteritis An inflammation of the stomach and intestines, normally caused by Norwalk and Norwalklike viruses, other caliciviruses, rotaviruses, and astroviruses.

Acyclovir A synthetic purine nucleoside derivative with antiviral activity against herpes simplex virus.

Acyl group Functional group derived from a carboxylic acid.

Adaptation A process in biological evolution as the result of natural selection where a species becomes better adjusted to the living conditions of its environment. In adaptation, individuals that have the most offspring contribute more of their genetic makeup to the next generation. Beneficial traits are favoured in this editing process and the next generation of a species or population is better adapted to new environmental conditions that caused certain individuals to have fewer offspring. Thus genes that are not optimal for certain conditions will become rarer as a result. Adaptation, as evolution in general, is studied at the level of a population of interbreeding individuals.

Adaptive mutation Bacteria and yeast cells in the stationary phase, have a way of producing only the mutations most appropriate for their making use of new substrates for growth.

Addition compound Complex compound. An addition compound contains two or more simpler compounds that can be packed in a definite ratio into a crystal. A dot is used to separate the compounds in the formula. For example, $ZnSO_4 \cdot 7\,H_2O$ is an addition compound of zinc sulphate and water. This represents a compound, and not a mixture, because there is a definite 1:7 ratio of zinc sulphate to water in the compound. Hydrates are a common type of addition compound.

Adenine A purine derivative, 6-aminopurine, found in nucleosides, nucleotides, coenzymes, and nucleic acids.

Figure Adenine

Adenosine 5-triphosphate (ATP) The triphosphate of the nucleoside adenosine, which is a high energy molecule or has high phosphate group transfer potential and serves as the cell's major form of energy currency.

Figure Adenosine 5-triphosphate

Adenosine deaminase deficiency A lack of an enzyme called adenosine deaminase. Its main characteristic is corresponding lack of immune defences against infection. Sufferers die shortly after birth unless kept in a germ-free environment.

Adenosine diphosphate The nucleoside diphosphate usually formed upon the breakdown of ATP when it provides energy for work.

Adhesion A molecular component on the surface of a microorganism that is involved in adhesion to a substratum or cell. Adhesion to a specific host tissue usually is a preliminary stage in pathogenesis, and adhesions are important virulence factors.

Adiabatic cooling The decrease in temperature of an expanding gas that involves no additional heat flowing out of the gas. It is the cooling from the energy lost by expansion.

Adiabatic heating The increase in temperature of compressed gas that involves no additional heat flowing into the gas. It is heating from the energy gained by compression.

Adiabatic process Adiabatic process is a thermodynamic process in which no heat enters or leaves the system. In general, an adiabatic change involves a fall or rise in temperature of the system.

Adjuvant Material added to an antigen to increase its immunogenicity. Common examples are alum, killed *Bordetella pertussis*, and an oil emulsion of the antigen, either alone or with killed mycobacteria.

Adsorption Adsorption is a process in which molecules of gas, of dissolved substances in liquids, or of liquids adhere in an extremely thin layer to surfaces of solid bodies with which they are in contact.

Adult stem cell A specialized cell that is needed for growth, wound healing and tissue regeneration. Adult stem cells are found in all tissues and organs of animals and plants.

Adult T-cell leukemia A type of white blood cell cancer caused by the HTLV-1 virus.

Aerobe An organism that grows in the presence of atmospheric oxygen.

Aerobic anoxygenic photosynthesis Photosynthetic process in which electron donors such as organic matter or sulfide, which do not result in oxygen evolution, are used under aerobic conditions.

Aerobic respiration A metabolic process in which molecules, often organic, are oxidized with oxygen as the final electron acceptor.

Aerosol Aerosols are colloidal dispersions of liquid or solid particles in a gas, as in a mist or smoke. The commonly used aerosol sprays contain an inert propellant liquefied under pressure. The pressure of the gas causes the mixture to be released as a fine spray or foam when a valve is opened.

Aerotolerant anaerobes Microorganisms that grow equally well whether or not oxygen is present.

Affinity constant The reciprocal of the dissociation constant; a measure of the binding energy of a ligand in a receptor.

Aflatoxins A polyketide secondary fungal metabolite that can cause liver cancer. They are natural carcinogens

Agar A complex sulphated polysaccharide, usually extracted from red algae, that is used as a solidifying agent in the preparation of culture media.

Agglutinates The visible aggregates or clumps formed by an agglutination reaction.

Agglutination reaction The formation of an insoluble immune complex by the cross-linking of cells or particles.

Agglutinin The antibody responsible for an agglutination reaction.

AIDS-related complex (ARC) A collection of symptoms such as lymphadenopathy, fever, malaise, fatigue, loss of appetite, and weight loss. It results from an HIV infection and may progress to frank AIDS.

Air mass A large, more or less uniform body of air with nearly the same temperature and moisture conditions throughout.

Air-borne noise This refers to noise which is fundamentally transmitted by way of the air and can be attenuated by the use of barriers and walls placed physically between the noise and receiver.

Airborne transmission The type of infectious organism transmission in which the pathogen is truly suspended in the air and travels over a metre or more from the source to the host.

Akinetes Specialized, nonmotile, dormant, thick-walled resting cells formed by some cyanobacteria.

ALARA As Low As Reasonably Achievable, economic and social factors being taken into account. This is the optimisation principle of radiation protection.

Alcoholic fermentation A fermentation process that produces ethanol and CO_2 from sugars.

Alcohols Alcohols are compounds in which a hydroxy group, -OH, is attached to a saturated carbon atom.

Aldehydes Aldehydes are broad class of organic compounds having the generic formula RCHO, and characterized by unsaturated carbonyl group (C=O). They are formed from alcohols by either dehydrogenation or oxidation. Their chemical derivation is indicated by the name *a* photosynthetic eucaryotic microor-ganisms lacking multicellular sex organs and conducting vessels.

Algicide An agent that kills algae.

Algology The scientific study of algae.

Aliphatic compounds Aliphatic compounds are acyclic or cyclic, saturated or unsaturated carbon compounds, excluding aromatic compounds.

Alkali metals Alkali metal is a term that refers to six elements: lithium (Li), sodium (Na), potassium (K), rubidium (Rb), caesium (Cs), and francium (Fr). These elements make up group 1 of the periodic table of elements. They all form singly charged positive ions, and are extremely reactive. They react violently with water, forming hydroxides and releasing hydrogen gas and heat. Caesium and francium are the most reactive and lithium is the least.

Alkaline earth An oxide of an alkaline earth metal, which produces an alkaline solution in reaction with water.

Alkaline earth metals Alkaline earth metal is a term that refers to six elements: beryllium (Be), magnesium (Mg), calcium (Ca), strontium (Sr), barium (Ba), and radium (Ra). These elements make up group 2 of the periodic table of elements. They all exhibit a single oxidation state, +2. They are all light and very reactive.

Barium and radium are the most reactive and beryllium is the least.

Chemists to denote slightly soluble metal oxides formerly used the term earth. The oxides of barium, strontium, and calcium resemble alumina, atypical earth, but form alkaline mixtures with water. For this reason barium, strontium, and calcium were called alkaline earth metals. This name has now been extended to include all of the elements of group 2.

Alkaloids Alkaloids are basic nitrogen organic compounds derived from plants and having diverse pharmacological properties. Alkaloids include morphine, cocaine, atropine, quinine, and caffeine, most of which are used in medicine as analgesics or anaesthetics. Some alkaloids are poisonous, e.g. Strychnine and coniine, and colchicine inhibit cell division.

Alkalophile A microorganism that grows best at pHs from about 8.5 to 11.5.

Alkanes Alkanes are acyclic branched or unbranched hydrocarbons having the general formula C_n consisting entirely of hydrogen atoms and saturated carbon atoms. In systematic chemical nomenclature alkane names end in the suffix -ane. They form a homologous series (the alkane series) methane (CH_4), ethane (C_2H_6), propane (C_3H_8), butane (C_4H_{10}), etc. The lower members of the series are gases; the high-molecular mass alkanes are waxy solid. Generaly the alkanes are fairly unreactive. They form haloalkanes with halogens when irradiated with ultraviolet radiation. Alkanes are present in natural gas and petroleum.

Allele One of two or more alternative forms of a gene. A person may have two copies of the same allele which would be called homozygous or two different forms which is heterozygous. Different alleles arise from changes in the base sequence of that gene through mutations. For example, the gene for eye colour has different alleles resulting in blue or brown eyes.

Allergen A substance capable of inducing allergy or specific susceptibility.

Allergic contact dermatitis An allergic reaction caused by haptens that combine with proteins in the skin to form the allergen that produces the immune response.

Allobar A form of an element that has isotopic abundances that are different from the naturally occuring form. For example, depleted uranium has had most of the Uranium-235 removed, and is an allobar of natural uranium.

Allograft A transplant between genetically different individuals of the same species.

Allosteric enzyme An enzyme whose activity is altered by the binding of a small effector or modulator molecule at a regulatory site separate from the catalytic site;

effector binding causes a conformational change in the enzyme and its catalytic site, which leads to enzyme activation or inhibition.

Allotrope Allotropy; allotropic; allotropism.

Some elements occur in several distinct forms called allotropes. Allotropes have different chemical and physical properties. For example, graphite and diamond are allotropes of carbon.

Allotropic forms Elements that can have several different structures with different physical properties, for example, graphite and diamond are two allotropic forms of carbon.

Allotype Allelic variants of antigenic determinant(s) found on antibody chains of some, but not all, members of a species, which are inherited as simple Mendelian traits.

Alpha decay The radioactive decay of a nucleus via emission of an alpha particle.

Alpha hemolysis A greenish zone of partial clearing around a bacterial colony growing on blood agar.

Alpha particle Alpha particle is a helium nucleus emitted spontaneously from radioactive elements both natural and manufactured. Its energy is in range 4-8 Mev and is dissipated in a very short path, i.e. A few centimetres of air or less than 0.005 mm of aluminium. As a helium nucleus consists of two protons and two neutrons bound together as a stable entity the loss of an alpha particle involves a decrease in nucleon number of 4 and decrease of 2 in the atomic number, e.g.

$$^{226}_{88}Ra \rightarrow ^{4}_{2}He + ^{222}_{86}Rn$$

A stream of alpha particles is known as an alpha ray or alpha-radiation.

Alpha process A process by which lighter elements capture helium nuclei (alpha particles) to form heavier elements. For example, when a carbon nucleus captures an alpha particle, a heavier oxygen nucleus is formed.

Alpha ray Alpha radiation. A stream of alpha particles. Alpha rays rapidly dissipate their energy as they pass through materials, and are far less penetrating than beta particles and gamma rays.

Alpha-proteobacteria One of the five subgroups of proteobacteria, each with distinctive 16S rRNA sequences. This group contains most of the oligotrophic proteobacteria; some have unusual metabolic modes such as methylotrophy, chemolithotrophy, and nitrogen fixing ability. Many have distinctive morphological features.

Alternating current An electric current that first moves one direction, then the opposite direction with a regular frequency.

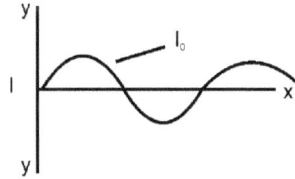

Figure An A.C. Wave

Alternative complement pathway An antibody-independent pathway of complement activation that includes the C_3-C_9 components of the classical pathway and several other serum protein factors.

Alveolar macrophage A vigorously phagocytic macrophage located on the epithelial surface of the lung alveoli where it ingests inhaled particulate matter and microorganisms.

Amantadine An antiviral compound used to prevent type A influenza infections.

Ambient sound The totally encompassing sound in a given situation at a given time, usually composed of sound from all sources near and far.

Amebiasis (amebic dysentery) An infection with amoebae, often resulting in dysentery; usually it refers to an infection by *Entamoeba histolytica*.

Amensalism A relationship in which the product of one organism has a negative effect on another organism.

Ames test A test that uses a special Salmonella strain to test chemicals for mutagenicity and potential carcinogenicity.

Amines Amines are compounds formally derived from ammonia by replacing one, two, or three hydrogen atoms by hydrocarbyl groups, and having the general structures RNH_2 (primary amines), R_2NH (secondary amines), R_3N (tertiary amines).

Amino acid activation The initial stage of protein synthesis in which amino acids are attached to transfer RNA molecules.

Amino acids Amino acids are compounds containing both a carboxylic acid group (-COOH) and an amino group (-NH_2). The most important are the α-amino acids, in which the -NH_2 group is attached to the C atom adjacent to the -COOH group. In the β-amino acids, there is an intervening carbon atom.

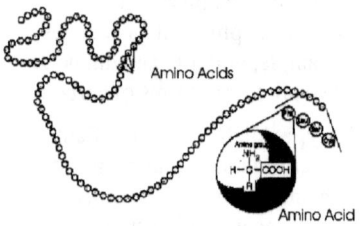

Figure Amino acid

Aminoacyl or acceptor site (A site) The site on the ribosome that contains an aminoacyl-tRNA at the beginning of the elongation cycle during protein synthesis; the growing peptide chain is transferred to the aminoacyl-tRNA and lengthens by an amino acid.

Aminoglycoside antibiotics A group of antibiotics synthesized by Streptomyces and Micromonospora, which contain a cyclohexane ring and amino sugars; all aminoglycoside antibiotics bind to the small ribosomal subunit and inhibit protein synthesis.

Ammeter A device for measuring electrical current.

Ammonia (NH$_3$) Pure NH$_3$ is a colourless gas with a sharp, characteristic odour. It is easily liquified by pressure, and is very soluble in water. Ammonia acts as a weak base. Aqueous solutions of ammonia are (incorrectly) referred to as "ammonium hydroxide".

Ammonium ion (NH$_4^+$) Ammonium. NH$_4^+$ is a cation formed by neutralization of ammonia, which acts as a weak base.

Amnesic shellfish poisoning The disease arising in humans and animals that eat seafood such as mussels contaminated with domoic acid from diatoms. The disease produces short-term memory loss in its victims.

Amniocentesis The most widely used technique of prenatal diagnosis from the 12th week of pregnancy onwards. A small quantity of fluid is removed for analysis from the fluid surrounding the developing fetus.

Amoeboid movement Moving by means of cytoplasmic flow and the formation of pseudopodia.

Amp Unit of electric current. It is equivalent to coulomb/sec.

Ampere Ampere (A) is the SI base unit of electric current.

The ampere is that constant current which, if maintained in two straight parallel conductors of infinite length, of negligible circular cross-section, and placed 1 metre apart in vacuum, would produce between these conductors a force equal to 2×10^{-7} newton per metre of length.

Amphibolic pathways Metabolic pathways that function both catabolically and anabolically.

Amphitrichous A cell with a single flagellum at each end.

Amphotericin B An antibiotic from a strain of *Streptomyces nodosus* that is used to treat systemic fungal infections; it also is used topically to treat candidiasis.

Amplitude (of waves) The maximum displacement of particles of the medium from their mean positions during the propagation of a wave is called the amplitude of the wave.

Anabolism The synthesis of complex molecules from simpler molecules with the input of energy.

Anaemia A condition that is due to a reduced number of red blood cells or reduced amounts of haemoglobin within them. This results in reduced oxygen carrying capacity and reduced aerobic activity in body cells.

Anaerobe An organism that grows in the absence of free oxygen.

Anaerobic digestion The microbiological treatment of sewage wastes under anaerobic conditions to produce methane.

Anaerobic respiration An energy-yielding process in which the electron transport chain acceptor is an inorganic molecule other than oxygen.

Anammox process The coupled use of nitrite as an oxidant and ammonium ion as a reductant under anaerobic conditions to yield nitrogen gas.

Anamnestic response The recall, or the remembering, by the immune system of a prior response to a given antigen.

Anaphylaxis An immediate (type I) hypersensitivity reaction following exposure of a sensitized individual to the appropriate antigen. Mediated by regain antibodies, chiefly $I_g E$.

Anaplerotic reactions Reactions that replenish depleted tricarboxylic acid cycle intermediates.

Anchor Embedded marker enabling authors to link to a specific part of a Web document.

Anergy A state of unresponsiveness to antigens. Absence of the ability to generate a sensitivity reaction to substances that are expected to be antigenic.

Angle of contact It is the angle which the tangent plane to the liquid surface makes with the tangent plane to the solid surface drawn into the liquid at any point on the line of contact between the liquid and the solid.

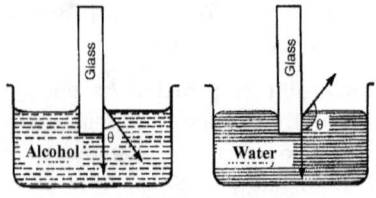

Figure Angle of contact

Angle of incidence Angle of an incident ray or particle to a surface; measured from a line perpendicular to the surface.

Angle of reflection Angle of a reflected ray or particle from a surface; measured from a line perpendicular to the surface.

Angstrom Angstrom is a unit of length equal to 10^{-10} m. The Angstrom is defined in terms of the wavelength of the emission spectra's red line of an atom of cadmium.

Angular acceleration The rate of change of angular velocity of a body moving along a circular path is called its angular acceleration. Angular acceleration is denoted by a.

Angular displacement The angle described at the center of the circle by a moving body along a circular path is called angular displacement. It is measured in radians.

Angular magnification The factor by which an image's apparent angular size is increased. *Cf.* magnification.

Angular momentum A property that an object, such as a planet revolving around the Sun, possesses by virtue of its rotation or circular motion. An object's angular momentum cannot change unless some force acts to speed up or slow down its circular motion. This principle, known as conservation of angular momentum, is why an object can indefinitely maintain a circular motion around an axis of revolution or rotation.

Angular momentum quantum number From quantum mechanics model of the atom, one of four descriptions of the energy state of an electron wave. The quantum number describes the energy sublevels of electrons within the main energy levels of an atom.

Angular velocity The rate of change of angular displacement is called angular velocity.

Anhydrous Anhydrous compound; anhydride. A compound with all water removed, especially water of hydration. For example, strongly heating copper(II) sulphate penta hydrate ($CuSO_4.5H_2O$) produces anhydrous copper(II) sulphate ($CuSO_4$).

Animal model A laboratory animal with a specific disease that researchers can experiment with, to find out more about that disease and how it occurs in humans. Animal models are used to learn more about the causes of a disease, its diagnosis in humans, and to investigate or trial new treatments or preventative actions. Animal models of disease may occur naturally in an animal population, or may be created using techniques such as genetic engineering, or by exposing animals to environments that induce that disease to develop.

Anion Anion is a negatively charged atomic or molecular particle.

Anion exchange An anionic resin has negative ions built into its structure and therefore exchanges positive ions. In anion exchange, the side groups are ionized basic groups, such as ($-NH_2$, $-NRH$, $-NR_2$, $-NR_3^+$) to which anions OH^- are attached. The exchange reaction is one in which different anions in the solution displace the OH^- from the solid.

Anisotropy Anisotropy is the property of molecules and materials to exhibit variations in physical properties along different molecular axes of the substance.

Annihilation A process in which a particle meets its corresponding antiparticle and both disappear. The energy appears in some other form, perhaps as a different particle and its antiparticle (and their energy), perhaps as many mesons, perhaps as a single neutral boson. The produced particles may be any combination allowed by conservation of energy and momentum and of all the charge types.

Annotation The process of determining the location of specific genes in a genome map after it has been produced by nucleic acid sequencing.

Anode The electrode at which oxidation occurs in a cell. Anions migrate to the anode.

Anogenital condylomata (venereal warts) Warts that are sexually transmitted and caused by types 6, 11, and 42 human papillomavirus. Usually occur around the cervix, vulva, perineum, anus, anal canal, urethra, or glans penis.

Anoxic Without oxygen present.

Anoxygenic photosynthesis Photosynthesis that does not oxidize water to produce oxygen; the form of photosynthesis characteristic of purple and green photosynthetic bacteria.

Antheridium A male gamete-producing organ, which may be unicellular or multicellular.

Anthrax An infectious disease of animals caused by ingesting *Bacillus anthracis* spores. Can also occur in humans and is sometimes called woolsorter's disease.

Anthropic principle Concept that states fundamentally that the Universe is the way it is because if it were different we would not exist to pose the question.

Anthropocentrism Anthropocentrism is a view that regards humans as the central element of the universe. Proponents of this believe that we should only protect and replenish the environment so that it serves human purposes such as producing food and drugs; and that the fate of animals and plants are not morally significant except in terms of sustaining human well being.

Antibiotic A microbial product or its derivative that kills susceptible microorganisms or inhibits their growth.

Antibodies Proteins produced by the immune system of humans and other vertebrates in response to the presence of a specific antigen.

Antibody A glycoprotein produced in response to the introduction of an antigen; it has the ability to combine with the antigen that stimulated its production. Also known as an immunoglobulin (Ig).

Antibody-dependent cell-mediated cytotoxicity (ADCC) The killing of antibody-coated target cells by cells with Fc receptors that recognize the Fc region of the bound antibody. Most ADCC is mediated by NK cells that have the Fc receptor or CD16 on their surface.

Antibody-mediated immunity See humoral immunity.

Anticoagulant Substance that prevents blood from clotting.

Anticodon A sequence of three bases in a molecule of transfer RNA (tRNA) that binds to a complementary codon in messenger RNA (mRNA). Each anticodon designates a specific amino acid to be added to a growing polypeptide.

Anticodon triplet The base triplet on a tRNA that is complementary to the triplet codon on mRNA.

Antigen A foreign (nonself) substance to which lymphocytes respond; also known as an immunogen because it induces the immune response.

Antigen-binding fragment (Fab) "Fragment antigen binding." A monovalent antigen-binding fragment of an immunoglobulin molecule that consists of one light chain and part of one heavy chain, linked by interchain disulfide bonds.

Antigenic shift A major change in the antigenic character of an organism that alters it to an antigenic strain unrecognized by host immune mechanisms.

Antigen presenting cells Antigen-presenting cells (APCs) are cells that take in protein antigens, process them, and present antigen fragments to B cells and T cells in conjunction with class II MHC molecules so that the cells are activated. Macrophages, B cells, dendritic cells, and Langerhans cells may act as apcs.

Antimatter Matter made up of elementary particles whose masses are identical to their normal-matter counterparts but whose other properties, such as electric charge, are reversed. The positron is the antimatter counterpart of an electron, with a positive charge instead of a negative charge. When an antimatter particle collides with its normal-matter counterpart, both particles are annihilated and energy is released.

Antimetabolite A compound that blocks metabolic pathway function by competitively inhibiting a key enzyme's use of a metabolite because it closely resembles the normal enzyme substrate.

Antimicrobial agent An agent that kills microorganisms or inhibits their growth.

Antioxidant A molecule that protects cells from oxidative damage of oxygen and free radical molecules that are chemically unstable and cause random reactions damaging proteins, nucleic acids, and cell membranes. Examples of dietary antioxidants are vitamins C, E, and K, and diverse plant products such as lycopene, a nutraceutical found in tomatoes.

Antiparticle For every fermion type there is another fermion type that has exactly the same mass but the opposite value of all other charges. This is called the antiparticle. For example, the antiparticle of an electron is a particle of positive electric charge called the positron. Bosons also have antiparticles except for those that have zero value for all charges, for example a photon or a composite boson made from a quark and its corresponding antiquark. In this case there is no distinction between the particle and the antiparticle, they are the same object.

Antiquark The antiparticle of a quark.

Antisense RNA A single-stranded RNA with a base sequence complementary to a segment of another RNA molecule that can specifically bind to the target RNA and inhibit its activity.

Antisepsis The prevention of infection or sepsis.

Antiseptic Chemical agents applied to tissue to prevent infection by killing or inhibiting pathogens.

Antiserum Serum containing induced antibodies.

Antitoxin An antibody to a microbial toxin, usually a bacterial exotoxin, that combines specifically with the toxin, in vivo and in vitro, neutralizing the toxin.

Aperiodic Refers to the lack of symmetry in molecular structures or functions. An important insight into the mechanism of biological structures is their aperiodic composition and distribution of atoms causing the extra-ordinary complexity of cells.

Apical complex A set of organelles characteristic of members of the phylum Apicomplexa: polar rings, subpellicular microtubules, conoid, rhoptries, and micronemes.

Apicomplexan A sporozoan protist that lacks special locomotor organelles but has an apical complex and a spore-forming stage. It is either an intra- or extracellular parasite of animals; a member of the phylum Apicomplexa.

Aplanospore A nonflagellated, nonmotile spore that is involved in asexual reproduction.

Apoenzyme The protein part of an enzyme that also has a nonprotein component.

Apoptosis Programmed cell death. The fragmentation of a cell into membrane-bound particles that are eliminated by phagocytosis. Apoptosis is a physiological suicide mechanism that preserves homeo-stasis and occurs during normal tissue turnover. It is responsible for cell death in pathological circums-tances, such as exposure to low concentrations of xenobiotics and infections by HIV and various other viruses. Apoptotic cells display profound structural changes such as plasma membrane blebbing and nuclear collapse. DNA is cleaved into short oligonucleosomal length DNA fragments. Apoptosis usually occurs after the activation of calcium-dependent endogenous endonuclease.

Aporepressor An inactive form of the repressor protein, which becomes the active repressor when the corepressor binds to it.

Ar Ar is symbol for element argon.

Arbuscular mycorrhizal (AM) fungi The mycorrhizal fungi in a symbiotic fungus-root association that penetrate the outer layer of the root, grow intracellularly, and form characteristic much-branched hyphal structures called arbuscules.

Arbuscules Branched, treelike structures formed in cells of plant roots colonized by endotrophic mycorrhizal fungi.

Arc degree A unit of angular measure in which there are 360 arc degrees in a full circle.

Arc second Abbreviated *arcsec*. A unit of angular measure in which there are 60 arc seconds in 1 arc minute and therefore 3600 arc seconds in 1 arc degree. One arc second is equal to about 725 km on the Sun.

Archaea A prokaryotic form of life that forms a domain in the tree of life. There are three domains: bacteria, archaea, and eukarya. Bacteria are also prokaryotic organisms. Eukaryotes include animals, plants, fungi, and protozoan and have very different cell structures, bigger and with internal membrane bound struc-tures. While bacteria and archaea look similar in structure, they have very different metabolic and genetic activity. One defining physiological characteristic of archaea is their ability to live in extreme environments. They are often called extremophiles and unlike bacteria and eukarya depend on either high salt, high or low temperature, high pressure, or high or low pH.

Are Are (a) is a unit of area equal to 100 m². The unit is still used in agriculture.

Arenes Arenes are monocyclic and polycyclic aromatic hydrocarbons. See aromatic compounds.

Aromatic A term used to describe cyclic pi-bonded structures of special stability.

Aromatic compounds Aromatic compounds are major group of unsaturated cyclic hydrocarbons containing one or more rings, typified by benzene, which has a 6-carbon ring containing three double bonds. All the bonds in benzene (C_6H_6) are the same length intermediate between double and single C-C bonds. The properties arise because the electrons in the p-orbitals are delocalised over the ring, giving extra stabilization energy of 150 kJ/mol over the energy of Kakule structure. Aromatic compounds are unsaturated compounds, yet they do not easily partake in addition reactions.

Historical use of the term implies a ring containing only carbon, but it is often generalized to include heterocyclic structures such as pyridine and thiophene.

Arthroconidium A thallic conidium released by the fragmentation or lysis of hypha. It is not notably larger than the parental hypha, and separation occurs at a septum.

Arthrospore A spore resulting from the fragmentation of a hypha.

Artificial insemination The placement of sperm inside the female reproductive tract to improve the chances of fertilisation and pregnancy occurring. Artificial inse-mination is also called intrauterine insemination.

Artificially acquired active immunity The type of immunity that results from immunizing an animal with a vaccine. The immunized animal now produces its own antibodies and activated lymphocytes.

Figure Aromatic compounds

Artificially acquired passive immunity The type of immunity that results from introducing into an animal antibodies that have been produced either in another animal or by in vitro methods. Immunity is only temporary.

Ascocarp A multicellular structure in ascomycetes lined with specialized cells called asci in which nuclear fusion and meiosis produce ascospores. An ascocarp can be open or closed and may be referred to as a fruiting body.

Ascogenous hypha A specialized hypha that gives rise to one or more asci.

Ascogonium The receiving (female) organ in ascomycetous fungi which, after fertilization, gives rise to ascogenous hyphae and later to asci and ascospores.

Ascomycetes A division of fungi that form ascospores.

Ascospore A spore contained or produced in an ascus.

Ascus A specialized cell, characteristic of the ascomycetes, in which two haploid nuclei fuse to produce a zygote, which immediately divides by meiosis; at maturity an ascus will contain ascospores.

Aspergillosis A fungal disease caused by species of Aspergillus.

Assembler A general purpose device for molecular manufacturing capable of guiding chemical reactions by positioning molecules.

Assessment period The period in a day over which assessments are made.

Assessment point A point at which noise measurements are taken or estimated.

Assimilatory reduction The reduction of an inorganic molecule to incorporate it into organic material. No energy is made available during this process.

Assisted reproductive technologies Assisted reproductive technologies (ART) refer to advanced fertility techniques such as in vitro fertilisation (IVF) which are used to bring eggs and sperm together to help achieve pregnancy.

Associative nitrogen fixation Nitrogen fixation by bacteria in the plant root zone.

Astronomical unit Astronomical unit (AU) is a unit of length employed in astronomy for describing planetary distance. It is the mean distance of the earth from the sun, equal to 1.4959787×10^{11} m.

Astrophysics The physics of astronomical objects such as stars and galaxies.

Atom The smallest unit of matter that possesses chemical properties. All atoms have the same basic structure: a nucleus containing positively charged protons with an equal number of negatively charged electrons orbiting around it. In addition to protons, most nuclei contain neutral neutrons whose mass is similar to that of protons. Each atom corresponds to a unique chemical element determined by the number of protons in its nucleus.

Atomic force microscope A type of scanning probe microscope that images a surface by moving a sharp probe over the surface at a constant distance; a very small amount of force is exerted on the tip and probe movement is followed with a laser.

Atomic mass The mass of an atom.

Atomic mass unit (amu) Exactly one twelfth the mass of a neutral atom of the most abundant isotope of carbon, ^{12}C. 1 amu = $1.66053873 \times 10^{-27}$ kg. Abbreviated as AMU or μ. Sometimes called the dalton, after John Dalton, architect of the first modern atomic theory.

Atomic nucleus Nucleus; nuclei; atomic nuclei. A tiny, incredibly dense positively charged mass at the heart of the atom. The nucleus is composed of protons and neutrons (and other particles). It contains almost all of the mass of the atom but occupies only a tiny fraction of the atom's volume.

Atomic number The number of protons in an atomic nucleus. The atomic number and the element symbol are two alternate ways to label an element. In nuclide symbols, the atomic number is a leading subscript; for example, in $_6C^{12}$, the 6 is the atomic number.

Atomic theory An explanation of chemical properties and processes that assumes that tiny particles called atoms are the ultimate building blocks of matter.

Atomic weight Atomic mass. The average mass of an atom of an element, usually expressed in atomic mass units. The terms mass and weight are used interchangeably in this case. The atomic weight given on the periodic table is a weighted average of isotopic masses found in a typical terrestrial sample of the element.

ATP Short for adenosine triphosphate, A nucleotide and universal energy currency for metabolism. Almost all caloric content of food is converted into ATP before it can be utilized for tissue growth, muscle work and other physiological processes.

ATP-binding cassette transporters Membrane protein complexes that use ATP energy to move substances across membranes without modifying the compound being transported. They require an ex-tracytoplasmic substrate-binding protein for proper function.

Attenuated vectors Micro-organisms or pieces of DNA such as plasmids which have certain infective components removed by recombinant DNA technology to destroy their virulence, thereby making them safer to use.

Attenuation 1. A mechanism for the regulation of transcription of some bacterial operons by aminoacyl-tRNAs.

2. A procedure that reduces or abolishes the virulence of a pathogen without altering its immunogenicity.

Attenuator A RhO-independent termination site in the leader sequence that is involved in attenuation.

Attractive Describes a force that tends to pull the two participating objects together. *Cf.* repulsive, oblique.

Audible range The limits of frequency which are audible or heard as sound. The normal ear in young adults detects sound having frequencies in the region 20 Hz to 20 kHz, although it is possible for some people to detect frequencies outside these limits.

Autoclave An apparatus for sterilizing objects by the use of steam under pressure. Its development tremendously stimulated the growth of microbiology.

Autogenous infection An infection that results from a patient's own microbiota, regardless of whether the infecting organism became part of the patient's microbiota subsequent to admission to a clinical care facility.

Autoignition temperature Autoignition temperature is the minimum temperature required to initiate or cause self-sustained combustion in any substance in the absence of a spark or flame. This varies with the test method.

Autoimmune disease A disease produced by the immune system attacking self-antigens. Autoimmune disease results from the activation of self-reactive T and B cells that damage tissues after stimulation by genetic or environmental triggers.

Autoimmunity Autoimmunity is a condition characterized by the presence of serum autoantibodies and self-reactive lymphocytes. It may be benign or pathogenic. Autoimmunity is a normal consequence of aging; is readily inducible by infectious agents, organisms, or drugs; and is potentially reversible in that it disappears when the offending "agent" is removed or eradicated.

Autolysins Enzymes that partially digest peptidoglycan in growing bacteria so that the peptidoglycan can be enlarged.

Automated engineering Engineering design done by a computer system, generating detailed designs from broad specifications with little or no human help.

Autosomal dominant 'Autosomal' refers to a nonsex chromosome. Autosomal dominance is when one particular form of a gene, one allele, dominates over other alleles and is always expressed when present in an individual whether they are homozygous for that allele or heterozygous.

Autosome In the human being, any one of the 22 matched pairs of chromosomes. One in each pair is inherited from the mother, the other from the father.

Auxotroph A mutated prototroph that lacks the ability to synthesize an essential nutrient and therefore must obtain it or a precursor from its surroundings.

Avian influenza Referred to as the "bird flu", this is a highly contagious influenza virus that can infect any bird.

Avogadro constant Avogadro constant is the number of elementary entities in one mole of a substance.

$$L = N/n$$

It has the value

$(6.022045 \pm 0.000\,031) \times 10^{23}$ mol^{-1}.

Avogadro's number The number of carbon-12 atoms in exactly 12.00 g of C that is 6.02×10^{23} atoms or other chemical units. It is the number of chemical units in one mole of a substance.

Axis An arbitrarily chosen point used in the definition of angular momentum. Any object whose direction changes relative to the axis is considered to have angular momentum. No matter what axis is chosen, the angular momentum of a closed system is conserved.

Axon The cell extension of a neuron that carries an electrical signal to synapses which are secreting chemical signaling molecules called neurotransmitters to stimulate/inhibit receiving cells. Some axons in the peripheral nervous system connecting to muscle cells or connecting sensory neurons from the skin, eye, or internal organs to the central nervous system can be quite long compared to the size of an average cell.

Axial filament The organ of motility in spirochetes. It is made of axial fibrils or periplasmic flagella that extend from each end of the protoplasmic cylinder and overlap in the middle of the cell. The outer sheath lies outside the axial filament.

Azeotrope Azeotrope is a mixture of two liquids that boils at constant composition, i.e. the composition of the vapour is the same as that of the liquid. Azeotropes occur because of deviations in Raoult's law leading to a maximum or minimum in the boiling point - composition diagram. The composition of an azeotrope depends on the pressure.

Azo compounds Azo compounds are organic compounds containing the group -N=N- linking two other groups. They can be formed by reaction of a diazonium ion with a benzene ring.

B

B cell (B lymphocyte) A type of lymphocyte derived from bone marrow stem cells that matures into an immunologically competent cell under the influence of the bursa of Fabricius in the chicken and bone marrow in nonavian species. Following interaction with antigen, it becomes a plasma cell, which synthesizes and secretes antibody molecules involved in humoral immunity.

Bacillus A rod-shaped bacterium.

Bacillus thuringiensis A species of soil bacterium that possess genes for a group of insecticides, the Bt toxins. Different strains of the bacterium produce different Bt toxins. Some organic farmers use this bacterium as an alternative to using chemicals to control pest insects. The genes for Bt toxins have been genetically engineered into cotton plants so that the plants produce the insecticides.

Background noise Background noise is the term used to describe the noise measured in the absence of the noise under investigation. It is described as the average of the minimum noise levels measured on a sound level meter and is measured statistically as the A-weighted noise level exceeded for ninety percent of a sample period. This is represented as the L_{90} noise level.

Background radiation The naturally-occurring ionising radiation which every person is exposed to, arising from the earth's crust and from cosmic radiation.

Bacteremia The presence of viable bacteria in the blood.

Bacteria A large group of single-celled organisms that do not have organelles enclosed in membranes and have most of their DNA in a chromosome and the remainder in small circular plasmids. They have a cell wall composed of protein and complex carbohydrate over a plasma membrane.

Bacterial artificial chromosome (BAC) A cloning vector constructed from the E. Coli F-factor plasmid that is used to clone foreign DNA fragments in E. Coli.

Bacterial vaginosis Bacterial vaginosis is a sexually transmitted disease caused by Gardnerella vaginalis, Mobiluncus spp., Mycoplasma hominis, and various anaerobic bacteria. Although a mild disease it is a risk factor for obstetric infections and pelvic inflammatory disease.

Bactericide An agent that kills bacteria.

Bacteriochlorophyll A modified chlorophyll that serves as the primary light-trapping pigment in purple and green photosynthetic bacteria.

Bacteriocin A protein produced by a bacterial strain that kills other closely related strains.

Bacteriophage (phage) typing A technique in which strains of bacteria are identified based on their susceptibility to a variety of bacteriophages.

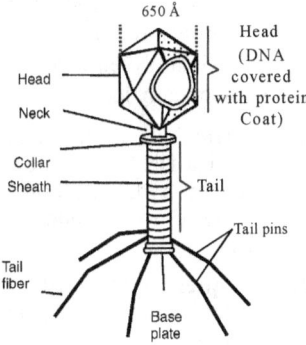

Figure Bacteriophage (phage)

Bacteriorhodopsin Pigmented protein found in the plasma membrane of a salt-loving bacterium, Halobacterium halobium; it pumps protons out of the cell in response to light.

Bacteriostatic Inhibiting the growth and reproduction of bacteria.

Bacteroid A modified, often pleomorphic, bacterial cell within the root nodule cells of legumes; after transformation into a symbiosome it carries out nitrogen fixation.

Baeocytes Small, spherical, reproductive cells produced by pleurocapsalean cyanobacteria through multiple fission.

Bagasse The dry, fibrous residue that remains after the stalks of sugar cane have been crushed and all the juice extracted. It can be used as a source of cellulose for some paper products.

Balanced forces When a number of forces act on a body, and the resultant force is zero, then the forces are said to be resultant forces.

Balanced growth Microbial growth in which all cellular constituents are synthesized at constant rates relative to each other.

Balanitis Inflammation of the glans penis usually associated with Candida fungi; a sexually transmitted disease.

Ball mills Ball mills, also known as centrifugal or planetary mills, are devices used to rapidly grind materials to colloidal fineness by developing high grinding energy via centrifugal and/or planetary action.

Balmer series A set of four line spectra, narrow lines of colour emitted by hydrogen atom electrons as they drop from excited states to the ground state.

Bandgap The range of energies between existing energy bands where no energy levels exist.

Bar Bar (bar) is a unit of pressure equal to 10^5 Pa. Its use is temporarily maintained with the SI. The millibar (100 Pa) is commonly used in meteorology.

Barometer An instrument that measures atmospheric pressure, used in weather forecasting and in determining elevation above sea level.

Barophilic or barophile Organisms that prefer or require high pressures for growth and reproduction.

Barotolerant Organisms that can grow and reproduce at high pressures but do not require them.

Barrel Barrel is an American unit of capacity usually employed in the petroleum industry and trading in fuels.

Baryon A hadron made from three quarks. The proton (uud) and the neutron (udd) are both baryons. They may also contain additional quark-antiquark pairs.

Basal Situated near the base. The basal surface of a cell is opposite the apical surface.

Basal body The cylindrical structure at the base of procaryotic and eucaryotic flagella that attaches them to the cell.

Basal lamina (basal laminae) Thin mat of extracellular matrix that separates epithelial sheets, and many types of cells such as muscle cells or fat cells, from connective tissue. Sometimes called a basement membrane.

Base Historically, base is a substance that yields an OH - ion when it dissociates in solution, resulting in a ph>7. In the Brönsted definition, a base is a substance capable of accepting a proton in any type of reaction. The more general definition, due to G.N. Lewis, classifies any chemical species capable of donating an electron pair as a base. Typically, bases are metal oxides, hydroxides, or compounds (such as ammonia) that give hydroxide ions in aqueous solution.

Base analogs Molecules that resemble normal DNA nucleotides and can substitute for them during DNA replication, leading to mutations.

Base load That part of electricity demand which is continuous, and does not vary over a 24-hour period. Approximately equivalent to the minimum daily load.

Base pair Two nucleotides in an RNA or a DNA molecule that are paired by hydrogen bonds - for example, G with C and A with T or U.

Base sequence The order of the chemical units (bases) adenine, thymine, cytosine and guanine in DNA that forms the genetic code. The sequence of the bases will determine what protein is produced.

Basic dyes Dyes that are cationic, or have positively charged groups, and bind to negatively charged cell structures. Usually sold as chloride salts.

Basidiocarp The fruiting body of a basidiomycete that contains the basidia.

Basidiomycetes A division of fungi in which the spores are born on club-shaped organs called basidia.

Basidiospore A spore born on the outside of a basidium following karyogamy and meiosis.

Basidium A structure that bears on its surface a definite number of basidiospores (typically four) that are formed following karyogamy and meiosis. Basidia are found in the basidiomycetes and are usually club-shaped.

Basophil A phagocytic leukocyte whose granules stain bluish-black with a basic dye. It has a segmented nucleus. The granules contain histamine and heparin.

Batch culture A culture of microorganisms produced by inoculating a closed culture vessel containing a single batch of medium.

B-cell antigen receptor A transmembrane immunoglobulin complex on the surface of a B cell that binds an antigen and stimulates the B cell. It is composed of a membrane-bound immunoglobulin, usually IgD or a modified IgM, complexed with another membrane protein.

Beam The particle stream produced by an accelerator usually clustered in bunches.

Bearing A mechanical device that permits the motion of a component (ideally, with minimal resistance) in one or more degrees of freedom while resisting motion (ideally, with a stiff restoring force) in all other degrees of freedom.

Beat Rhythmic increases and decreases of volume from constructive and destructive interference between two sound waves of slightly different frequencies.

Becquerel Becquerel (Bq) is the SI derived unit, with a special name, for radioactivity, equal to s^{-1}. It describes a radioactivity of an amount of radionuclide decaying at the rate, on average, of one spontaneous nuclear transition per second. The unit is named after the French scientist A. H. Becquerel (1852-1908), equal to s^{-1}.

Beer's law Beer's law is the functional relationship between the quantity measured in an absorption method (A) and the quantity sought, the analyte concentration (c). As a consequence of interactions between the photons and absorbing particles, the power of the beam is attenuated from P_0 to P. Beer's law can be written

$$A = \log (P_0/P) = abc$$

Where a is a proportionality constant called the absorptivity and b is the path length of the radiation through the absorbing medium. Also called the Beer-Lambert law.

Benthic Pertaining to the bottom of the sea or another body of water.

Beta decay The radioactive decay of a nucleus via the reaction

$$n \longrightarrow p + e^- + \text{ or } p \longrightarrow n + e^+ + n;$$

so called because an electron or antielectron is also known as a beta particle.

Beta hemolysis A zone of complete clearing around a bacterial colony growing on blood agar. The zone does not change significantly in colour.

Beta particles Beta particle is a charged particle emitted from a radioactive atomic nucleus either natural or manufactured. The energies of beta particles range from 0 to 4 mev. They carry a single charge; if this is negative, the particle is identical with an electron; if positive, it is a positron.

An unstable atomic nucleus changes into a nucleus of the same mass number but different proton number with the emission of an electron and an antineutrino (or a positron and a neutrino)

$$_{6}^{14}C \rightarrow _{7}^{14}N + e^{-} + \overline{v}$$

Beta radiation Streams of beta particles are known as beta ray or beta radiation. Beta rays may cause skin burns and are harmful within the body. A thin sheet of metal can afford protection to the skin.

Beta-proteobacteria One of the five subgroups of proteobacteria, each with distinctive 16S rRNA sequences. Members of this subgroup are similar to the alpha-proteobacteria metabolically, but tend to use substances that diffuse from organic matter decomposition in anaerobic zones.

B-factory An accelerator designed to maximize the production of B mesons. The properties of the B mesons are then studied with special detectors.

Big bang theory Current model of galactic evolution in which the universe was created from an intense and brilliant explosion from a primeval fireball.

Bile The digestive juice released from liver into the digestive tract to help solubilize and absorb fat soluble nutrients. Bile contains bile acids, biochemical derivatives of cholesterol. Bile acids serve as intestinal detergents for the proper homogenization and uptake of dietary lipids.

Binal symmetry The symmetry of some virus capsids that is a combination of icosahedral and helical symmetry.

Binary compound A compound that contains two different elements. NaC_1 is a binary compound; NaC_{10} is not.

Binary fission Asexual reproduction in which a cell or an organism separates into two cells.

Binding energy The energy required to break a nucleus into its constituent protons and neutrons; also the energy equivalent released when a nucleus is formed.

Binomial system The nomenclature system in which an organism is given two names; the first is the capitalized generic name, and the second is the uncapitalized specific epithet.

Biochemical oxygen demand (BOD) The amount of oxygen used by organisms in water under certain standard conditions; it provides an

Biocide Any chemical agent that can kill a living organism. For example, pesticides that kill insects.

Biocontainment A process aimed at keeping biological organisms within a limited space or area. For example, if an outbreak of a cow disease is found on one farm, a biocontainment process would aim at stopping the disease from spreading to other farms.

Biodegradable A property of molecules or chemicals that refers to their usefulness as food because they can be metabolized by organism.

Biodegradation The breakdown of a complex chemical through biological processes that can result in minor loss of functional groups, fragmentation into larger constituents, or complete breakdown to carbon dioxide and minerals. Often the term refers to the undesired microbial-mediated destruction of materials such as paper, paint, and textiles.

Biodiesel An alternative fuel for use in diesel engines that is made from natural renewable sources such as animal fats or vegetable oils and does not contain petroleum. It has similar properties to petroleum but releases fewer environmental pollutants in its emissions. Biodiesel can be used in diesel engines with little or no modifications, either as a diesel fuel substitute, or added to petroleum-based fuels to reduce their polluting effect. Examples include oils such as soyabeans, rapeseed, sunflowers or animal tallow.

Biodiversity The diversity of variety, species, families, genera etc. of living organisms in a particular place.

Biodynamic agriculture An organic farming system which treats the earth as a living organism in the context of the whole cosmos. It is therefore a holistic approach which works not only with soil, weather and seasons, as external factors, but also with the movements of planetary bodies, in particular the moon against the background of the stars. The farms are treated as individualities and as far as possible as self-contained units in that external inputs are kept to an absolute minimum if not zero. This is the most rigorous definition possible for a sustainable agri-culture. It includes the development of local breeds and varieties suited to the natural conditions of a locality.

Bioelectricity The term bioelectricity refers to the use of charged molecules and elements (= ions) in biological systems. The movement and placement of charges has a great influence on molecular interactions between molecules and thus affects structure and function of proteins, DNA, and cell membranes. The latter are able to stabilize local charge separation in form of ion gradients which are a form of energy storage but also serve as information processing device.

Bioethics The study of the ethical and moral implications of applications of biomedical research and biotechnology.

Biofilms Organized microbial systems consisting of layers of microbial cells associated with surfaces, often with complex structural and functional characteristics. Biofilms have physical/chemical gradients that influence microbial metabolic processes. They can form on inanimate devices and also cause fouling.

Biofouling When living organisms attach to and start living on any object that is submerged in the sea. This is commonly seen as barnacles attached to the hulls of ships.

Biogas Biogas is a mixture of methane and carbon dioxide resulting from the anaerobic decomposition of such waste materials as domestic, industrial, and agricultural sewage. Methanogenic bacteria carry out the decomposition; these obligate anaerobes produce methane, the main component of biogas, which can be collected and used as an energy source for domestic processes, such as heating, cooking, and lighting.

Biogeochemical cycling The oxidation and reduction of substances carried out by living organisms and/or abiotic processes that results in the cycling of elements within and between different parts of the ecosystem.

Bioinsecticide A pathogen that is used to kill or disable unwanted insect pests. Bacteria, fungi, or viruses are used, either directly or after manipulation, to control insect populations.

Biologic transmission A type of vector-borne transmission in which a pathogen goes through some morphological or physiological change within the vector.

Biological control The control of a population of one organism by another organism. Generally the controlling organism is a predator or disease-causing organism of the species being controlled.

Biological shield A mass of absorbing material placed around a reactor or radioactive material to reduce the radiation to a level safe for humans.

Biological value (of proteins) The biological value of a protein refers to, how much of the nitrogen content of food is retained by the body. The biological value of proteins ranges from 50 to 100 percent and is a measure of how much dietary protein source can support growth. Animal proteins have biological values of 70 percent or higher, and plant proteins have biological values of 50 to 70.

Bioluminescence The production of light by living cells, often through the oxidation of molecules by the enzyme luciferase.

Biomagnification The increase in concentration of a substance in higher-level consumer organisms.

Biopesticide The use of a microorganism or another biological agent to control a specific pest.

Bioremediation The use of biologically mediated processes to remove or degrade pollutants from specific environments. Bioremediation can be carried out by modification of the environment to accelerate biological processes, either with or without the addition of specific microorganisms.

Biosensor The coupling of a biological process with production of an electrical signal or light to detect the presence of particular substances.

Biotechnologists Scientists who use biological processes to develop novel products.

Biotechnology 1. A broad term generally used to describe the use of biology in industrial processes such as agriculture, brewing and drug development. The term also refers to the production of genetically modified organisms or the manu-facture of products from genetically modified organisms.

2. The use of plants, animals and micro-organisms to create products or processes. Traditional applications include animal breeding, brewing beer with yeast, and cheese making with bacteria. Recent developments include the use of enzymes or bacteria in a wide range of applications, including waste management, industrial production, food production and remediation of contaminated land. Modern biotechnology also includes the use of gene technology, which allows us to move genetic material from one species to another.

Bioterrorism The intentional or threatened use of viruses, bacteria, fungi, or toxins from living organisms to produce death or disease in humans, animals, and plants.

Biotransformation or microbial transformation The use of living organisms to modify substances that are not normally used for growth.

Biotreatment The treatment of a waste or hazardous substance using organisms such as bacteria, fungi and protozoa.

Black body In radiation physics, an ideal blackbody is a theoretical object that absorbs all the radiant energy falling upon it and emits it in the form of thermal radiation. Planck's radiation law gives the power radiated by a unit area of blackbody, and the Stefan-Boltzman law expresses the total power radiated.

Black body radiation Black body radiation is the radiation emitted by a perfect black body, i.e., a body which absorbs all radiation incident on it and reflects none. The wavelength dependence of the radiated energy density ρ (energy per unit volume per unit wavelength range) is given by the Planck formula

$$\rho = \frac{8\pi hc}{\lambda^5 (e^{hc/\lambda kT} - 1)}$$

Where λ is the wavelength, h is Planck's constant, c is the speed of light, k is the Boltzmann constant, and T is the temperature.

Black body temperature The temperature at which a black body would emit the same radiation as emitted by a given radiator at a given temperature. It generally covers the entire wave length range.

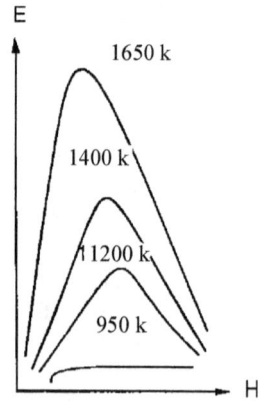

Figure Black body Temperature

Black hole A body whose escape velocity is greater than the speed of light, causing gravity to pull back toward the body any light it would otherwise emit.

Black peidra A fungal infection caused by Piedraia hortae that forms hard black nodules on the hairs of the scalp.

Blastocyst After a mammalian ovum is fertilised it begins to divide. The blastocyst is an early stage of this process which consists of a sphere that is fluid-filled and surrounded by a layer of cells, surrounding a fluid-filled cavity. There is a mass of cells at one side which will become the embryo. The blastocyst is formed before implantation into the uterus.

Blastomycosis A systemic fungal infection caused by Blastomyces dermatitidis and marked by suppurating tumors in the skin or by lesions in the lungs.

Blastospore A spore formed by budding from a hypha.

Bohr magneton Bohr magneton (μ_b) is the atomic unit of magnetic moment, defined as

$$M_b = eh/4\pi m_e = 9.274 \times 10^{-24} \text{ A m}^2$$

Where h is Planck's constant, m_e the electron mass, and e the elementary charge. It is the moment associated with a single electron spin.

Bohr model Model of the structure of the atom that attempted to correct the deficiencies of the solar system model and account for the Balmer series.

Boiling point Boiling point is the temperature at which the liquid and gas phases of a substance are in equilibrium at a specified pressure. The normal boiling point is the boiling point at normal atmospheric pressure.

Boiling water reactor (BWR) A common type of light water reactor (LWR), where water is allowed to boil in the core thus generating steam directly in the reactor vessel.

Boltzmann constant Boltzmann constant (k) is the molar gas constant R divided by Avogadro's

B-oxidation pathway

constant. It has the value 1.380658×10^{-23} J/K.

Bond Two atoms are said to be bonded when the energy required to separate them is substantially larger than the van der Waals attraction energy. Ionic bonds result from the electrostatic attraction between ions; covalent and metallic bonds result from the sharing of electrons among atoms; hydrogen bonds are weaker and result from dipole interactions and limited electron sharing. When used without modification, "bond" usually refers to a covalent bond.

Born-Haber cycle Born-Haber cycle is a cycle of reactions used for calculating the lattice energies of ionic crystalline solids. For a compound MX, the lattice energy is the enthalpy of the reaction

$$M^+(g) + X^-(g) \rightarrow M^+X^-(s) \; \Delta H_L$$

The standard enthalpy of formation of the ionic solid is the enthalpy of the reaction

$$M(s) + 1/2 X_2(g) \rightarrow M^+X^-(s) \; \delta h_f$$

The cycle involves equating this enthalpy to the sum of the enthalpies of a number of steps proceeding from the elements to the ionic solid. The steps are: 1. Atomization of the metal

$$M(s) \rightarrow M(g) \; \Delta H_1$$

2. Atomization of the nonmetal

$$1/2 X_2(g) \rightarrow X(g) \; \Delta H_2$$

3. Ionization of the metal

$$M(g) \rightarrow M^+(g) + e^- \; \Delta H_3$$

This is obtained from the ionization potential.

4. Ionization of the nonmetal

$$X(g) + e^- \rightarrow X^-(g) \; \Delta H_4$$

This is electron affinity.

5. Formation of the ionic solids

$$M^+(g) + X^-(g) \rightarrow M^+X^-(s) \; \Delta H_L$$

Equation the enthalpies gives

$$\Delta h_f = \Delta H_1 + \Delta H_2 + \Delta H_3 + \Delta H_4 + \Delta H_L$$

From which ΔH_L can be found.

Boson A particle that has integer intrinsic angular momentum (spin) measured in units of h-bar (spin =0, 1, 2,). All particles are either fermions or bosons. The particles associated with all the fundamental interactions (forces) are bosons. Composite particles with even numbers of fermion constituents (quarks) are also bosons.

Bottom quark The fifth flavour of quark, with electric charge of -1/3.

Botulism A form of food poisoning caused by a neurotoxin (botulin) produced by Clostridium botulinum serotypes A-G; sometimes found in improperly canned or preserved food.

Boundary The division between two regions of differing physical properties.

B-oxidation pathway The major pathway of fatty acid oxidation to produce NADH, $FADH_2$, and acetyl coenzyme A.

Boyle's law Boyle's law is the empirical law, exact only for an ideal gas, which states that the volume of a gas is inversely proportional to its pressure at constant temperature.

Bragg angle Bragg angle (θ) is defined by the equation

$$n\lambda = 2d \sin \theta$$

Which relates the angle θ between a crystal plane and the diffracted x-ray beam, the wavelength λ of the x-rays, the crystal plane spacing d, and the diffraction order n.

Breed To form fissile nuclei, usually as a result of neutron capture, possibly followed by radioactive decay.

Breeder reactor *See* Fast Breeder Reactor and Fast Neutron Reactor.

Bremsstrahlung Radiation that is emitted when a free electron is deflected by an ion, but the free electron is not captured by the ion. Generally, it is a type of radiation emitted when high energy electrons are accelerated.

Bright-field microscope A microscope that illuminates the specimen directly with bright light and forms a dark image on a brighter background.

British thermal unit The amount of energy or heat needed to increase the temperature of one pound of water one degree Fahrenheit.

Broad-spectrum drugs Chemotherapeutic agents that are effective against many different kinds of pathogens.

Bronchial asthma An example of an atopic allergy involving the lower respiratory tract.

Bronchial-associated lymphoid tissue (BALT) The type of defensive tissue found in the lungs. Part of the nonspecific immune system.

Brosted acid A material that gives up hydrogen ions in a chemical reaction.

Brosted base A material that accepts hydrogen ions in a chemical reaction.

Brownian assembly Brownian motion in a fluid brings molecules together in various positions and orientations. If molecules have suitable comple-mentary surfaces, they can bind, assembling to form a specific structure.

Brownian motion 1. Brownian motion is the continuous random movement of small particles suspended in a fluid, which arise from collisions with the fluid molecules. First observed by the British botanist R. Brown (1773-1858) when studying pollen particles. The effect is also visible in particles of smoke suspended in a still gas.

2. Motion of a particle in a fluid owing to thermal agitation, observed in 1827 by Robert Brown.

***Bt* crops** Crop plants that contain genes for Bt toxins. Examples are Bollgard cotton and Ingard cotton.

***Bt* toxins** Insecticidal proteins produced by the soil microorganism called *Bacillus thurin-*

giensis. *Bt* is an abbreviation of the name *Bacillus thuringiensis*.

Bubo A tender, inflamed, enlarged lymph node that results from a variety of infections.

Budding A vegetative outgrowth of yeast and some bacteria as a means of asexual reproduction; the daughter cell is smaller than the parent.

Buffer Buffer is a solution designed to maintain a constant *ph* when small amounts of a strong acid or base are added. Buffers usually consist of a fairly weak acid and its salt with a strong base. Suitable concentrations are chosen so that the pH of the solution remains close to the pk_a of the weak acid.

Bulk technology Technology in which atoms and molecules are manipulated in bulk, rather than individually.

Bulking sludge Sludges produced in sewage treatment that do not settle properly, usually due to the development of filamentous microorganisms.

Burnable poison A neutron absorber included in the fuel which progressively disappears and compensates for the loss of reactivity as the fuel is consumed.

Burnup Measure of thermal energy released by nuclear fuel relative to its mass, typically Gigawatt days per tonne (GWd/tU).

Bursa of Fabricius Found in birds; the blind saclike structure located on the posterior wall of the cloaca; it performs a thymuslike function. A primary lymphoid organ where B-cell maturation occurs. Bone marrow is the equivalent in mammals.

Burst size The number of phages released by a host cell during the lytic life cycle.

Butanediol fermentation A type of fermentation most often found in the family Enterobacteriaceae in which 2,3-butanediol is a major product; acetoin is an intermediate in the pathway and may be detected by the Voges-Proskauer test.

C

C kinase Ca^{2+}-dependent protein kinase that, when activated by diacylglycerol and an increase in the concentration of Ca^{2+}, phosphorylates target proteins on specific serine and threonine residues.

Ca^{2+}-release channel Ion channel in the membrane of the endoplasmic reticulum and sarcoplasmic reticulum that releases Ca^{2+} into the cytosol when activated.

Cadherin Member of a family of proteins that mediate Ca^{2+}-dependent cell-cell adhesion in animal tissues.

Caged compound Organic molecule designed to change into an active form when irradiated with light of a specific wavelength. An example is caged ATP.

Calandria A cylindrical reactor vessel which contains the heavy water moderator. It is penetrated from end to end by hundreds of calandria tubes which accommodate the pressure tubes containing the fuel and coolant.

Calicivirus The virus that causes Rabbit Calicivirus Disease, RCD, in rabbits. It is spread by mosquitoes and fleas.

Calmodulin Ubiquitous Ca^{2+} binding protein whose binding to other proteins is governed by changes in intracellular Ca^{2+} concentration. Its binding modifies the activity of many target enzymes and membrane transport proteins.

Calomel electrode Calomel electrode is a type of half cell in which the electrode is mercury coated with calomel (Hg_2Cl_2) and the electrolyte is a solution of potassium chloride and saturated calomel. In the calomel half cell the overall reaction is

$$Hg_2Cl_2(s) + 2e^- \rightleftarrows 2Hg(l) + 2Cl^-$$

Calorie Unit of heat. One calorie (small "c") is the amount of heat needed to raise the temperature of 1 gram of water by 1°C. A kilocalorie is the unit used to describe the energy content of foods.

Calutron A device that separates isotopes by ionizing the sample, accellerating the ions in a strong electric field, and then passing them through a strong magnetic field. The magnetic field bends the trajectories of the ions with high charge-to-mass ratio more, allowing ions to be separated by mass and collected.

Calvin cycle The main pathway for the fixation of CO_2 into organic

Carbon

material by photoautotrophs during photosynthesis; it also is found in chemolithoautotrophs.

Cancer A malignant tumor that expands locally by invasion of surrounding tissues, and systemically by metastasis.

Candela Candela (cd) is the SI base unit of luminous intensity. The candela is the luminous intensity, in a given direction, of a source that emits monochromatic radiation of frequency 540×10^{12} Hz and that has a radiant intensity in that direction of 1/683 watt per steradian.

Candidal vaginitis Vaginitis caused by *Candida species*.

Candidiasis An infection caused by *Candida* species of dimorphic fungi, commonly involving the skin.

CANDU Canadian deuterium uranium reactor, moderated and cooled by heavy water.

CAP (catabolite gene activator protein) Gene regulatory protein in procaryotes that, when glucose is absent, activates genes responsible for the breakdown of alternative carbon sources.

Capacitance An element in an electrical circuit capable of separating charges and storing electrical energy. In cells, membranes have capacitor properties contributing to the storage of electrochemical energy.

Capsid 1. The protein coat or shell that surrounds a virion's nucleic acid. 2. Protein coat of a virus, formed by the self-assembly of one or more protein subunits into a geometrically regular structure.

Capsomer The ring-shaped morphological unit of which icosahedral capsids are constructed.

Capsule A layer of well-organized material, not easily washed off, lying outside the bacterial cell wall.

Carbanion A highly reactive anionic chemical species with an even number of electrons and an unshared pair of electrons on a tetravalent carbon atom.

Carbene A highly reactive chemical species containing an electrically neutral, divalent carbon atom with two nonbonding valence electrons; a prototype is CH_2.

Carbohydrates Biochemical name for sugar containing molecules including single sugar like glucose and galactose, but also polysaccharides like starch, cellulose, chitin, and more complex carbohydrate components part of lipids and proteins such as blood serum glycoproteins. All microorganisms contain carbohydrate surfaces being the major determinants of immunogenic reactions during infections.

Carbon The element that defines the chemical properties of all life. All molecules that contain carbon are known as organic molecules and studies by organic chemistry. Carbon is the third most common element in cells, after hydrogen and oxygen, which are the most common biological elements because they are found in water. Also water makes up to 70% of a cells weight, it is not an organic molecule, since it lacks carbon.

Carbon dioxide cycle Large amount of cabon dioxide is being formed as a result of combustion and formation of plants and plant products. Animals also breathe in oxygen present in air and exhale carbon dioxide (Respiration). Decay of animals after death gives carbon dioxide. In spite of this, percentages of carbon dioxide and oxygen remain practically constant in air. This is due to a never ending carbon-dioxide cycle in nature. During day time, plants covert carbon dioxide from air to oxygen (photosynthesis).

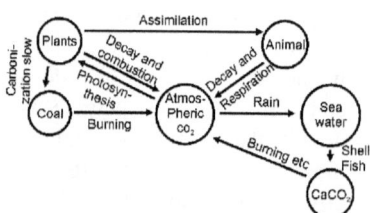

Figure Carbon dioxide cycle

Carbonium ion A highly reactive cationic chemical species with an even number of electrons and an unoccupied orbital on a carbon atom.

Carbonyl A chemical moiety consisting of O with a double bond to C. If the C is bonded to N, the resulting structure is termed an amide; if it is bonded to O, it is termed a carboxylic acid or an ester linkage.

Carboxylic acids Carboxylic acids are organic compounds characteri-zed by the presence of one or more RC(=O)OH groups (the carboxyl group). In systematic chemical nomenclature carboxylic acids names end in the suffix -oic (e.g. Ethanoic acids, CH_3COOH). The carbon of the terminal group being counted as part of the chain. They are generally weak acids. Carboxylic acids include the large and important class of fatty acids and may be either saturated or unsaturated. There are also some natural aromatic carboxylic acids (benzoic, salicylic).

Carboxysomes Polyhedral inclusion bodies that contain the CO_2 fixation enzyme ribulose 1,5-bisphosphate carboxylase; found in cyanobacteria, nitrifying bacteria, and thiobacilli.

Caries Tooth decay.

Carnot cycle Carnot cycle is the most efficient cycle of operations for a reversible heat engine. Published in 1824 by N. L. S. Carnot (1796-1832), it consists of four operations on the working substance in the engine:

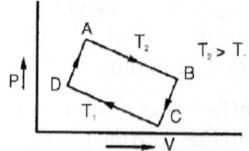

Figure Carnot cycle

A. Isothermal expansion at thermodynamic temperature T_1 with heat q_1 taken in. B. Adiabatic expansion with a fall of temperature to T_2. C. Isothermal compression at temperature T_2

with heat q_2 given out. D. Adiabatic compression at temperature back to T_1.

According to the Carnot principle, the efficiency of any reversible heat engine depends only on the temperature range through which it works, rather than the properties of the working substances.

Carotenoids Pigment molecules, usually yellowish in colour, that are often used to aid chlorophyll in trapping light energy during photosynthesis.

Carrier An infected individual who is a potential source of infection for others and plays an important role in the epidemiology of a disease.

Caseous lesion A lesion resembling cheese or curd; cheesy. Most caseous lesions are caused by M. Tuberculosis.

Casual carrier An individual who harbours an infectious organism for only a short period.

Catabolism That part of metabolism in which larger, more complex molecules are broken down into smaller, simpler molecules with the release of energy.

Catabolite repression Inhibition of the synthesis of several catabolic enzymes by a metabolite such as glucose.

Catalyst Catalyst is a substance that increases the rate of a chemical reaction without itself undergoing any permanent chemical change. Catalyst that have the same phase as the reactants are homogeneous catalysts. Those that have a different phase are heterogeneous catalyst.

The catalyst provides an alternative pathway by which the reaction can proceed, in which the activation energy is lower. Thus it increases the rate at which the reaction comes to equilibrium, although it does not alter the position of the equilibrium.

Catheter A tubular surgical instrument for withdrawing fluids from a cavity of the body, especially one for introduction into the bladder through the urethra for the withdrawal of urine.

Cathode Cathode is a negative electrode of an electrolytic cell; to which positively charged ions (cations) migrate when a current is passed as in electroplating baths.

In a primary or secondary cell the cathode is the electrode that spontaneously becomes negative during discharge, and from which therefore electrons emerge.

In vacuum electronic devices, electrons are emitted by the cathode and flow to the anode.

Cathode ray The mysterious ray that emanated from the cathode in a vacuum tube; shown by Thomson to be a stream of particles smaller than atoms.

Cation Cation is a positively charged atomic or molecular particle.

Cation exchange A cationic resin has positive ions built into its structure and therefore exchanges negative ions. In cation exchange, the side groups are ionized acidic groups, such as ($-SO_3H$, $-COOH$, $-OH$) to which cations H^+ are attached. The exchange reaction is one in which different cations in the solution displace the H^+ from the solid.

Cat-scratch disease (CSD) A loosely defined syndrome caused by either of the following gram-negative bacilli: *Bartonella* (Rochalimaea) *henselae* or *Afipia felis*. The typical case of CSD is self-limiting, with abatement of symptoms over a period of days to weeks.

CD95 pathway The CD95 receptor is found on many nucleated eucaryotic cells. When the receptor is bound to a specific ligand (CD95L), the CD95-CD95L complex activates several cytoplasmic proteins that initiate a cellular suicide cascade leading to apoptosis.

CEC Process in which a chemical reaction precedes and follows the electron-transfer process.

Cell A cell is the basic unit of life in all organisms which can reproduce itself. It is a small, water-filled compartment filled with chemicals and small structures called organelles. It also contains a complete copy of the organism's genome in the organelle called the nucleus.

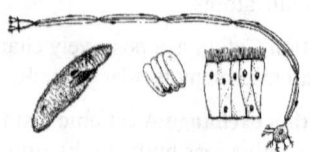

Figure Various Cells

Cell cycle The sequence of events in a cell's growth-division cycle between the end of one division and the end of the next. In eucaryotic cells, it is composed of the G1 period, the S period in which DNA and histones are synthesized, the G2 period, and the M period (mitosis).

Cell line A culture of cells which can be kept alive indefinitely through the appropriate supply of nutrients.

Cell pharmacology Delivery of drugs by medical nanomachines to exact locations in the body.

Cell surgery Modifying cellular structures using medical nanomachines.

Cell wall The strong layer or structure that lies outside the plasma membrane; it supports and protects the membrane and gives the cell shape.

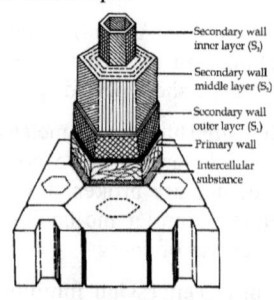

Figure Cell wall

Cell-based therapies Therapies involving the transplantation of stem cells into damaged tissues to regenerate the various cell types of that tissue. For example, bone marrow transplants are a form of cell-based therapy that has been used for over 30 years to treat leukaemia. New stem cell research may lead to cell-based therapies to treat a range of conditions, including heart disease, spinal injuries, diabetes and Parkinson disease.

Cell-mediated immunity The type of immunity that results from T cells coming into close contact with foreign cells or infected cells to destroy them; it can be transferred to a nonimmune individual by the transfer of cells.

Cellular automaton A program that applies a simple rule of what to do repeatedly. Depending on the rule of what to do next, the pattern or behavior generated can look (i) repetitive, simple, and symmetric, (ii) nested (fractal), (iii) random and without any symmetry or repetition whatsoever, or (iv) complex with local patterns but overall broken symmetry.

Cellular slime molds Slime molds with a vegetative phase consisting of amoeboid cells that aggregate to form a multicellular pseudoplasmodium; they belong to the division Acrasiomycota.

Cellulitis A diffuse spreading infection of subcutaneous skin tissue caused by streptococci, staphylococci, or other organisms. The tissue is inflamed with edema, redness, pain, and interference with function.

Cellulose A long-chain, branched polysaccharide that forms the cell walls of plants.

Celsius (Centigrade) Temperature Scale A temperature scale on which the freezing point of water is 0° C and the boiling point is 100° C.

Celsius scale of temperature In the Celsius scale of temperature, the ice-point is taken as the lower fixed point (0 deg C) and the steam-point is taken as the upper fixed point (100 deg C). The interval between the ice point and steam point is divided into 100 equal divisions. Thus, the unit division on this scale is 1degC. This scale was earlier called the centigrade scale. 1 deg C = 9/5 deg F.

Center of charge Geometric point in the reference frame of a physical body where that body's net charge can be said to reside for physical purposes.

Center of mass The balance point of an object.

Centigrade Alternate name for the Celsius scale.

Central processor unit The central processing unit of a computer, responsible for executing instructions to process information.

Centrifugal force An apparent outward force on an object following a circular path that this force is a consequence of the third law of motion.

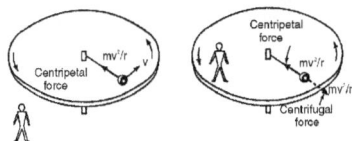

Figure Centrifugal force

Centripetal force The force required to pull an object out of its natural straight-line path and into a circular path; centripetal means.

Centromere The most condensed and constricted region of a chromo-some which joins the two chromatids of the chromosome together. It is also the attachment point of spindle fibres during cell division when the two chromatids separate.

Cephalosporin A group of b-lactam antibiotics derived from the fungus Cephalosporium, which share the 7-aminocephalosporanic acid nucleus.

Ceramics Ceramics are an inorganic material of very high melting point. Ceramics are metal silicates, oxides, nitrides, etc.

CERN The major European international accelerator laboratory located near Geneva, Switzerland.

CGS Centimeter-Gram-Second. The system of measurement that uses these units for distance, mass, and time.

CGS system of units CGS system of units is a system of units based upon the centimetre, gram, and second. The International System has supplanted the CGS system.

Chain reaction A self-sustaining reaction where some of the products are able to produce more reactions of the same kind; in a nuclear chain reaction neutrons are the products that produce more nuclear reactions in a self-sustaining series.

Figure Chain reaction

Chalcogens Chalcogens are the Group 16 elements: oxygen (O), sulphur (S), selenium (Se), tellurium (Te), and polonium (Po). Compounds of these elements are called chalcogenides.

Chancre The primary lesion of syphilis, occurring at the site of entry of the infection.

Chancroid A sexually transmitted disease caused by the gram-negative bacterium *Haemophilus ducreyi*. Worldwide, chancroid is an important cofactor in the transmission of the AIDS virus. Also known as genital ulcer disease due to the painful circumscribed ulcers that form on the penis or entrance to the vagina.

Channel (ion channel) A membrane protein that allows the passive flow of ions across a cell membrane. Ion channels are usually selective for a specific ion type and or either open or closed. These are two structural states of the protein and the change from the open to the closed state (gating) is regulated by the cell. Several regulatory mechanisms have been described including voltage-gating, ligand-gating, heat, and mechano-sensation. Channels are a category of transporters.

Character, acoustic The total of the qualities making up the individuality of the noise. The pitch or shape of a sound's frequency content (spectrum) dictate a sound's character.

Charge A quantum number carried by a particle. Determines whether the particle can participate in an interaction process. A particle with electric charge has electrical interactions; one with h2 charge has h2 interactions, etc.

Charge conservation The observation that electric charge is conserved in any process of transformation of one group of particles into another.

Charles' law The volume of a fixed mass of gas at constant pressure expand by constant fraction of its volume at 0°C for each Celsius degree or kelvin its temperature is raised. For any ideal gas fraction is approximately 1/273. This can expressed by the equation

$$V = V_0 \cdot \left(1 + \frac{t}{273}\right)$$

where V_0 is the volume at 0°C and V is its volume at t°C.

This is equivalent to the statement that the volume of a fixed mass of gas at constant pressure is proportional to its thermodynamic temperature

$$V = kt$$

This law also known as Gay-Lussac's law.

Charm quark (c) The fourth quark (in order of increasing mass), with electric charge +2/3.

Chelate Chelate is a compound characterized by the presence of bonds from two or more bonding sites within the same ligand to a central metal atom.

Chemical bond Bond; bonding; chemical bonding. A chemical bond is a strong attraction between two or more atoms. Bonds hold atoms in molecules and crystals together. There are many types of chemical bonds, but all involve electrons which are either shared or transferred between the bonded atoms.

Chemical change Reaction; chemical reaction.

Chemical compound A pure substance consisting of atoms or ions of two or more different elements. The elements are in definite proportions. A chemical compound usually possesses properties unlike those of its constituent elements. For example, table salt is a chemical compound made up of the elements chlorine and sodium.

Chemical equation Chemical equation is a way of denoting a chemical reaction using the symbol for the participating particles (atoms, molecules, ions, etc.); for example,

$$A\text{a} + b\text{b} \rightleftarrows c\text{c} + d\text{d}$$

The single arrow is used for an irreversible reaction; double arrows are used for reversible reactions. When reactions involve different phases it is usual to put the phase in brackets after the symbol.

s = solid

l = liquid

g = gas

aq = aqueous

The numbers *a*, *b*, *c*, and *d*, showing the relative numbers of molecules reacting, are called the stoichiometric coefficients. The convention is that stoichiometric coefficients positive for reactants and negative for products. If the sum of the coefficients is zero the equation is balanced.

Chemical evolution The chemical changes that transformed simple atoms and molecules into the more complex chemicals needed for the origin of life. For example, hydrogen atoms in the cores of stars combine through nuclear fusion to form the heavier element helium.

Chemical oxygen demand (COD) The amount of oxygen required to convert organic matter in water and wastewater to CO_2.

Chemical potential For a mixture of substances, the chemical potential of constituent B (μ_b) is defined as the partial derivative of the Gibbs energy *G* with respect to the amount (number of moles) of B, with temperature, pressure, and amounts of all other constituents held constant.

$$\mu_B = \frac{\partial G}{\partial n}$$

Also called partial molar Gibbs energy. Components are in equilibrium if their chemical potentials are equal.

Chemiosmotic hypothesis The hypothesis that a proton gradient and an electrochemical gradient are generated by electron transport and then used to drive ATP synthesis by oxidative phosphorylation.

Chemolithotrophic autotrophs Microorganisms that oxidize reduced inorganic compounds to derive both energy and electrons; CO_2 is their carbon source. Also called chemolithoautotrophs.

Chemoorganotrophic heterotrophs Organisms that use organic compounds as sources of energy, hydrogen, electrons, and carbon for biosynthesis.

Chemoreceptors Special protein receptors in the plasma membrane or periplasmic space that bind chemicals and trigger the appropriate chemotaxic response.

Chemostat A continuous culture apparatus that feeds medium into the culture vessel at the same rate as medium containing microorganisms is removed; the medium in a chemostat contains one essential nutrient in a limiting quantity.

Chemotaxis The pattern of microbial behavior in which the microorganism moves toward chemical attractants and/or away from repellents.

Chemotherapeutic agents Compounds used in the treatment of disease that destroy pathogens or inhibit their growth at concentrations low enough to avoid doing undesirable damage to the host.

Chemotrophs Organisms that obtain energy from the oxidation of chemical compounds.

Chickenpox A highly contagious skin disease, usually affecting 2- to 7-year-old children; it is caused by the varicella-zoster virus, which is acquired by droplet inhalation into the respiratory system.

Chimera A recombinant plasmid containing foreign DNA, which is used as a cloning vector in genetic engineering.

Chiral Having handedness: consisting of one or another stereo-chemical form.

Chiral molecule Chiral molecule is a molecule which cannot be superimposed on its mirror image. A common example is an organic molecule containing a carbon atom to which four different atoms or groups are attached. Such molecules exhibit optical activity, i.e., they rotate the plane of a polarized light beam.

Chitin A tough, resistant, nitrogen-containing polysaccharide forming the walls of certain fungi, the exoskeleton of arthropods, and the epidermal cuticle of other surface structures of certain protists and animals.

Chlamydiae Members of the genus Chlamydia: gram-negative, coccoid cells that reproduce only within the cytoplasmic vesicles of host cells using a life cycle that alternates between elementary bodies and reticulate bodies.

Chlamydial pneumonia A pneumonia caused by *Chlamydia pneumoniae*. Clinically, infections are mild and 50% of adults have antibodies to the chlamydiae.

Chlamydospore An asexually produced, thick-walled resting spore formed by some fungi.

Chloramphenicol A broad-spectrum antibiotic that is produced by *Streptomyces venezuelae* or synthetically; it binds to the large ribosomal subunit and inhibits the peptidyl transferase reaction.

Chlorophyll The green photosynthetic pigment that consists of a large tetrapyrrole ring with a magnesium atom in the center.

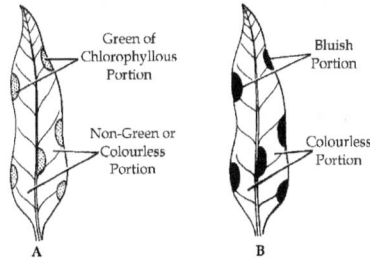

Figure Chlorophyll

Chloroplast An eucaryotic plastid that contains chlorophyll and is the site of photosynthesis.

Cholera An acute infectious enteritis, endemic and epidemic in Asia, which periodically spreading to the Middle East, Africa, Southern Europe, and South America; caused by *Vibrio cholerae*.

Choleragen The cholera toxin; an extremely potent protein molecule elaborated by strains of *Vibrio cholerae* in the small intestine after ingestion of feces-contaminated water or food. It acts on epithelial cells to cause hypersecretion of chloride and bicarbonate and an outpouring of large quantities of fluid from the mucosal surface.

Cholesterol Important lipid found only in animals. Cholesterol is important as cell membrane component, but also serves as a biosynthetic precursor for steroid hormones (e.g. sex hormones) and the active gall bladder ingredients bile acids. The human liver can synthesize all the necessary levels of cholesterol and will reduce its own synthesis if cholesterol is taken in during a meal. 'Bad' and 'Good' cholesterol refers to special transport particles of lipids in our blood serum called lipoprotein particles. The low density form or LDL is high in cholesterol and chronically high concentration of LDL in blood results in insoluble deposits that can clog arteries and restrict blood flow contributing to heart problems.

Chorionic villus sampling (CVS) A small piece of tissue from part of the placenta which shared the genetic make up of the fetus is removed for prenatal diagnosis.

Chromatin The DNA-containing portion of the eucaryotic nucleus; the DNA is almost always complexed with histones. It can be very condensed or more loosely organized and genetically active.

Chromatography Chromatography is a method for separation of the components of a sample in which the components are distributed between two phases, one of which is stationary while the other moves. In gas chromatography, the gas moves over a liquid or solid stationary phase. In liquid chromatography, the liquid mixture moves through another liquid, a solid, or a gel. The mechanism of separation of components may be adsorption, differential solubility, ion-exchange, permeation, or other mechanisms.

Chromoblastomycosis A chronic fungal infection of the skin, producing wartlike nodules that may ulcerate. It is caused by the black molds *Phialophora verrucosa or Fonsecaea pedrosoi*.

Chromogen A colourless substrate that is acted on by an enzyme to produce a coloured end product.

Chromophore group A chemical group with double bonds that absorbs visible light and gives a dye its colour.

Chromosome A microscopic particle containing thousands of genes (DNA) found in the nucleus of the cell. The human being has 23 pairs of chromosomes in each somatic body cell. 22 are matching pairs called autosomes. The two remaining are sex chromosomes: in females two X chromosomes, in males an X and a Y chromosome. One chromosome of each pair plus one sex chromosome come from the mother, the other 23 from the father. Each chromosome is a double strand of DNA packaged in protein.

Chromosphere The layer of the solar atmosphere that is located above the photosphere and beneath the transition region and the corona. The chromosphere is hotter than the photosphere but not as hot as the corona.

Chronic carrier An individual who harbours a pathogen for a long time.

Chrysolaminarin The polysaccharide storage product of the chrysophytes and diatoms.

Chyme Digested content of the stomach released for further digestion in the small intestine.

Chymosin One of the enzymes which causes milk to clot and turn into curds and whey during cheese making.

Chytrids A group of chytridio-mycetes, which are simple terrestrial and aquatic fungi that produce motile zoospores with single, posterior, whiplash flagella. Also considered protists.

Cilia Threadlike appendages extending from the surface of some protozoa that beat rhythmically to propel them; cilia are membrane-bound cylinders with a complex internal array of microtubules, usually in a 9 1 2 pattern.

Circuit An electrical device in which charge can come back to its starting point and be recycled rather than getting stuck in a dead end.

Circular motion The motion of a body along a circular path is called circular motion.

Cladding The metal tubes containing oxide fuel pellets in a reactor core.

Clapeyron equation Clapeyron equation is a relation between pressure and temperature of two phases of a pure substance that are in equilibrium,

$$\frac{dp}{dT} = \frac{\Delta_{trs}S}{\Delta_{trs}V}$$ where $\delta_{trs}s$ is the difference in entropy between the phases and $\delta_{trs}v$ the corresponding difference in volume.

Classical complement pathway The antibody-dependent pathway of complement activation; it leads to the lysis of pathogens and stimulates phagocytosis and other host defenses.

Classical mechanics Classical mechanics describes a mechanical system as a set of particles having a well-defined geometry at any given time, and undergoing motions determined by applied forces and by the initial positions and velocities of the particles. The forces themselves may have electromagnetic or quantum mechanical origins. Classical statistical mechanics uses the same physical model, but treats the geometry and velocities as uncertain, statistical quantities subject to random thermally-induced fluctuations. Classical mechanics and classical statistical mechanics give a good account of many mechanical properties and behaviours of molecules; but for describing the electronic properties and behaviours of molecules, they are often useless.

Classification The arrangement of organisms into groups based on mutual similarity or evolutionary relatedness.

Climax Stage of relative stability attained by a community of organisms, often the culminating development of a natural succession.

Climax community A self-perpetuating, more-or-less stable community of organisms that continues as long as environmental conditions under which it developed prevail. The final stage in an ecological succession.

Cline A pattern of directional, often gradual, change in phenotype or genotype of populations across a geographic transect.

Clitellum The region of an annelid responsible for secreting mucus around two worms in copula and for secreting a cocoon to protect developmental stages.

Cloaca Posterior chamber of digestive tract in many vertebrates, receiving feces and urogenital products. In certain invertebrates, a terminal portion of digestive tract that serves also as respiratory, excretory, or reproductive tract.

Clone A series of identical cells or individuals that have developed from a single cell or individual.

Closed canopy A forest where tree crowns spread over 20 per cent of the ground; has the potential for commercial timber harvests.

Closed circulatory system A circulatory system in an animal in which blood is confined to vessels throughout its circuit.

Closed system A physical system on which no outside influences act; closed so that nothing gets in or out of the system and nothing from outside can influence the system's observable behavior or properties.

Obviously we could never make measurements on a closed system unless we were in it, for no information about it could get out of it. In practice we loosen up the condition a bit, and only insist that there be no interactions with the outside world which would affect those properties of the system which are being studied.

Besides, when the experimenter is a part of the system, all sorts of other problems arise. This is a dilemma physicists must deal with: the fact that if we take measurements, we are a part of the system, and must be very certain that we carry out experiments so that fact doesn't distort or prejudice the results.

Cloud chamber A chamber in which charged subatomic particles appear as trails of liquid droplets.

Cloud forests High mountain forests where temperatures are uniformly cool and fog or mist keeps vegetation wet all the time.

Clouds of electrons The distribution of electrons in space around the atomic nucleus.

Cnidaria The phylum of animals whose members are characterized by radial or biradial symmetry, diploblastic organization, a gastrovascular cavity, and nematocysts. Jellyfish, sea anemones, and their relatives.

Cnidocil Modified cilium on nematocyst bearing cnidocytes in cnidarians; triggers nematocyst.

Cnidocyte Modified interstitial cell that holds the nematocyst; during development of the nematocyst, the cnidocyte is a cnidoblast.

Coacervate An aggregate of colloidal droplets held together by electrostatic forces.

Coagulation Process in which a series of enzymes are activated, resulting in clotting of blood.

Coal gasification The heating and partial combustion of coal to release volatile gases, such as methane and carbon monoxide; after pollutants are washed out, these gases become efficient, clean-burning fuel.

Coal washing Coal technology that involves crushing coal and washing out soluble sulfur compounds with water or other solvents.

Coanda effect The effect that indicates that a fluid tends to flow along a surface, rather than flow through free space.

Coarctate pupa Pupa in which the last larval cuticle is retained as a puparium.

Coastal management The use of coastal resources with the intention of preserving them.

Coastal plain estuary An estuary created by flooding a coastal river valley with seawater.

Coastal shelf The shallow region of the ocean surrounding a large landmass.

Coastal Zone Management Act Legislation of 1972 that gave federal money to thirty seacoast and Great Lakes states for development and restoration projects.

Coat In reference to the eggshell of many cestodes, the portion contributed by the outer envelope, derived from embryonic blastomeres.

Coccolith A small calcareous plate imbedded in the cell wall of coccolithophores, a type of phytoplankton.

Coccolithophorids Unicellular, eukaryotic members of the phytoplankton that have calcareous, button-like structures, or coccoliths.

Coccus Any of various spherical-shaped bacteria.

Cochlea A tubular cavity of the inner ear containing the essential organs of hearing; occurs in crocodiles, birds, and mammals; spirally coiled in mammals.

Co-composting Microbial decomposition of organic materials in solid waste into useful soil additives and fertilizer; often, extra organic material in the form of sewer sludge, animal manure, leaves, and grass clippings are added to solid waste to speed the process and make the product more useful.

Cocoon Protective covering of a resting or developmental stage, sometimes used to refer to both the covering and its contents; for example, the cocoon of a moth or the protective covering for the developing embryos in some annelids.

Codominance A condition in which both alleles of a heterozygous pair are expressed independently.

Codon A sequence of three bases on messenger RNA that specifies the position of an amino acid in a protein.

Coefficient of relationship The fraction of genes identical by common descent shared between two individuals.

Coelacanths A group of lobed-fin fossil fishes. Latimeria was discovered alive in 1952.

Coelenteron Internal cavity of a cnidarian; gastrovascular cavity; archenteron.

Coelom A fluid-filled body cavity, lined by mesodermlying between the gut and the outer body wall musculature that is lined with derivatives of the embryonic mesoderm.

Coelomic fluid The fluid that fills the coelom of echinoderms and other invertebrates.

Coelomocyte Another name for amebocyte; primitive or undifferentiated cell of the coelom and the water-vascular system.

Coelomoduct A duct that carries gametes or excretory products (or both) from the coelom to the exterior.

Coelozoic Living in the lumen of a hollow organ, such as the intestine.

Coenecium, coenoecium The common secreted investment of an ectoproct colony; may be chitinous, gelatinous, or calcareous.

Coenenchyme Extensive mesogleal tissue between the polyps of an alcyonarian (phylum Cnidaria) colony.

Coenocyte Organisms possessing a large mass of cytoplasm with many nuclei.

Coenocytic A tissue in which the nuclei are not separated by cell membranes; syncytial.

Coenosarc The inner, living part of hydrocauli in hydroids.

Coenurus Tapeworm metacestode in the family Taeniidae, in which several scolices bud from an internal germinative membrane; not enclosed in an internal secondary cyst.

Coenzyme An organic nonprotein molecule, frequently a phosphoryla-ted derivative of a water-soluble vitamin, that binds with the protein molecule (apoenzyme) to form the active enzyme (holoenzyme). Examples include biotin, NAD^+, and coenzyme A.

Coevolution The change in gene frequencies resulting from two species, acting as strong selective forces on one another.

Cofactor A metal ion or inorganic ion with which an enzyme must unite in order to function.

Cogeneration The simultaneous production of electricity and steam or hot water in the same plant.

Cognition The processes in the minds of animals or their general mental functions, including perception, representation, and memory.

Coherence The property of two wave trains with identical wavelengths and a constant phase relationship.

Cohesion Tendency of like molecules to stick together, usually due to hydrogen bonds.

Cold front A moving boundary of cooler air displacing warmer air.

Coleoptile The meristematic growing tip of a grass.

Coleorhiza Sheath surrounding the radicle (embryonic root) of monocotyledons.

Coliform bacteria Bacteria that live in the intestines (including the colon) of humans and other animals; used as a measure of the presence of feces in water or soil.

Collagen A tough, fibrous protein occurring in vertebrates as the chief constituent of collagenous connective tissue; also occurs in invertebrates, for example, the cuticle of nematodes.

Collenchyme A gelatinous mesenchyme containing undifferentiated cells; found in cnidarians and ctenophores.

Collencyte A type of cell in sponges that is star shaped and apparently contractile.

Colleterial glands Female accessory glands in insects that produce a substance to cement eggs together or material for an ootheca.

Colliculus collis = hill; ulus = diminutive. Eye and ear reflex centers in the brain.

Colligation The formation of a covalent bond by the combination or recombination of two radicals (the reverse of unimolecular homolysis).

Colloblast A glue-secreting cell on the tentacles of ctenophores.

Colloid A two-phase system in which particles of one phase are suspended in the second phase.

Colonial A multicellular organism that produces a colony of cells, usually referring to colonial algae.

Colonial hypothesis A hypothesis formulated to explain the origin of multicellularity from protist ancestors; animals may have been derived when protists associated together and cells became specialized and interdependent.

Colonization The pioneer establishment of vegetation on a previously unvegetated area.

Colonizer An organism that initiates the biological "conquest" of soil or rock.

Colony A cluster of genetically identical individuals formed asexually from a single colonizing individual.

Colour The visual perception of light associated with its frequency or wave length.

Colostrum The first secretion of the mammary glands following the birth of an infant.

Columella Central pillar in gastropod shells.

Columnar In the form of a column.

Comb jellies The invertebrates with a gelatinous body, radial symmetry, and eight rows of ciliary combs.

Comb plate One of the plates of fused cilia that are arranged in rows for ctenophore locomotion.

Comb rows Rows of cilia that serve as the locomotor organs of ctenophorans.

Commensalism A relationship in which one individual lives close to or on another and benefits, and the host is unaffected; often symbiotic.

Common misuse We often hear non-scientists say such things as "The car was going at a high rate of speed." This is redundant at best, since it merely means "The car was moving at high speed." It is the sort of mistake made by people who don't think while they talk.

Common name A regional name for well-known plants; in the language of the region, rather than in Latin, and not necessarily paralleling any scientific name.

Commonality In learning, the inference of a phyletic, evolutionary relationship among the species exhibiting a particular type of learning.

Communal nesting More than one female in a nest raising the young of more than one female.

Communal resource management systems Resources managed by a community for long term sustainability.

Communication Act on the part of one organism (or cell) that alters the probability of patterns of behavior in another organism (or cell) in an adaptive fashion.

Community An assemblage of organisms that are associated in a common environment and interact with each other in a self-sustaining and self-regulating relation.

Community diversity The number of different kinds of organisms living in an area.

Community ecology The study of interactions of all populations living in the ecosystem of a given area.

Commutator A split ring in a d-c generator, each segment of which is connected to an end of a corresponding armature loop.

Companion cell Phloem cell associated with a sieve tube member.

Comparative anatomy The study of animal structure in an attempt to deduce evolutionary pathways in particular animal groups.

Comparative embryology The study of animal development in an attempt to deduce evolutionary pathways in particular animal groups.

Comparative method A comparison of the behaviour of two or more species for the purpose of either elucidating some common aspects of the ecology and evolution of behavior or exploring the mechanisms underlying behavior.

Comparative psychologist An ethologist who studies the genetic, neural, and hormonal bases of animal behaviour.

Comparative psychology A branch of psychology involving the study of animals. Some comparative psychologists are more concerned with learning, cognition, and intelligence in human and non-human animals, while others are indistinguishable from other animal behaviourists in that they explore the causation, development, evolution, and functional aspects of behavior in a broad range of species.

Compartmentalization The division of labour in living cells such that enzymes related to a particular function are packaged and separated from the other cell contents, usually by a membrane.

Compensation effect In a considerable number of cases plots of $t s$ vs. h, for a series of reactions, e.g. For a reaction in a range of different solvents, are straight lines of approximately unit slope. Therefore, the terms h and $t s$ in the expression partially compensate, and $g = h - t s$ often is a much simpler function of solvent (or other) variation than h or $t s$ separately.

Compensation point The condition in a living system in which the uptake of CO_2 equals the release of CO_2; that is, photosynthesis equals respiration.

Competition Some degree of overlap in ecological niches of two populations in the same community, such that both depend on the same food source, shelter, or other resources, and negatively affect each other's survival.

Competitive exclusion A theory that no two populations of different species will occupy the same niche and compete for exactly the same resources in the same habitat for very long; disputed by some ecologists who see biological communities as highly individualistic and variable.

Complement fixation test Immunological method used to detect presence of antibodies that bind (or fix) complement; a standard diagnostic test for many infections.

Complementary DNA (cDNA) DNA prepared by transcribing the base sequence from mRNA into DNA by reverse transcriptase; also called copy DNA.

Complementary strand Two polynucleotide chains in which the pairing of adenine is always with thymine (in DNA) or uracil (in RNA), and guanine is always paired with cytosine.

Complete flower A flower with all four floral whorls (sepals, petals, stamens, and carpels).

Complete linkage Two genes positioned so close to one another on the same chromosome that recombination between them does not occur.

Complete protein A protein that has all of the essential amino acids and in the correct proportions.

Complete vibration Back-and-forth motion of an object describing simple harmonic motion.

Complex A molecular entity formed by loose association involving two or more component molecular entities (ionic or uncharged), or the corresponding chemical species. The bonding between the components is normally weaker than in a covalent bond.

The term has also been used with a variety of shades of meaning in different contexts: it is therefore best avoided when a more explicit alternative is applicable. In inorganic chemistry the term "coordination entity" is recommended instead of "complex".

Complex camera eye The type of image-forming eye found in squids and octopuses.

Complexity (ecological) The number of species at each trophic level and the number of trophic levels in a community.

Component One of the several vectors that can be combined geometrically to find a resultant vector.

Composite reaction A chemical reaction for which the expression for the rate of disappearance of a reactant (or rate of appearance of a product) involves rate constants of more than a single elementary reaction. Examples are "opposing reactions" (where rate constants of two opposed chemical reactions are involved), "parallel reactions" (for which the rate of disappearance of any reactant is governed by the rate constants relating to several simultaneous reactions to form different respective products from a single set of reactants), and stepwise reactions.

Composite signal A signal formed by combining two or more simpler signals.

Composition of forces The combining of two or more component forces into a single resultant force.

Composting The biological degradation of organic material under aerobic (oxygen-rich) conditions to produce compost, a nutrient-rich soil amendment and conditioner.

Compound A substance composed of atoms of two or more elements joined by chemical bonds and chemically united in fixed proportions.

Compound eye An eye consisting of many individual lens systems (ommatidia). Present in many members of the phylum Arthropoda.

Compound fruit A fruit consisting of several individual fruits held together (a multiple fruit) or in which separate carpels of a flower stay together (an aggregate fruit).

Compound leaf A leaf composed of two or more completely independent blade units called leaflets.

Compound pistil A pistil composed of more than one carpel.

Compression A fossil formed when carbonized plant material is still present in the original shape but is greatly compressed and reduced in size by pressure.

Compression wood The reaction wood produced along the lower side of leaning trees, straightening the trunk by expanding and pushing the tree upright.

Compton effect An effect that demonstrates that photons (the quantum of electromagnetic radiation) have momentum. A photon fired at a stationary particle, such as an electron, will impart momentum to the electron and, since its energy has been decreased, will experience a corresponding decrease in frequency.

Concave Surface with center of curvature on the same side as the observer.

Concave lens A lens that diverges parallel light rays (assuming the outside refractive index to be smaller).

Concave mirror A mirror that converges parallel light rays incident on its surface.

Concentration Concentration is the amount of given substance in a stated unit of a mixture, solution, or ore.

$$C_A = \frac{n_A}{V}$$

The concentration of an atom, ion, or molecule in a solution may be symbolized by the use of square brackets, as $[Ca^{2+}]$.

Concentration gradient The difference in concentration in two parts of a system.

Concentricycloidea The class of echinoderms whose members are characterized by two concentric water-vascular rings encircling a disklike body; no digestive system; and internal brood pouches. Sea daisies.

Concerted process Two or more primitive changes are said to be concerted (or to constitute a concerted process) if they occur within the same elementary reaction. Such changes will normally (though perhaps not inevitably) be "energetically coupled". (In the present context the term "energetically coupled" means that the simultaneous progress of the primitive changes involves a transition state of lower energy than that for their successive occurrence.) In a concerted process the primitive changes may be synchronous or asynchronous.

Conchae Thin bones in the nasal chamber.

Concomitant immunity Premunition.

Concurrent forces Forces with lines of action that pass through the same point.

Condensation The aggregation of water molecules from vapour to liquid or solid when the saturation concentration is exceeded.

Condensation nuclei Tiny particles that float in the air and facilitate the condensation process.

Condensation reaction A (usually stepwise) reaction in which two or more reactants (or remote reactive sites within the same molecular entity) yield a single main product with accompanying formation of water or of some other small molecule, e.g. ammonia, ethanol, acetic acid, hydrogen sulphide.

The mechanism of many condensa-tion reactions has been shown to comprise consecutive addition and elimination reactions, as in the base-catalysed formation of (E)-but-2-enal (crotonaldehyde) from acetaldehyde, via 3-hydroxy-butanal (aldol). The overall reaction in this example is known as the aldol condensation. The term is sometimes also applied to cases where the formation of water or another simple molecule does not occur, as in "benzoin condensation".

Conditioned response (CR) The behavior pattern that becomes conditioned during classical conditioning.

Conditioned stimulus (CS) The previously neutral stimulus that, through classical conditioning, now elicits the conditioned response.

Conditioning A form of learning in which a behavior is associated with a reward such as food.

Conduct The conduction of electricity refers to the process of electrical charge flowing through a material. The conduction of the charge carriers is the electrical current.

Conduction The conveyance of energy, such as heat, sound, or electricity. The direct transfer of thermal motion (heat) between molecules of the environment and those on the body surface of an animal.

Conductor A material which has a small energy gap is a conducting material. A conductor conducts electricity very well; it conducts better than either an insulator or a semi-conductor.

Condyles Bearing surfaces between arthropod joints that provide the fulcra on which the joints move.

Cone A vertebrate photoreceptor cell with a tapered outer segment; unlike rod cells, cone cells are usually sensitive

Cone cell A color-sensitive photoreceptor cell concentrated in the retina.

Conformation A molecular geometry that differs from other geometries chiefly by rotation about single or triple bonds; distinct conformations are associated with distinct potential wells. Typical biomolecules and products of organic synthesis can interconvert among many conformations; typical diamondoid structures are locked into a single potential well, and thus lack conformational flexibility.

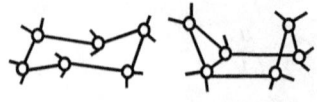

Chair form   Boat form
Figure Conformations of Cyclohexane

Confusion effect The reduced capture efficiency experienced by a predator caused by high densities or swarms of prey.

Conidiophore Hyphae on which one or many conidia are produced.

Conidiosporangium A structure that produces conidiospores.

Conidiospore An asexual spore produced singly.

Conidium Asexual reproductive spores of some ascomycetes and imperfect fungi.

Conifer Any of a group of plants that produce a strobilus or cone as a reproductive structure.

Coniferous forest A community type dominated by cone-bearing gymnosperms mostly in the northern hemisphere.

Conifers Needle-bearing trees that produce seeds in cones.

Conjugate acid-base pair The Brönsted acid BH^+ formed on protonation of a base B is called the conjugate acid of B, and B is the conjugate base of BH^+. (The conjugate acid always carries one unit of positive charge more than the base, but the absolute charges of the species are immaterial to the definition.) For example: the Brönsted acid HCl and its conjugate base Cl^- constitute a conjugate acid-base pair.

Conjugated system, conjugation In the original meaning a conjugated system is a molecular entity whose structure may be represented as a system of alternating single and multiple bonds. In such systems, conjugation is the interaction of one p-orbital with another across an intervening sigma bond in such structures (in appropriate molecular entities d-orbitals may be involved). The term is also extended to the analogous interaction involving a p-orbital containing an unshared electron pair.

Conjugation Temporary union of two ciliate protozoa while they are exchanging chromatin material and undergoing nuclear phenomena resulting in binary fission. Also, formation of cytoplasmic bridges between bacteria for transfer of plasmids.

Connective tissue A basic type of tissue that includes bone, cartilage, and various fibrous tissues. Connective tissue serves to support and bind tissues together.

Connectivity In a chemical context, the information content of a line formula, but omitting any indication of bond multiplicity.

Conoid Truncated cone of spiral fibrils located within the polar rings of the suborder Eimeriina.

Conservation To protect, conserve the natural world and all its components.

Conservation of angular momentum The total angular momentum of a closed system remains constant. There are several other laws that deal with particle physics, such as conservation of baryon number, of strangeness, etc., which are conserved in some fundamental interactions (such as the electromagnetic interaction) but not others (such as the weak interaction).

Conservation of electric charge The total electric charge of a closed system remains constant.

Conservation of linear momentum The total linear momentum of a closed system remains constant.

Conservation of mass-energy The total mass-energy of a closed system remains constant.

Conservation of matter In any chemical reaction, matter changes form; it is neither created nor destroyed.

Conservative forces Forces for which the law of conservation of mechanical energy holds true; gravitational forces and electrostatic forces.

Conserved A quantity is said to be conserved if under specified conditions it's value does not change with time.

Example: In a closed system, the charge, mass, total energy, linear momentum and angular momentum of the system are conserved. (Relativity theory allows that mass can be converted to energy and vice-versa, so we modify this to say that the mass-energy is conserved.)

Conspecific A member of the same species.

Constant proportions, rule of A principle that states that the relative amounts of ions in seawater are always the same.

Constitution The description of the identity and connectivity (and corresponding bond multiplicities) of the atoms in a molecular entity (omitting any distinction from their spatial arrangement).

Constraints In optimality models, the limits placed on an animal because of its inherent abilities.

Consumer A heterotroph. A primary consumer feeds directly on a primary producer, whereas a secondary consumer feeds on a primary consumer.

Consummatory behaviour Actions of an animal completing a behaviour sequence, as in consuming food, mating, etc.

Consumption The fraction of withdrawn water that is lost in transmission or that is evaporated, absorbed, chemically transformed, or otherwise made unavailable for other purposes as a result of human use.

Contagious Capable of being transmitted through direct contact. Also used to describe population distributions that are aggregated, such as in an area.

Contaminative antigen Antigen borne by the parasite that is common to both the host and the parasite but that genetically is of host origin.

Context In communication, stimuli other than the signal that are impinging on the receiver that might alter the meaning of a signal.

Contiguity The association of events in time with particular reference here to classical conditioning.

Continental boundary current A surface ocean current flowing generally north or south along a continental edge.

Continental drift The breakup and movement of land masses of the earth. The earth had a single landmass about 250 million years ago. This mass broke apart into continents, which have moved slowly to their present positions.

Continental margin The edge of a continent; the zone between a continent and the deep-sea floor.

Continental rise The gently sloping area at the base of the continental slope.

Continental shelf The shallow, gently sloping section of the continental margin that extends from the shore to the point where the slope gets steeper.

Continental slope The relatively steep portion of the sea bottom between the outer edge of the continental shelf and the deep ocean basin.

Continuous feeder Usually slow-moving sessile animals that feed all of the time.

Continuous spectrum A spectrum without dark lines or bands or in which there is an uninterrupted change from one colour to another.

Continuous variable One that can assume any value whatsoever between certain limits, versus a discrete variable that can assume only specific values.

Contour feathers Feathers that cover the body, wings, and tail of a bird. Contour feathers provide flight surfaces and are responsible for plumage colours.

Contour plowing Plowing along hill contours; reduces erosion.

Contractile root A specialized root, common in bulbs, that contracts, pulling the stem deeper into the ground.

Contractile vacuole A clear fluid-filled cell vacuole in protozoa and a few lower metazoa; takes up water and releases it to the outside in a cyclical manner, for osmoregulation and some excretion.

Control group An observed, unmanipulated set of test subjects. In an experimental manipulation, we must also perform the actions involved in that manipulation on a second test group of organisms in order to ascertain whether any effects of the experimental treatment are due to that treatment and not to the actions involved in providing the treatment.

Control rods Neutron-absorbing material inserted into spaces between fuel assemblies in nuclear reactors to regulate fission reaction.

Conurbation An area with more than one million people that is formed by the merger of two or more population centers and that meets other specified requirements.

Convection The act of conveying or transmission. The movement of air (or a liquid) over the surface of a body and contributes to heat loss (if the air is cooler than the body) or heat gain (if air is warmer than the body).

Convection currents Rising or sinking air currents that stir the atmosphere and transport heat from one area to another. Convec-tion currents also occur in water.

Convective mixing The vertical mixing of water masses driven by wind stresses or density changes at the sea surface.

Conventional pollutants The seven substances (sulphur dioxide, carbon monoxide, particulates, hydrocarbons, nitrogen oxides, photochemical oxidants, and lead) that make up the largest volume of air quality degradation; identified by the Clean Air Act as the most serious threat of all pollutants to human health and welfare; also called criteria pollutants.

Convergent evolution Groups of unrelated organisms becoming similar in appearance because of evolutionary change in response to similar environments.

Converging lens A lens that is thicker in the middle than it is at the edge and bends incident parallel rays toward a common point.

Convex Surface with center of curvature on the opposite side from the observer.

Convex lens A lens that converges parallel light rays (assuming the outside refractive index to be smaller)

Convex mirror A mirror that diverges parallel light rays incident on its surface.

Cool deserts Deserts such as the American Great Basin characterized by cold winters and sagebrush.

Cooperation Behavior patterns that are mutually beneficial to the cooperators.

Cooperative breeding A breeding system in which nonparents share in rearing the young.

Coordinate system In order to describe where things are, one needs to lay out the basic directions (equivalent to North, South, East, and West on a map). This is a coordinate system. There are two main differences between the directions on a map and in a coordinate system: First, a coordinate system has an origin — a place from which every other place is referenced; the map-equivalent would be if everything were measured from city hall - "The bank is three blocks south of city hall." "The grocery store is two block east and one block north of city hall." etc. Second, a mathematical coordinate system would treat the north-south pair as a single dimension. One would be the "positive direction" and the other would be the "negative direction." (It is arbitrary which is which, but there is usually a convention) i.e. If we call north the "positive North-South direction," then south is the negative North-South direction." Similarly, if east is the "positive East-West direction," then west is the "negative East-West direction." Finally, it is important in mathematics that the dimensions of a coordinate system be perpendicular. (North-South is perpendicular to East-West.)

Coordination The formation of a covalent bond, the two shared electrons of which have come from only one of the two parts of the molecular entity linked by it, as in the reaction of a Lewis acid and a Lewis base to form a Lewis adduct; alternatively, the bonding formed in this way. In the former sense, it is the reverse of unimolecular heterolysis. "Coordinate covalence" and "coordinate link" are synonymous (obsolescent) terms. The synonym "dative bond" is obsolete. The term is also used to describe the number of ligands around a central atom without necessarily implying two-electron bonds.

Coordination number The coordination number of a specified atom in a chemical species is the number of other atoms directly linked to that specified atom. For example, the coordination number of carbon in methane is four, and it is five in protonated methane, CH_5^+. (The term is used in a different sense in the crystallographic description of ionic crystals.)

Coordinatively saturated A transition metal complex that has formally 18 outer shell electrons at the central metal atom.

Coordinatively unsaturated A transition metal complex that possesses fewer ligands than exist in the coordinatively saturated complex. These complexes usually have fewer than 18 outer shell electrons at the central metal atom.

Copepodid Juvenile stage that succeeds the naupliar stages in copepods, often quite similar in body form to the adult.

Copepods Small, mostly planktonic crustaceans.

Copernican principle The idea, suggested by Copernicus, that the sun, not the earth, is at the center of the universe. We now know that neither idea is correct (the sun is not even located at the center of our galaxy, much less the universe), but it set into effect a long chain of demotions of earth's and our place in the universe, to where it is now: on an unimpressive planet orbiting a mediocre star in a corner of a typical galaxy, lost in the universe.

Coprolite Fossilized fecal material.

Coprophagy Feeding on dung or excrement as a normal behavior among animals; reinjestion of feces.

Copulation Sexual union to facilitate the reception of sperm by the female.

Coracidium Larva with a ciliated epithelium hatching from the egg of certain cestodes; a ciliated free-swimming oncosphere.

Coral knoll A column of coral within the lagoon of an atoll.

Coral reefs Prominent oceanic features composed of hard, limy skeletons produced by coral animals; usually formed along edges of shallow, submerged ocean banks or along shelves in warm, shallow, tropical seas.

Coral rubble Coral fragments.

Coralline algae Any red alga that is impregnated with calcium carbonate. Coralline algae often contribute to coral reefs.

Corallite The calcareous skeletal cup in which a coral polyp sits.

Cord grasses Salt-tolerant grasses, species of Zostera, that inhabit salt marshes.

Core The dense, intensely hot mass of molten metal, mostly iron and nickel, thousands of kilometres in diameter at the earth's center.

Core area The area of heaviest use within the home range.

Core region The primary industrial region of a country; usually located around the capital or largest port; has both the greatest population density and the greatest economic activity of the country.

Corepressor A substance that inhibits production of a particular enzyme.

Coriolis effect The apparent change in direction of a moving object (to the left in the Southern Hemisphere and to the right in the Northern Hemisphere) due to the rotation of the earth.

Coriolis pseudoforce A pseudoforce which arises because of motion relative to a frame which is itself rotating relative to second, inertial frame. The magnitude of the coriolis "force" is dependent on the speed of the object relative to the noninertial frame, and the direction of the "force" is orthogonal to the object's velocity.

Corium The deep layer of the skin; dermis.

Cork Suberized cells on the outer surface of woody stems and roots; produced by the cork cambium.

Cork cambium Meristematic tissue that produces cork cells on its outer surface and phelloderm on its inner surface.

Corm Underground, enlarged, food-storing stem covered by papery leaves.

Cornea The outer transparent coat of the eye.

Corneum Epithelial layer of dead, keratinized cells. Stratum corneum.

Cornified Adjective for conversion of epithelial cells into nonliving, keratinized cells.

Cornucopian fallacy The belief that nature is limitless in its abundance and that perpetual growth is not only possible but essential.

Corolla Collective term for the petals of a flower.

Corona A crown; an encircling structure. The ciliated organ at the anterior end of rotifers used for swimming or feeding.

Coronary Encircling as a crown. 1. Vessels encircling the heart. 2. A condition caused by a decreased blood flow to the heart muscle. 3. Specifically, a blocked coronary artery or a branch of a coronary artery.

Correlation analysis The use of empirical correlations relating one body of experimental data to another, with the objective of finding quantitative estimates of the factors underlying the phenomena involved. Correlation analysis in organic chemistry often uses linear free-energy relations for rates or equilibria of reactions, but the term also embraces similar analysis of physical (most commonly spectroscopic) properties and of biological activity.

Corridor A strip of natural habitat that connects two adjacent nature preserves to allow migration of organisms from one place to another.

Cortex The outer layer of a structure. Ground tissue located between the vascular bundles and epidermis of stems and roots.

Cortisol A glucocorticoid secreted by the adrenal cortex.

Cortisone An animal hormone not synthesized by plants.

Cosmic censorship conjecture The conjecture, so far totally undemonstra-ted within the context of general relativity, that all singularities (with the possible exception of the big bang singularity) are accompanied by event horizons which completely surround them at all points in time. That is, problematic issues with the singularity are rendered irrelevant, since no information can ever escape from a black hole's event horizon.

Cosmic rays High-energy nuclear particles apparently originating from outer space.

Cosmological redshift An effect where light emitted from a distant source appears redshifted because of the expansion of spacetime itself.

Cosmopolitan Worldwide in distribution.

Cosmotron A high-energy synchrotron.

Cost of meiosis The reduction in numbers of alleles passed on to subsequent generations as a result of reproducing sexually compared to asexually.

Cost/benefit analysis An evaluation of large-scale public projects by comparing the costs and benefits that accrue from them.

Costa Prominent striated rod in some flagellate protozoa that courses from one of the kinetosomes along the cell surface beneath the recurrent flagellum and undulating membrane.

Costal Pertaining to a rib.

Cotyledon A seed leaf; the first leaf formed in a seed.

Cotylocidia Larva of Aspidobothria.

Coulomb's law The primary law for electrostatics, analogous to Newton's law of universal gravitation. It states that the force between two point charges is proportional to the algebraic product of their respective charges as well as proportional to the inverse square of the distance between them.

Coulomb's law of electrostatics The force between two point charges is directly proportional to the product of their magnitudes and inversely proportional to the square of the distance between them.

Coulomb's law of magnetism The force between two magnetic poles is directly proportional to the strengths of the poles and inversely proportional to the square of their distance apart.

Counteracting osmolyte strategy An osmolyte (ion) that counteracts another ion.

Countercurrent An ocean current that flows directly back into another current; also, in some animals, paired blood vessels containing blood flowing in opposite directions.

Countercurrent exchange mechanism The passive exchange of something between fluids moving in opposite directions past each other.

Counterillumination The emission of light by midwater animals to match the background light.

Countershading Contrasting coloration that helps conceal the animal (e.g., the darkly pigmented top and lightly pigmented bottom of frog embryos).

Couple Two forces of equal magnitude acting in opposite directions in the same plane, but not along the same line.

Courtship behaviour Behaviour related to the attraction of the opposite sex and mating.

Covalent bond A region of relatively high electron density between nuclei which arises at least partly from sharing of electrons and gives rise to an attractive force and characteristic internuclear distance.

Cover crops Plants, such as rye, alfalfa, or clover, that can be planted immediately after harvest to hold and protect the soil.

Coxa, coxopodite The proximal joint of an insect or arachnid leg; in crustaceans, the proximal joint of the protopod.

Coxae The hip.

Coxal glands Excretory organs of arachnids, consisting of a sac, tubule, and opening on the coxa.

Crack Form of purified cocaine with widespread street use.

Crasulacean acid metabolism A variation of the C4 pathway that functions in a number of cacti and succulents; allows for the fixation of carbon dioxide during the night, then in the daytime the carbon dioxide is transferred to the Calvin Cycle.

Creatine phosphate. High-energy phosphate compound found in the muscle of vertebrates and some invertebrates, used to regenerate stores of ATP.

Creeping eruption Skin condition caused by hookworm larvae not able to mature in a given host.

Cremaster Suspender.

Crepuscular Daily cycles with peak activity around dusk and/or dawn.

Crest A region of upward displacement in a transverse wave.

Cretin A human with severe mental, somatic, and sexual retardation resulting from hypothyroidism during early stages of development.

Cricoid A ring, circle.

Crinoidea The class of echinoderms whose members are attached by a stalk of ossicles or are free living. Possess a reduced central disk. Sea lilies and feather stars.

Crista A crest or ridge on a body organ or organelle; a platelike projection formed by the inner membrane of mitochondrion.

Cristae The folded-membrane inner structure of mitochondria.

Critical angle That limiting angle of incidence in the optically denser medium that results in an angle of refraction of 90°.

Critical depth The depth at which photosynthesis equals cell respiration.

Critical factor The single environmental factor closest to a tolerance limit for a given species at a given time.

Critical mass The amount of a particular fissionable material required to make a fission reaction self-sustaining.

Critical micelle concentration (CMC) There is a relatively small range of concentrations separating the limit below which virtually no micelles are detected and the limit above which virtually all additional surfactant molecules form micelles. Many properties of surfactant solutions, if plotted against the concentration, appear to change at a different rate above and below this range. By extrapolating the loci of such a property above and below this range until they intersect, a value may be obtained known as the critical micellization concentration (critical micelle concentration), symbol CM, abbreviation CMC. As values obtained using different properties are not quite identical, the method by which the CMC is determined should be clearly stated.

Critical period A discrete portion of a sensitive period during development, during which the probability for forming and reinforcing the behaviour is greatest.

Critical point The upper limit of the temperature-pressure curve of a substance.

Critical pressure The pressure needed to liquefy a gas at its critical temperature.

Critical temperature The temperature to which a gas must be cooled before it can be liquefied by pressure.

Critical velocity Velocity below which an object moving in a vertical circle will not describe a circular path.

Croplands Lands used to grow crops.

Cropper A deep-sea animal in which the roles of predator and deposit feeder have merged

Crossing-over The exchange of material between homologous chromosomes, during the first meiotic division, resulting in a new combination of genes.

Cross-pollinated Pertaining to a flower having pollen deposited on it from a different flower of another plant.

Crown A molecular entity comprising a monocyclic ligand assembly that contains three or more binding sites held together by covalent bonds and capable of binding a guest in a central (or nearly central) position. The adducts formed are sometimes known as "coronates". The best known members of this group are macrocyclic polyethers, such as "18-crown-6", containing several repeating units -CR_2-CR_2O- (where R is most commonly H), and known as crown ethers.

Crude birth rate The number of births in a year divided by the midyear population.

Crude death rate The number of deaths per thousand persons in a given year; also called crude mortality rate.

Crura Branches of the intestine of a flatworm.

Crust The cool, lightweight, outermost layer of the earth's surface that floats on the soft, pliable underlying layers; similar to the "skin" on a bowl of warm pudding.

Crustacea The subphylum of mandibulate arthropods whose members are characterized by having two pairs of antennae, one pair of mandibles, two pairs of maxillae, and biramous appendages. Crabs, crayfish, lobsters.

Crustaceans (subphylum Crustacea) Arthropods that have two pairs of mandibles.

Cryptand A molecular entity comprising a cyclic or polycyclic assembly of binding sites that contains three or more binding sites held together by covalent bonds, and which defines a molecular cavity in such a way as to bind (and thus "hide" in the cavity) another molecular entity, the guest (a cation, an anion or a neutral species), more strongly than do the separate parts of the assembly (at the same total concentration of binding sites). Corresponding monocyclic ligand assemblies (crowns) are sometimes included in this group, if they can be considered to define a cavity in which a guest can hide. The terms "podand" and "spherand" are used for certain specific ligand assemblies. Coplanar cyclic polydentate ligands, such as porphyrins, are not normally regarded as cryptands.

Cryptic coloration A colour pattern that allows an organism to blend with the surroundings.

Cryptobiotic Living in concealment; refers to insects and other animals that live in secluded situations, such as underground or in wood; also tardigrades and some nematodes, rotifers, and others that survive harsh environmental conditions by assuming for a time a state of very low metabolism.

Cryptogonochorism Separate sexes joined or associated to form the appearance of hermaphroditism.

Cryptomonads (phylum crypto-phyta) Unicellular, eukaryotic members of the phytoplankton that have two flagella and no skeleton.

Cryptoniscus Intermediate, free-swimming larval stage of the isopod suborder Epicaridea, developing after microniscus; attaches to definitive host.

Cryptozoite Preerythrocytic schizont of Plasmodium spp.

Crystal A solid that consists of a regular pattern of molecules.

Crystalline style A proteinaceous, rodlike structure in the digestive tract of a bivalve (Mollusca) that rotates against a gastric shield and releases digestive enzymes.

Crystallized song The final stage in song development, when the song variation (repertoire) has decreased and become more fixed.

Ctene Bands of cilia found on the body surfaces of ctenophores.

Ctenidia Comb-like structures, especially gills of molluscs; also applied to comb plates of Ctenophora.

Ctenidium Series of stout, peglike spines on the head (genal ctenidium) and first thoracic tergite (pronotal ctenidium) of many fleas.

Ctenoid scales Thin, overlapping dermal scales of the more advanced fishes; exposed posterior margins have fine, toothlike spines.

Ctenophora The phylum of animals whose members are characterized by biradial symmetry, diploblastic organization, colloblasts, and meridionally arranged comb rows. Comb jellies.

Cubozoa The class of cnidarians whose members have prominent cuboidal medusae with tentacles that hang from the corner of the medusa. Small polyp, gametes gastrodermal in origin. Chironex.

Culm Hollow, jointed stem of grasses.

Cultivar Abbreviation for cultivated variety of plant.

Cultural eutrophication An increase in biological productivity and ecosystem succession caused by human activities.

Cupula Small inverted cup-like structure housing another structure; gelatinous matrix covering hair cells in lateral line and equilibrium organs.

Curare A variety of poisonous plant extracts from the bark, roots, stems, and tendrils of several woody lianas, including Chondodendron tomentosum.

Curie The quantity of any radioactive nuclide that has a disintegration rate of 3.7×10^{10} becquerels.

Curie constant A characteristic constant, dependent on the material in question, which indicates the proportionality between its susceptibility and its thermodynamic temperature.

Curie-Weiss law A more general form of Curie's law, which states that the susceptibility, χ, of a paramagnetic substance is related to its thermodynamic temperature T by the equation.

Currency The resource that is being maximized in an optimality model; usually assumed to be energy in an optimal foraging model.

Current The time rate at which charge passes through a circuit element or through a fixed place in a conducting wire, $I = dq/dt$.

Current sensitivity Current per unit scale division of an electric meter.

Current, electrical The flow (usually, the motion through a wire) of electrical charge (referred to as charge carriers). While current is simply the flow of charge, in general, people also refer to AC and DC. Any moving charge is a current; there are a variety of convenient ways to move a charge. AC (alterna-ting current) is what comes from the outlets in your house. This is where the electrical charges oscillate back and forth rather than flow throughout the wires. DC (direct current) is what comes from batteries; this is where the electrical charges flow through the wire from one battery terminal to the other battery terminal. (Notice that the notion "AC current" is redundant, because "AC current" means "Alternating Current current") Although in a wire, it is a flow of electrons which causes the current, technically, the current is the flow of positive charge. It can be shown that positive charge moving to the right has the same effect as negative charge moving to the left. Both of these describe a current to the right. Electrical current is expressed in units of ampere which were named for Andre Marie Ampere.

Curtin-Hammett principle In a chemical reaction that yields one product (X) from one conformational isomer (A') and a different product (Y) from another conformational isomer (A") (and provided these two isomers are rapidly interconvertible relative to the rate of product formation, whereas the products do not undergo interconversion) the product composition is not in direct proportion to the relative concentrations of the conformational isomers in the substrate; it is controlled only by the difference in standard free energies (dG) of the respective transition states. It is also true that the product composition is formally related to the relative concentrations of the conformational isomers A' and A" (i.e. the conformational equilibrium constant) and the respective rate constants of their reactions; these parameters are generally - though not invariably - unknown.

Cutaneous Pertaining to the skin (e.g., a skin infection).

Cutaneous respiration Exchange of gases across thin, moist surfaces of the skin. Also cutaneous exchange or integumentary exchange.

Cut-off bias The smallest negative grid voltage, for a given plate voltage, that causes a vacuum tube to cease to conduct.

Cuticle Anoncellular, protective, organic layer secreted by the external epithelium (hypodermis) of many invertebrates; refers to the epidermis or skin in higher animals. Waterproof layer of cutin on leaves and nonwoody stems.

Cuticulin Protein component of arthropod exoskeletons.

Cutin Waxy material secreted by epidermal cells.

Cyanobacteria A large group of bacteria that carry out oxygenic photosynthesis using a system like that present in photosynthetic eucaryotes.

Cycle A complete vibration.

Cyclic photophosphorylation The formation of ATP when light energy is used to move electrons cyclically through an electron transport chain during photosynthesis; only photosystem I participates.

Cycloaddition A reaction in which two unsaturated molecules (or moieties within a molecule) join, forming a ring.

Cycloalkanes Cycloalkanes are cyclic saturated hydrocarbons containing a ring of carbon atoms joined by single bonds. They have the general formula C_nH_{2n}, for example cyclohexane, C_6H_{12}. In general, they behave like the alkanes but are rather less reactive.

Cyst A general term used for a specialized microbial cell enclosed in a wall. Cysts are formed by protozoa and a few bacteria. They may be dormant, resistant structures formed in response to adverse conditions or reproductive cysts that are a normal stage in the life cycle.

Cystic fibrosis An inherited disease that results in abnormal mucus secretion that produces severe respiratory problems, incomplete digestion and increased salt secretion in sweat.

Cytochromes Heme proteins that carry electrons, usually as members of electron transport chains.

Cytokine A general term for nonantibody proteins, released by a cell in response to inducing stimuli, which are mediators that influence other cells, and produced by lymphocytes, mono-cytes, macrophages, and other cells.

Cytomegalovirus inclusion disease An infection caused by the cytomegalovirus and marked by nuclear inclusion bodies in enlarged infected cells.

Cytopathic effect The observable change that occurs in cells as a result of viral replication. Examples include ballooning, binding together, clustering, or even death of the cultured cells.

Cytoplasmic matrix The protoplasm of a cell that lies within the plasma membrane and outside any other organelles. In bacteria it is the substance between the cell membrane and the nucleoid.

Cytoproct Site on a protozoan where undigestible matter is expelled.

Cytosine A pyrimidine 2-oxy-4-aminopyrimidine found in nucleosides, nucleotides, and nucleic acids.

Cytoskeleton A fibrous network made of proteins that contributes to the structure and internal organization of eukaryotic cells. The cytoskeleton is found in the cytoplasm of cells and has three major fiber types: microfilaments made of actin protein, intermediate filaments made of various kinds of proteins, and microtubules made of tubulin. The three fiber types serve different functions; actin filaments are often associated to changes in cell size and structure, contractility such as in muscle cells, and cell division, growth and motility. Microtubules are major filaments for internal transport and movement of chromosomes and organelles during cell division. Intermediate filaments contribute to flexibility, elasticity, and stiffness of cells and tissues.

Cytostome A permanent site in the protozoan ciliate body through which food is ingested.

Cytotoxic T (TC) cell A cell that is capable of recognizing virus-infected cells through the major histocompatability molecules and developing into an activated cell that destroys the infected cells.

Cytotoxic T lymphocyte (CTL) The activated T cell that can attack and destroy virus-infected cells, tumor cells, and foreign cells.

Cytotoxin A toxin or antibody that has a specific toxic action upon cells; cytotoxins are named according to the cell for which they are specific.

Damping The dissipation of a vibration's energy into heat energy, or the frictional force that causes the loss of energy.

Dane particle A 42 nm spherical particle that is one of three that are seen in hepatitis B virus infections. The Dane particle is the complete virion.

Dark matter Matter that is in space but is not visible to us because it emits no radiation by which to observe it. The motion of stars around the centers of their galaxies implies that about 90% of the matter in a typical galaxy is dark. Physicists speculate that there is also dark matter between the galaxies but this is harder to verify.

Dark reactivation The excision and replacement of thymine dimers in DNA that occurs in the absence of light.

Dark-field microscopy Microscopy in which the specimen is brightly illuminated while the background is dark.

Darwinian fitness The true measure of evolutionary change of an organism. Darwinian fitness refers to the numerical advantage of having offspring. The individual with the most offspring has the higher fitness. The reasons can be chance or natural selection and are not important to measure fitness. It is often equated with survival of the fittest, which is often meant to be the strongest or best adapted individual. However, this interpretation is wrong, if it does not explain why a certain individual has the most offspring. Overall, the genetic variation of the individuals with the most offspring will dominate the genepool of a population. The change in genetic variability in a population from generation to generation is the true measure of (micro-) evolution.

Dative bond A dipolar bond.

Daughterless carp Carp which only produce male fish. This slows the growth of the population with the aim of reducing overall carp numbers. Since all fish embryos start life as males, the technology works by silencing or switching off the gene responsible for stimulating the development of female embryos.

Deamination The removal of amino groups from amino acids.

Death phase The decrease in viable microorganisms that occurs after the completion of growth in a batch culture.

Decay Disintegration of atomic nuclei resulting in the emission of alpha or beta particles (usually with gamma radiation). Also the exponential decrease in radioactivity of a material as nuclear disintegrations take place and more stable nuclei are formed.

Decibel [dB] The level of noise is measured objectively using a Sound Level Meter. This instrument has been specifically developed to mimic the operation of the human ear. The human ear responds to minute pressure variations in the air. These pressure variations can be likened to the ripples on the surface of water but of course cannot be seen. The pressure variations in the air cause the eardrum to vibrate and this is heard as sound in the brain. The stronger the pressure variations, the louder the sound is heard.

The range of pressure variations associated with everyday living may span over a range of a million to one. On the top range may be the sound of a jet engine and on the bottom of the range may be the sound of a pin dropping.

Instead of expressing pressure in units ranging from a million to one, it is found convenient to condense this range to a scale 0 to 120 and give it the units of decibels. The following are examples of the decibel readings of every day sounds;

0dB the faintest sound we can hear.

30dB a quiet library or in a quiet location in the country.

45dB typical office space. Ambience in the city at night.

60dB Restaurent at lunch time.

70dB the sound of a car passing on the street.

80dB loud music played at home.

90dB the sound of a truck passing on the street.

100dB the sound of a rock band.

115dB limit of sound permitted in industry.

120dB deafening.

Decibel scale A nonlinear scale of loudness based on the ratio of the intensity level of a sound to the intensity at the threshold of hearing.

Decimal reduction time The time required to kill 90% of the microorganisms or spores in a sample at a specified temperature.

Decommissioning Removal of a facility (e.g. reactor) from service, also the subsequent actions of safe storage, dismantling and making the site available for unrestricted use.

Decomposer An organism that breaks down complex materials into simpler ones, including the release of simple inorganic products. Often a decomposer such as an insect or earthworm physically reduces the size of substrate particles.

Defensin Specific peptides produced by neutrophils that permeabilize the outer and inner membranes of certain microorganisms, thus killing them.

Defined medium Culture medium made with components of known composition.

Degenerate Not a moral judgment but an adjective that describes multiple states that amount to the same thing: different triplet combinations of nucleotide bases that code for the same amino acid, for example.

Degradation A gradual wearing down or away. Also with regard to soil a lowering of the nutrient content and associated ability to support continuing crop growth.

Degree of polymerisation Degree of polymerisation is the number of monomeric units in a macromolecule or an oligomer molecule.

Delta agent A defective RNA virus that is transmitted as an infectious agent, but cannot cause disease unless the individual is also infected with the hepatitis B virus. See hepatitis D.

Delta-proteobacteria One of the five subgroups of proteobacteria, each with distinctive 16S rRNA sequences. Chemoorganotrophic bacteria that usually are either predators on other bacteria or anaerobes that generate sulphide from sulphate and sulphite.

Denaturation 1. A change in the shape of an enzyme that destroys its activity; the term is also applied to changes in nucleic-acid shape.

2. Dramatic change in conformation of a protein or nucleic acid caused by heating or by exposure to chemicals and usually resulting in the loss of biological function.

Dendrite Extension of a nerve cell, typically branched and relatively short, that receives stimuli from other nerve cells.

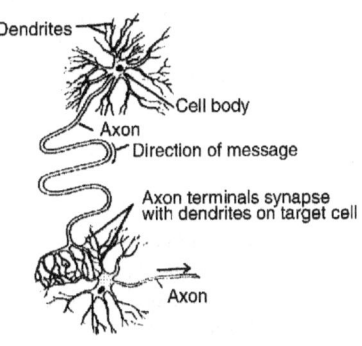

Figure A Dendrite

Dendritic cell An antigen-presenting cell that has long membrane extensions resembling the dendrites of neurons. These cells are found in the lymph nodes, spleen, and thymus; skin; and other tissues. Express MHC class II and B7 costimulatory molecules and thus are efficient presenters of antigens to T-helper cells.

Dendrogram A treelike diagram that is used to graphically summarize mutual similarities and relationships between organisms.

Denitrification The reduction of nitrate to gas products, primarily nitrogen gas, during anaerobic respiration.

Density In the most common usage, density (ρ) is mass density or mass per unit volume.

$\rho = m/V$

More generally, the amount of some quantity. Divided by a length, area, or volume.

Relative density is the ratio of the density of a substance to the density of some reference substance. For liquids or solids, it is the ratio of the density to the density of water at 4°C. This quantity was formerly called specific gravity.

Density of states The density of electronic states per unit energy and per unit volume.

Dental plaque (plak) A thin film on the surface of teeth consisting of bacteria embedded in a matrix of bacterial polysaccharides, salivary glycoproteins, and other substances.

Deoxyribonucleic acid The nucleic acid that constitutes the genetic material of all cellular organisms. It is a polynucleotide composed of deoxyribonucleotides connected by phosphodiester bonds.

Depleted uranium Uranium having less than the natural 0.7% U-235. As a by-product of enrichment in the fuel cycle it generally has 0.25-0.30% U-235, the rest being U-238. Can be blended with highly-enriched uranium to make reactor fuel.

Depolarization A process of changing the membrane potential from negative to more positive values. The sign of the potential refers to the inside of the cell. Depolarization causes action potentials in neurons and muscle cells. Depolarization is the result of inward currents carried by Na^+ and Ca^{++} ions.

Dermatomycosis A fungal infection of the skin; the term is a general term that comprises the various forms of tinea, and it is sometimes used to specifically refer to athlete's foot.

Dermatophyte A fungus parasitic on the skin.

Desensitization To make a sensitized or hypersensitive individual insensitive or nonreactive to a sensitizing agent.

Desert crust A crust formed by microbial binding of sand grains in the surface zone of desert soil; crust formation primarily involves cyanobacteria.

Designer foods Foods that are enriched with nutraceuticals, antioxidants, and secondary metabolites to improve the physical performance of the body.

Desmosome Specialized cell-cell junction, usually formed between two epithelial cells, characterized by dense plaques of protein into which intermediate filaments in the two adjoining cells insert.

Destructive interference The condition in which two waves arriving at the same point at the same time out of phase add amplitudes to create zero total disturbance.

Detergent An organic molecule, other than a soap, that serves as a wetting agent and emulsifier; it is normally used as cleanser, but some may be used as antimicrobial agents.

Dielectric constant

Deuterium "Heavy hydrogen", a stable isotope having one proton and one neutron in the nucleus. It occurs in nature as 1 atom to 6500 atoms of normal hydrogen.

Deuteromycetes In some classification systems, the deuteromycetes or Fungi Imperfecti are a class of fungi. These organisms either lack a sexual stage or it has not yet been discovered.

Dew Condensation of water vapour into droplets of liquid on surfaces.

Dew point temperature The temperature at which condensation begins.

Diamagnetism In diamagnetism the magnetization is in the opposite direction to that of applied field, i.e. Susceptibility is negative. It results from changes induced in the orbits of electrons in the atoms of a substance by the applied field, the direction of the change opposing the applied flux.

Diamondoid As used in this volume, this term describes structures that resemble diamond in a broad sense: strong, stiff structures containing dense, three-dimensional networks of covalent bonds, formed chiefly from first and second row atoms with a valence of three or more. Many of the most useful diamondoid structures will in fact be rich in tetrahedrally coordinated carbon. Diamondoid is used more narrowly elsewhere in the literature.

Diatomic molecule. A molecule that contains only two atoms. All of the noninert gases occur as diatomic molecules; e. g. hydrogen, oxygen, nitrogen, fluorine, and chlorine are H_2, O_2, N_2, F_2, and C_{12}, respectively.

Diatoms Algal protists with siliceous cell walls called frustules. They constitute a substantial subfraction of the phytoplankton.

Diauxic growth A biphasic growth pattern or response in which a microorganism, when exposed to two nutrients, initially uses one of them for growth and then alters its metabolism to make use of the second.

Diazo compounds Diazo compounds are compounds having the divalent diazo group, $=N^+=N^-$, attached to a carbon atom. The term includes azo compounds, diazonium compounds, and also such compounds as diazomethane, $CH_2=N_2$.

Dielectric constant Dielectric constant or permittivity (ε) is an index of the ability of a substance to attenuate the transmission of an electrostatic force from one charged body to another. The lower the value, the greater the attenuation. The standard measurement apparatus utilizes a vacuum whose dielectric constant is 1. In reference to this, various materials interposed between the charged terminal have the following value at 20°C:

Air 1.00058

glass 3

benzene 2.3

acetic acid 6.2

ammonia 15.5

ethanol 25
glycerol 56
water 81

The exceptionally high value for water accounts for its unique behaviour as a solvent and in electrolytic solutions. Dielectric constant values decrease as the temperature rises.

Dienes Dienes are unsaturated organic compounds that contain two fixed double bonds between carbon atoms. Dienes in which the two double-bond units are linked by one single bond are termed conjugated.

Differential interference contrast (DIC) microscope A light microscope that employs two beams of plane polarized light. The beams are combined after passing through the specimen and their interference is used to create the image.

Differential media Culture media that distinguish between groups of microorganisms based on differences in their growth and metabolic products.

Differential staining procedures Staining procedures that divide bacteria into separate groups based on staining properties.

Differentiation A process of development whereby properties of a cell or tissue become specialised for its particular task.

Diffraction The behaviour of a wave when it encounters an obstacle or a nonuniformity in its medium; in general, diffraction causes a wave to bend around obstacles and make patterns of strong and weak waves radiating out beyond the obstacle.

Diffuse reflection Light rays reflected in many random directions, as opposed to the parallel rays reflected from a perfectly smooth surface such as a mirror.

Diffusely adhering *E. coli* (DAEC) DAEC strains of *E. coli* adhere over the entire surface of epithelial cells and usually cause diarrheal disease in immunologically naive and malnourished children.

Diffusion coefficient D The diffusion coefficient D describes the relation-ship between a concentration gradient DC/Dx and the flow of matter per unit area.

Diffusion Diffusion is the spontaneous mixing of one substance with another when in contact or separated by a permeable membrane. Diffusion is a result of the random motions of their component atoms, molecules, ions, or other particles. Diffusion occurs most readily in gases, less so in liquids, and least in solids. The rate of diffusion is proportional to the concentration of the substance and increases with temperature. The theoretical principles are stated in Fick's laws.

Dikaryotic stage In fungi, having pairs of nuclei within cells or compartments. Each cell contains two separate haploid nuclei, one from each parent.

Dinoflagellate An algal protist characterized by two flagella used in swimming in a spinning pattern. Many are bioluminescent and an important part of marine phytoplankton, some also are important marine pathogens.

Diphtheria An acute, highly contagious childhood disease that generally affects the membranes of the throat and less frequently the nose. It is caused by *Corynebacterium diphtheriae*.

Dipicolinic acid A substance present at high concentrations in the bacterial endospore. It is thought to contribute to the endospore's heat resistance.

Diplococcus A pair of cocci.

Diploid The presence of two chromosomes of a pair in a cell.

Dipolar bond A covalent bond in which one atom supplies both bonding electrons, and the other atom supplies an empty orbital in which to share them. Also termed as dative bond.

Dipole Dipole is a pair of separated opposite electric charges. Electric dipole is an assemblage of atoms or subatomic particles having equal electric charges of opposite sign separated by a finite distance. In the case of HCl, the electrons are attracted towards the more electronegative chlorine atom.

Dipole moment Electric dipole moment (μ) is the product of the positive charge and the distance between the charges. Dipole moments are often stated in debyes; The SI unit is the coulomb metre. In a diatomic molecule, such as HCl, the dipole moment is a measure of the polar nature of the bond; i.e. the extent to which the average electron charges is displaced towards one atom (in the case of HCl, the electrons are attracted towards the more electronegative chlorine atom). In a polyatomic molecule, the dipole moment is the vector sum of the dipole moments of the individual bonds. In a symmetrical molecule, such as tetrafluoromethane (CF_4) there is no overall dipole moment, although the individual C-F bonds are polar.

Direct current An electrical current that always moves in one direction.

Direct proportion When two variables increase or decrease together in the same ratio.

Directed- or adaptive mutation A mutation that seems to be chosen so the organism can better adapt to its surroundings.

Disaccharides Disaccharides are compounds in which two monosaccharides are joined by a glycosidic bond. For example, sucrose comprises one glucose molecule and one fructose molecule bonded together.

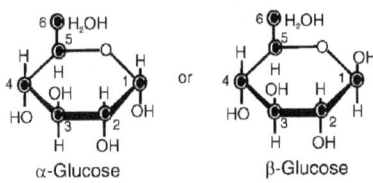

Figure Disaccharides

Disease A deviation or interruption of the normal structure or

function of any part of the body that is manifested by a characteristic set of symptoms and signs.

Disease syndrome A set of signs and symptoms that are characteristic of the disease.

Disinfectant An agent, usually chemical, that disinfects; normally, it is employed only with inanimate objects.

Disinfection The killing, inhibition, or removal of microorganisms that may cause disease. It usually refers to the treatment of inanimate objects with chemicals.

Dispersion The effect of spreading colours of light into a spectrum with a material that has an index of refraction that varies with wavelength.

Displacement The change in the position of an object in a particular direction is called displacement. Displacement may also be defined as the shortest distance between the initial and final position of a moving body. It is a vector quantity.

Dissimilatory nitrate reduction The process in which some bacteria use nitrate as the electron acceptor at the end of their electron transport chain to produce ATP. The nitrate is reduced to nitrite or nitrogen gas.

Dissimilatory reduction The use of a substance as an electron acceptor in energy generation. The acceptor is reduced but not incorporated into organic matter during biosynthetic processes.

Dissociation Dissociation is the process by which a chemical combination breaks up into simpler constituents as a result of either added energy, or the effect of a solvent on a dissolved polar compound. It may occur in the gaseous, solid, or liquid state, or in solution.

An example of dissociation is the reversible reaction of hydrogen iodide at high temperatures.

$$2HI(g) \rightleftharpoons H_2(g) + I_2(g)$$

The term dissociation is also applied to ionisation reactions of acids and bases in water.

Dissociation constant 1. Dissociation constant is a constant whose numerical value depends on the equilibrium between the undissociated and dissociated forms of a molecule. A higher value indicates greater dissociation.

The term dissociation is also applied to ionisation reactions of acids and bases in water. For example

$$HCN + H_2O \rightleftharpoons H_2O^+ + CN^-$$

Which is often regarded as a straightforward dissociation into ions.

$$HCN \rightleftharpoons H^+ + CN^-$$

The equilibrium constant of such a dissociation is called the acid dissociation constant or acidity constant, given by

$$K_a = \frac{[H^+].[CN^-]}{[HCN]}$$

The concentration of water [H_2O] can be taken as constant.

Similarly, for a base, the equilibrium

$$NH_2 \rightleftharpoons NH_4^+ + OH^-$$

is also a dissociation; with the base dissociation constant or basicity constant, given by

$$K_b = \frac{[NH_4^+].[OH^-]}{[NH_3]}$$

K_a (K_b) is a measure of the strength of the acid (base).

2. For systems in which ligands of a particular kind bind to a receptor in a solvent there will be a characteristic frequency with which existing ligand-receptor complexes dissociate as a result of thermal excitation, and a characteristic frequency with which empty receptors bind ligands as a result of Brownian encounters, forming new complexes. The frequency of binding is proportional to the concentration of the ligand in solution. The dissociation constant is the magnitude of the ligand concentration at which the probability that the receptor will be found occupied is 1/2.

Distance The actual length of the path travelled by a body irrespective of the direction is called the distance travelled. It is a scalar quantity.

Distillation Distillation is the process of boiling a liquid and condensing and collecting the vapour. The liquid collected is the distillate. The usual purpose of distillation is purification or separation of the components of a mixture. This is possible because the composition of the vapour is usually different from that of liquid mixture from which it is obtained. Gasoline, kerosene, fuel oil, and lubricating oil are produced from petroleum by distillation.

Diurnal oxygen shifts The changes in oxygen levels that occur in waters when algae produce and use oxygen on a cyclic basis during day and night.

DNA (deoxyribonucleic acid) A large molecule that contains all genetic information in the cell.

DNA carriers 1. Substances or particles that can transfer genes into a cell. These include viruses, liposomes and artificial chromosomes that can transport large amounts of DNA.

2. An individual who carriers one copy of a recessive gene for a hereditary condition.

DNA fingerprinting / profiling A genetic tool used to compare and contrast DNA sequences using electrophoresis. Profiling is used in forensic science and to help in establishing parentage.

DNA ligase An enzyme that joins two DNA fragments together through the formation of a new phosphodiester bond.

DNA microarrays (DNA chips) Solid supports that have DNA attached in highly organized arrays and are normally used to evaluate gene expression.

DNA polymerase 1. An enzyme that synthesizes new DNA using a parental DNA strand as a template.

2. An enzyme that makes DNA in the presence of a DNA primer and a mixture of the four nucleotides.

DNA primer A short stretch of DNA needed to start the DNA polymerase reaction.

DNA vaccine A vaccine that contains DNA which encodes antigenic proteins. It is injected directly into the muscle; the DNA is taken up by the muscle cells and encoded protein antigens are synthesized. This produces both humoral and cell-mediated responses.

Domains 1. Compact, self-folding, structurally independent regions of proteins (usually around 100-300 amino acids in length); large proteins may have two or more domains connected by less structured stretches of polypeptide. In the antibody molecule, they are the loops, along with about 25 amino acids on each side, that form compact, globular sections.

2. The primary taxonomic groups above the kingdom level; all living organisms may be placed in one of three domains.

Dominant gene or allele Most genes in the human body come in pairs. The pair's members can have codes which match each other or be different. If they are different, one is usually dominant, the other is described as 'recessive'. This means that it is this gene which is expressed in the phenotype.

Dominant When referring to genes, a dominant gene is one that almost always will be expressed and lead to a specific physical characteristic. A dominant trait is the one that will be expressed in individuals that are both homozygous and heterozygous.

Donor An atom which is likely to give off one or more electrons when placed in a crystal.

Doppler effect The change in the wavelength of sound or light waves caused when the object emitting the waves moves toward or away from the observer; also called Doppler Shift. In sound, the Doppler Effect causes a shift in sound frequency or pitch. In light, an object's visible colour is altered and its spectrum is shifted toward the blue region of the spectrum for objects moving toward the observer and toward the red for objects moving away.

Dose The energy absorbed by tissue from ionising radiation. One gray is one joule per kg, but this is adjusted for the effect of different kinds of radiation, and thus the sievert is the unit of dose equivalent used in setting exposure standards.

Double bond Two atoms sharing electrons as in a single bond may also share electrons in an orbital with a node passing through the two atoms. This adds a second, weaker bonding interaction; the combination is termed as double bond. A twisting motion that forces the nodal plane at one atom to become perpendicular to the nodal plane on the other atom eliminates the overlap between the atomic orbitals, destroying the pi bond. The energy required to do this creates a large barrier to rotation about the bond.

Double diffusion agar assay An immunodiffusion reaction in which both antibody and antigen diffuse through agar to form stable immune complexes, which can be observed visually.

Double helix Twin, parallel spirals which form the backbone of DNA. This backbone is formed from alternating sugar and phosphate groups.

Doublet The electronic state of a molecule having one unpaired spin is termed as doublet. This term is derived from spectroscopy: an unpaired spin can be either up or down with respect to a magnetic field, and these states have different energy, resulting in field-dependent pairs, or doublets, of spectral lines.

Down quark (d) The second flavour of quark, with electric charge -1/3.

Down's syndrome A genetic disability in which characteristic physical features are accompanied by learning difficulty. The disorder is the consequence of a chromosome abnormality and is often called trisomy-21 because most commonly there is an additional copy of chromosome 21 present.

DPT (diphtheria-pertussis-tetanus) vaccine A vaccine containing three antigens that is used to immunize people against diphtheria, pertussis or whooping cough, and tetanus.

Drift Motion of carriers caused by an electric field.

Driving force 1. A terminology used in thermodynamics expressing the availability of energy to 'drive' a process such as mechanical work or chemical synthesis. Driving forces exist where a potential gradient exist. A potential gradient can be in form of a temperature gradient causing heat to flow, an electrical gradient causing electrons or ions to flow, or a concentration gradient causing diffusion.

2. An external force that pumps energy into a vibrating system.

Droplet nuclei Small particles that represent what is left from the evaporation of larger particles called droplets.

Duality The concept that electrons behave both as classical particles and as waves depending on how they are observed.

Duchenne muscular dystrophy A single gene disorder which affects 1 in 5000 boys. The condition produces progressive weakness of proximal muscles, beginning in early childhood. Most affected children become chairbound before adulthood. The inheritance is X-linked i.e. it is transmitted from heterozygous females who are unaffected and are described as carriers, to sons who are affected, and to daughters who, like their mothers, are unaffected carriers.

Early mRNA Messenger RNA produced early in a virus infection that codes for proteins needed to take over the host cell and manufac-ture viral nucleic acids.

Ebola virus hemorrhagic fever An acute infection caused by a virus that produces varying degrees of hemorrhage, shock, and sometimes death.

Ebullioscopic constant Ebullioscopic constant (E_b) is the constant that expresses the amount by which the boiling point T_b of a solvent is raised by a nondissociating solute, through the relation

$$\Delta t_b = E_b\, b$$

Where b is the molality of the solute.

Echo A reflected sound that can be distinguished from the original sound, which usually arrives 0.1 sec or more after the original sound.

Eclipse period The initial part of the latent period in which infected host bacteria do not contain any complete virions.

Eco centrism A view that considers the whole environment or ecosphere as being important and deserving of consideration, not just that of organisms such as animals and humans. It states that all elements of the environment have worth and should be valued and cared for.

Ecosystem A self-regulating biological community and its associated physical and chemical environment.

Ectomycorrhizal Referring to a mutualistic association between fungi and plant roots in which the fungus surrounds the root tip with a sheath.

Ectoparasite A parasite that lives on the surface of its host.

Ectoplasm The outer stiffer portion or region of the cytoplasm in a protozoan, which may be differentiated in texture from the inner portion or endoplasm.

Ectosymbiosis A type of symbiosis in which one organism remains outside of the other organism.

Effacing lesion The type of lesion caused by enteropathogenic strains of *E. coli* (EPEC) when the bacteria attach to and destroy the brush border of intestinal epithelial cells. The term AE *E. coli* is now used to designate true EPEC strains that are an important cause of diarrhea in children from developing countries and in traveller's diarrhea.

Electrical energy

Effective mass In a vibrating system, a particular vibrational mode can be described as a harmonic oscillator with some mass and stiffness. Given some measure of vibrational amplitude, there exists a unique choice of mass and stiffness that yields the correct values for both frequency and energy; these are the effective mass and effective stiffness.

Efflorescent Efflorescence; effloroscing. Efflorescent substances lose water of crystallization to the air. The loss of water changes the crystal structure, often producing a powdery crust.

Ehrlichiosis A tick-borne rickettsial disease caused by *Ehrlichia chaffeensis*. Once inside leukocytes, a nonspecific illness develops that resembles Rocky Mountain spotted fever.

Elastic An object behaves elastically if it returns to its original shape after a force is applied and then removed. In an elastic system, the internal potential energy is a function of shape alone, independent of past forces and deformations.

Elastic strain An adjustment to stress in which materials recover their original shape after a stress is released.

Electric charge Charge. A property used to explain attractions and repulsions between certain objects. Two types of charge are possible: negative and positive. Objects with different charge attract; objects with the same charge repel each other.

Electric circuit Consists of a voltage source that maintains an electrical potential, a continuous conducting path for a current to follow, and a device where work is done by the electrical potential; a switch in the circuit is used to complete or interrupt the conducting path.

Electric current The flow of electric charge electric field force field produced by an electrical charge.

Electric dipole An object that has an imbalance between positive charge on one side and negative charge on the other; an object that will experience a torque in an electric field.

Electric field The force per unit charge exerted on a test charge at a given point in space.

Electric field lines A map of an electric field representing the direction of the force that a test charge would experience; the direction of an electric field shown by lines of force.

Electric generator A mechanical device that uses wire loops rotating in a magnetic field to produce electromagnetic induction in order to generate electricity.

Electric potential energy Potential energy due to the position of a charge near other charges.

Electrical conductors Materials that have electrons that are free to move throughout the material; for example, metals.

Electrical energy A form of energy from electromagnetic interactions;

one of five forms of energy-mechanical, chemical, radiant, electrical, and nuclear.

Electrical force A fundamental force that results from the interaction of electrical charge and is billions and billions of times stronger than the gravitational force.

Electrical insulators Electrical nonconductors, or materials that obstruct the flow of electric current.

Electrical nonconductors Materials that have electrons that are not moved easily within the material-for example, rubber; electrical nonconductors are also called electrical insulators.

Electrical resistance The property of opposing or reducing electric current.

Electrical resistivity Electrical resistivity (ρ) is electric field strength divided by current density when there is no electromotive force in the conductor. Resistivity is an intrinsic property of a material. For a conductor of uniform cross section with area A and length L, and whose resistance is R, the resistivity is given by

$$\rho = R\frac{A}{l}$$

The SI unit is Ωm.

Electro negativity The comparative ability of atoms of an element to attract bonding electrons.

Electrochemical gradient Driving force that causes an ion to move across a membrane due to the combined influence of a difference in its concentration on the two sides of the membrane and the electrical charge difference across the membrane.

Electrochemical series Electrochemical series is a series of chemical elements arranged in order of their standard electrode potentials. The hydrogen electrode

$$H^+(aq) + e^- \rightleftarrows 1/2H_2(g)$$

is taken as having zero electrode potential. An electrode potential is, by definition, a reduction potential.

Elements that have a greater tendency than hydrogen to lose electrons to their solution are taken as electropositive; those that gain electrons from their solution are below hydrogen in the series and are called electronegative.

The series shows the order in which metals replace one another from their salts; electropositive metals will replace hydrogen from acids.

Electrode potential Electrode potential is defined as the potential of a cell consisting of the electrode in question acting as a cathode and the standard hydrogen electrode acting as an anode. Reduction always takes place at the cathode, and oxidation at the anode. According to the IUPAC convention, the term electrode potential is reserved exclusively to describe half-reactions written as reductions. The sign of the half-cell in question determines the sign of an electrode potential when it is coupled to a standard hydrogen

Electromagnetic waves

electrode.

Electrode potential is defined by measuring the potential relative to a standard hydrogen half cell.

$H_2(g) \rightleftharpoons 2H^+(aq) + 2e^-$

The convention is to designate the cell so that the oxidized form is written first. For example

$Pt(s)|H_2(g)|H^+(aq)||Zn^{2+}(aq)|Zn(s)$

The e.m.f. of this cell is

$E.m.f. = E_{right} - E_{left}$

By convention, at $p(H_2) = 101325$ Pa and $a(H^+) = 1.00$, the potential of the standard hydrogen electrode is 0.000 V at all temperatures. As a consequence of this definition, any potential developed in a galvanic cell consisting of a standard hydrogen electrode and some other electrode is attributed entirely to the other electrode

$E.m.f. = E(Zn^{2+}/Zn)$

Electrolysis Electrolysis is the decomposition of a substance as a result of passing an electric current between two electrodes immersed in the sample.

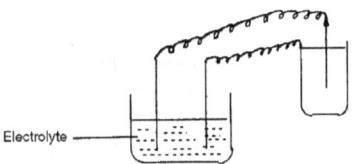

Figure Electrolysis

Electrolyte Water solution of ionic substances that conducts an electric current.

Electromagnet A magnet formed by a solenoid that can be turned on and off by turning the current on and off.

Electromagnetic force A fundamental force that governs all interactions among electrical charges and magnetism. Essentially, all charged particles attract oppositely charged particles and repel identically charged particles. Similarly, opposite poles of magnets attract and like magnetic poles repel.

Electromagnetic induction Process in which current is induced by moving a loop of wire in a magnetic field or by changing the magnetic field.

Electromagnetic interaction The interaction due to electric charge; this includes magnetic interactions.

Electromagnetic radiation Radiation that travels through vacuous space at the speed of light and propagates by the interplay of oscillating electric and magnetic fields. This radiation has a wavelength and a frequency.

Electromagnetic spectrum The entire range of all the various kinds or wavelengths of electromagnetic radiation, including gamma rays, x-rays, ultraviolet, optical, infrared, and radio waves.

Electromagnetic waves The waves which are due to oscillating electrical and magnetic fields and do not need any material medium for their propagation are called electro-magnetic waves. These waves can, however, travel through material medium also. Light waves, radio waves are examples of electro-magnetic waves. All electro-magnetic waves travel in vacuum with a speed of 3×10^8 m/s.

Electromagnetism The science dealing with the physical relationship between electricity and magnetism. The principle of an electromagnet, a magnet generated by electrical current flow, is based on this phenomenon.

Electromotive force Electromotive force is the difference in electric potential that exists between two dissimilar electrodes immersed in the same electrolyte or otherwise connected by ionic conductors.

Electron acceptor Atom or molecule that takes up electrons readily, thereby gaining an electron and becoming reduced.

Electron Electron is discovered by J.J. Thompson in 1896. The electron is an elementary particle with a negative electric charge of $(1.602\ 189\ 2 \pm 0.000\ 004\ 6) \times 10^{-19}$ C and a mass of 1/1837 that of a proton, equivalent to $(9.109\ 534 \pm 0.000\ 047) \times 10^{-31}$ kg. Electrons are arranged in from one to seven shells around the nucleus; the maximum number of electrons in each shell is strictly limited by the laws of physics ($2n^2$). The outer shells are not always filled: sodium has two electrons in the first shell ($2 \times 1^2 = 2$), eight in the second ($2 \times 2^2 = 8$), and only one in the third ($2 \times 3^2 = 18$). A single electron in the outer shell may be attracted into an incomplete shell of another element, leaving the original atom with a net positive charge. Valence electrons are those that can be captured by or shared with another atom.

Electrons can be removed from the atoms by heat, light, electric energy, or bombardment with high-energy particles. Decaying radioactive nuclei spontaneously emits free electrons, called β particles.

Electron affinity Electron affinity (E_A) is the energy change occurring when an atom or molecule gains an electron to form a negative ion. For an atom or molecule X, it is the energy released for the electron-attachment reaction.

$$X(g) + e^- \rightleftharpoons X^-(g)$$

Often this is measured in electronvolts. Alternatively, the molar enthalpy change, ΔH, can be used.

Electron carrier Molecule such as cytochrome c that transfers an electron from a donor molecule to an acceptor molecule.

Electron configuration The arrangement of electrons in orbits and sub-orbits about the nucleus of an atom.

Electron current Opposite to conventional current; that is, considers electric current to consist of a drift of negative charges that flows from the negative terminal to the positive terminal of a battery.

Electron density The location of an electron is not fixed, but is instead described by a probability density function. The sum of the probability densities of all the electrons in a region is the electron density in that region.

Electron donor Molecule that easily gives up an electron, becoming oxidized in the process.

Electron flux The rate of flow of electrons through a reference surface. In CGS units, measured in electrons s^{-1}, or simply s^{-1}.

Electron pair A pair of electrons with different spin quantum numbers that may occupy an orbital.

Electron spin Electron spin (s) is the quantum number, equal to 1/2, that specifies the intrinsic angular momentum of the electron.

Electron transport chain A series of electron carriers that operate together to transfer electrons from donors such as NADH and $FADH_2$ to acceptors such as oxygen.

Electron transport Movement of electrons from a higher to a lower energy level along a series of electron carrier molecules, as in oxidative phosphorylation and photosynthesis.

Electron volt A unit of energy that is equal to the energy that an electron gains as it moves through a potential difference of one volt. This very small amount of energy is equal to 1.602×10^{-19} joules. Because an electron volt is so small, engineers and scientists sometimes use the terms MeV and GeV electron volts.

Electronegativity Electronegativity is a parameter originally introduced by L. Pauling which describes, on a relative basis, the power of an atom to attract electrons. For example, in hydrogen chloride, the chlorine atom is more electronegative than the hydrogen and the molecule is polar, with negative charge on the chlorine atom.

There are various ways of assigning values for the electronegativity of an element. Pauling electronegativities are based on bond dissociation energies using a scale in which fluorine, the most electronegative element, has value 4 and francium, the lowest electronegative element, has value 0.7.

Electrophoresis Electrophoresis is a technique for the analysis and separation of colloids, based on the movement of charged colloidal particles in an electric field. The migration is toward electrodes of charge opposite to that of the particles. The rate of migration of the particles depends on the field, the charge on the particles, and on other factors, such as the size and shape of the particles.

Electrophoresis is important in the study of proteins. The acidity of the solution can be used to control the direction in which a protein moves upon electrophoresis.

Electrophysiology The technique of recording and stimulating currents and voltages across cell membranes using microelectrodes. Electrodes can be used to measure membrane potentials and inject currents. The latter charges the membrane and changes the membrane potentials. If the recorded voltage change is fed back to the stimulating electrode, the current can be adjusted such that the measured membrane potential stays constant. This is called the 'voltage-clamp' technique and has largely been responsible to elucidate the mechanism underlying the electrical phenomena of neurons and muscle tissue.

Electroporation The application of an electric field to create temporary pores in the plasma membrane in order to insert DNA into the cell and transform it.

Electrostatic charge An accumulated electric charge on an object from a surplus or deficiency of electrons.

Electroweak interaction In the Standard Model, electromagnetic and weak interactions are related; physicists use the term electro-weak to encompass both of them.

Element A substance composed of a particular kind of atom. All atoms with the same number of protons in the nucleus are examples of the same element and have identical chemical properties. For example, gold (with 79 protons) and iron (with 26 protons) are both elements, but table salt is not because it is made from two different elements: sodium and chlorine. The atoms of a particular element have the same number of protons in the nucleus and exhibit a unique set of chemical properties. There are about 90 naturally occurring elements on Earth.

Element Compare with compound and mixture An element is a substance composed of atoms with identical atomic number. The older definition of element was made obsolete by the discovery of isotopes.

Element symbol An international abbreviation for element names, usually consisting of the first one or two distinctive letters in element name. Some symbols are abbreviations for ancient names.

Elementary body A small, dormant body that serves as the agent of transmission between host cells in the chlamydial life cycle.

Elementary particles Particles smaller than atoms that are the basic building blocks of the universe. The most prominent examples are photons, electrons, and quarks.

Elongation cycle The cycle in protein synthesis that results in the addition of an amino acid to the growing end of a peptide chain.

Elongation factor Protein required for the addition of amino acids to growing polypeptide chains on ribosomes.

Embden-Meyerhof pathway A pathway that degrades glucose to pyruvate; the six-carbon stage converts glucose to fructose 1,6-bisphosphate, and the three-carbon stage produces ATP while changing glyceraldehyde 3-phosphate to pyruvate.

Embryo Early developmental stage of a plant or animal after fertilisation.

Embryogenesis Development of an embryo from a fertilized egg, or zygote.

Embryonic stem cell The pluripotent stem cells in animals at the very early embryonic development. They have the potential to grow into a complete adult organism.

Empirical formula Simplest formula. Empirical formulas show which elements are present in a compound, with their mole ratios indicated as subscripts. For example, the empirical formula of glucose is CH_2O, which means that for every mole of carbon in the compound, there are 2 moles of hydrogen and one mole of oxygen.

Emulsion Emulsion is colloidal system in which the dispersed and continuous phases are both liquids. Such systems require an emulsifying agent to stabilize the dispersed particles.

Enabling science and technologies Areas of research relevant to a particular goal, such as nanotechnology.

Enantiomers Enantiomers are a chiral molecule and its non-superposable mirror image. The two forms rotate the plane of polarized light by equal amounts in opposite directions. Also called optical isomers.

Encystation The formation of a cyst.

Endangered A species with such a low population number, that the population is in danger of extinction.

Endemic A form of typhus fever caused by the rickettsia Rickettsia typhi that occurs sporadically in individuals who come into contact with rats and their fleas.

Endemic disease A disease that is commonly or constantly present in a population, usually at a relatively steady low frequency.

Endergonic reaction A reaction that does not spontaneously go to completion as written; the standard free energy change is positive, and the equilibrium constant is less than one.

Endocrine cell Specialized animal cell that secretes a hormone into the blood; usually part of a gland, such as the thyroid or pituitary gland.

Endocytosis The process in which a cell takes up solutes or particles by enclosing them in vesicles pinched off from its plasma membrane.

Endoergic A transformation is termed endoergic if it absorbs energy; such a reaction increases molecular potential energy.

Endogenote The recipient bacterial cell's own genetic material into which the donor DNA can integrate.

Endogenous infection An infection by a member of an individual's own normal body microbiota.

Endogenous pyrogen A substance such as the lymphokine interleukin-1, which is produced by host cells and induces a fever response in the host. It also is called simply a pyrogen.

Endomycorrhizal Referring to a mutualistic association of fungi and plant roots in which the fungus penetrates into the root cells and arbuscules and vesicles are formed.

Endoparasite A parasite that lives inside the body of its host.

Endophyte A microorganism living within a plant, but not necessarily parasitic on it.

Endoplasm The central portion of the cytoplasm in a protozoan.

Endoplasmic reticulum A system of membranous tubules and flattened sacs (cisternae) in the cytoplasmic matrix of eucaryotic cells. Rough or granular endoplasmic reticulum bears ribosomes on its surface; smooth or agranular endoplasmic reticulum lacks them.

Endosome A membranous vesicle formed by endocytosis.

Endospore An extremely heat- and chemical-resistant, dormant, thick-walled spore that develops within bacteria.

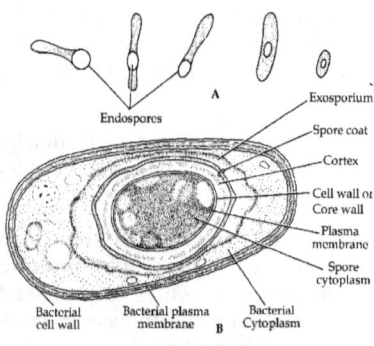

Figure Endospore

Endosymbiont An organism that lives within the body of another organism in a symbiotic association.

Endosymbiosis A type of symbiosis in which one organism is found within another organism.

Endosymbiotic theory or hypothesis The theory that eucaryotic organelles such as mitochondria and chloro-plasts arose when bacteria established an endosymbiotic relationship with the eucaryotic ancestor and then evolved into eucaryotic organelles.

Endothelium Single sheet of highly flattened cells that forms the lining of all blood vessels. Regulates exchanges between the bloodstream and surrounding tissues and is usually surrounded by a basal lamina.

Endothermic A transformation is termed endothermic if it absorbs energy in the form of heat. A typical endothermic reaction increases both entropy and molecular potential energy.

Endotoxin The heat-stable lipopolysaccharide in the outer membrane of the cell wall of gram-negative bacteria that is released when the bacterium lyses, or sometimes during growth, and is toxic to the host.

Energy Energy (E, U) is the characteristic of a system that enables it to do work. Like work itself, it is measured in joules (J).

The internal energy of a body is the sum of the potential energy and the kinetic energy of its component atoms and molecules.

Potential energy is the energy stored in a body or system as a consequence of its position, shape, or state (this includes gravitational energy, electrical energy, nuclear energy, and chemical energy).

Kinetic energy is energy of motion and is usually defined as the work that will be done by body possessing the energy when it is brought to rest. For a body of mass m having a speed v, the kinetic energy is $mv^2/2$. Kinetic energy is most clearly exhibited in gases, in which molecules have much greater freedom of motion than in liquids and solids.

Energy band A collection of closely spaced energy levels.

Energy flux The rate of flow of energy through a reference surface. In CGS units, measured in erg s^{-1}. Also measured in watts, where 1 watt = 1 × 10^7 erg s^{-1}. *Flux density*, the flux measured per unit area, is also often referred to as "flux".

Energy level The energy which an electron can have.

Enology The science of wine making.

Enriched uranium Uranium in which the proportion of U-235 has been increased above the natural 0.7%. Reactor-grade uranium is usually enriched to about 3.5% U-235, weapons-grade uranium is more than 90% U-235.

Enrichment Physical process of increasing the proportion of U-235 to U-238. See also SWU.

Enteric bacteria Members of the family Enterobacteriaceae; also used for bacteria that live in the intestinal tract.

Enterohemorrhagic E. Coli (EHEC) EHEC strains of E. Coli (0157:H7) produce several cytotoxins that provoke fluid secretion in traveler's diarrhea; however, their mode of action is unknown.

Enterotoxigenic E. Coli (ETEC) ETEC strains of E. Coli produce two plasmid-encoded enterotoxins (which are responsible for traveler's diarrhea) and are distinguished by their heat stability: heat-stable enterotoxin (ST) and heat-labile enterotoxin (LT).

Enterotoxin A toxin specifically affecting the cells of the intestinal mucosa, causing vomiting and diarrhea.

Enthalpy Enthalpy (H) is a thermodynamic property of a system defined by

$$H = U + pv$$

Where U is the internal energy of the system, p *its* pressure, and V *its* volume. J.W. Gibbs put the concept of an ensemble forward in 1902. In a chemical reaction carried out in the atmosphere the pressure remains constant and the enthalpy of reaction (ΔH), is to equal

$$\Delta H = \Delta U + p\delta v$$

For an exothermic reaction ΔH is taken to be negative.

Entner-Doudoroff pathway A pathway that converts glucose to pyruvate and glyceraldehyde 3-phosphate by producing 6-phosphogluconate and then dehydrating it.

Entropy A measure of uncertainty regarding the state of a system: for example, a gas molecule at an unknown location in a large volume has a higher entropy than one known to be confined to a smaller volume. Free energy can be extracted in converting a low-entropy state to a high-entropy state: the (time-average) pressure exerted by a gas molecule can do useful work as a small volume is expanded to a larger volume. In the classical configura-tion space picture, any molecular system can be viewed as a single-particle gas in a high-dimensional space. In the quantum mechanical picture, entropy is described as a function of the probabilities of occupancy of different members of a set of alternative quantum states. Increased information regarding the state of a system reduces its entropy and thereby increases its free energy, as shown by the resulting ability to extract more work from it.

An illustrative contradiction in the simple textbook view of entropy as a local property of a material can be shown as follows: The third law of thermodynamics states that a perfect crystal at absolute zero has zero entropy; this is true regardless of its size. A piece of disordered material, such as a glass, has some finite entropy $G0 > 0$ at absolute zero. In the local-property view, N pieces of glass, even (or especially) if all are atomically identical, must have an entropy of $NG0$. If these N pieces of glass are arranged in a regular three-dimensional lattice, however, the resulting structure constitutes a perfect crystal; at absolute zero, the third law states that this crystal has zero entropy, not $NG0$. To understand the informational perspective on entropy, it is a useful exercise to consider 1. what the actual entropy of such crystal is as a function of N, with and without information describing the structure of the unit cell,

2. how the third law can be phrased more precisely, and

3. what this more precise statement implies for the entropy of well-defined aperiodic structures. Note that any one unit cell in the crystal can be regarded as a description of all the rest.

Envelope 1. All the structures outside the plasma membrane in bacterial cells.

2. In virology it is an outer membranous layer that surrounds the nucleocapsid in some viruses.

Environmental stewardship This is a view that humans have a duty to manage and care for the whole natural environment. That we are responsible for the continued health of the whole ecosystem, not just the parts that benefit the human race. It involves integrating and applying environmental values into a process.

Enzootic The moderate prevalence of a disease in a given animal population.

Enzyme Enzyme is a protein that acts as a catalyst in biochemical reactions. Each enzyme is specific to a particular reaction or group of similar reactions. Many require the association of certain nonprotein cofactors in order to function. The molecule undergo-ing reaction binds to a specific active site on the enzyme molecule to form a short-lived intermediate: this greatly increases the rate at which the reaction proceeds to form the product.

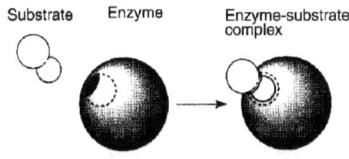

Figure Enzyme Substrate complex

Enzyme-linked immunosorbent assay (ELISA) A technique used for detecting and quantifying specific antibodies and antigens.

Eosinophil A polymorphonuclear leukocyte that has a two-lobed nucleus and cytoplasmic granules that stain yellow-red. A mobile phagocyte that is highly antiparasitic.

Epidemic (louse-borne) typhus A disease caused by Rickettsia prowazekii that is transmitted from person to person by the body louse.

Epidemiologist A person who specializes in epidemiology.

Epidemiology The study of the factors determining and influencing the frequency and distribution of disease, injury, and other health-related events and their causes in defined human populations.

Episome A plasmid that can exist either independently of the host cell's chromosome or be integrated into it.

Epitheca The larger of two halves of a diatom frustule (shell).

Epitope An area of the antigen molecule that stimulates the production of, and combines with, specific antibodies; also known as the antigenic determinant site.

Epizootic A sudden outbreak of a disease in an animal population.

Epizootiology The field of science that deals with factors determining the frequency and distribution of a disease within an animal population.

Epoxy resin Epoxy resins are thermosetting resins produced by copolymerising epoxide compounds with phenols. They contain ether linkages (-O-) and form a tight, cross-linked polymer network. Toughness, good adhesion, corrosive-chemical resistance, and good dielectric properties characterize epoxy resins. Most epoxy resins are two-part type which harden when blended.

Epsilon-proteobacteria One of the five subgroups of proteobacteria, each with distinctive 16S rRNA sequences. Slender gram-negative rods, some of which are medically important.

Equation of state Equation of state is an equation relating the pressure, volume, and temperature of a substance or system. Equation of state for ideal gas.

$Pv = nrt$

Where p is pressure, V molar volume, T temperature, and R the molar gas constant (8.314 $JK^{-1}mol^{-1}$).

Equilibrium (chemical) At equilibrium, the state of a system does not change over time, although internal fluctuation may exist. Thermodynamically, the equilibrium is the physical state of a system that has the lowest total energy content. To lower the energy content, a system may give up energy in form of heat or work or entropy, and usually it is a combination of all three. The laws of thermodynamic dictate that the total amount of energy cannot be changed and whatever energy in a system is lost, is taken up by the surroundings. The second law dictates that at equilibrium the entropy portion of the energy content of a system must be at its maximum. Interestingly, life is characterized by avoiding equilibrium states and minimizing entropy. This is used as an explanation of how life can maintain highly organized structures at the expense of the environment, whose entropy or disorder increases. Importantly, the energy content of a system and its surroundings are interdependent and the equilibrium state of a system can be changed by changing the internal composition or external conditions. This shift from one equilibrium (state 1) to a second equilibrium (state 2) is often characterized as chemical equilibrium describing the relationship between two states of a system that exist under slightly different conditions. Mathematically, the equilibrium can be described with the equilibrium constant where both states are equally probable. This constant allows the quantification of system properties such as the binding of a drug to its receptor protein.

Equilibrium constant The equilibrium constant (K) was originally introduced in 1863 by Norse chemists C.M. Guldberg and P. Waage using the law of mass action. For a reversible chemical reaction represented by the equation

$a\text{a} + b\text{b} \rightleftarrows c\text{c} + d\text{d}$

Chemical equilibrium occurs when the rate of the forward reaction equals the rate of the back reaction, so that the concentrations of products and reactants reach steady-state values.

The equilibrium constant is the ratio of chemical activities of the species A, B, C, and D at equilibrium.

$$K = \frac{a_C^c \cdot a_D^d}{a_A^a \cdot a_B^b}$$

To a certain approximation, the activities can be replaced by concentrations.

$$K_c = \frac{[C]^c \cdot [D]^d}{[A]^a \cdot [B]^b}$$

For gas reactions, partial pressures are used rather than concentrations

$$K_p = \frac{P_C^c \cdot P_D^d}{P_A^a \cdot P_B^b}$$

The units of K_p and K_c depend on the numbers of molecules appearing in the stoichiometric equation (a, b, c, and d).

The value equilibrium constant depends on the temperature. If the forward reaction is exothermic, the equilibrium constant decreases as the temperature rises. The equilibrium constant shows the position of equilibrium. A low value of K indicates that [C] and [D] are small compared to [A] and [B]; i.e. That the back reaction predominates.

The equilibrium constant is related to $d_r g°$, the standard Gibbs free energy change in the reaction, by

$RT \ln k = -\delta_r g°$

Erg A CGS unit of energy equal to work done by a force of 1 dyne acting over a distance of 1 cm. 10^7 (ten million) erg s^{-1} (ergs per second) = 1 watt. Also, 1 Calorie = 4.2×10^{10} (42 billion) ergs.

Ergot The dried sclerotium of Claviceps purpurea. Also, an ascomycete that parasitizes rye and other higher plants causing the disease called ergotism.

Ergotism The disease or toxic condition caused by eating grain infected with ergot; it is often accompanied by gangrene, psychotic delusions, nervous spasms, abortion, and convulsions in humans and in animals.

Erysipelas An acute inflammation of the dermal layer of the skin, occurring primarily in infants and persons over 30 years of age with a history of streptococcal sore throat.

Erythema infectiosum A disease in children caused by the parvovirus B19. This disease is common in children between 4 and 11 years of age and is sometimes called fifth disease, since it was the fifth of six erythematous rash diseases in children in an older classification.

Erythromycin An intermediate spectrum macrolide antibiotic produced by *Streptomyces erythreus*.

Erythropoietin A hormone released from the kidneys and the liver in response to low oxygen concentrations in the blood. It controls the rate of red blood cell production.

Escape velocity The minimum velocity with which an object must be thrown upwards so as to overcome the gravitational pull and escape into space, is called escape velocity (V esc). The escape velocity depends upon the mass and radius of the planet/star. It does not depend upon the mass of the body thrown up. The escape velocity of earth is given by.

Eschar A slough produced on the skin by a thermal burn, gangrene, or the anthrax bacillus.

Essential amino acids or fatty acids An amino acid or fatty acid that cannot be synthesized by our own cells and need to be part of our diet to stay healthy.

Ester A molecule containing an ester linkage, a carbonyl group bonded to an O that is in turn bonded to a C.

Ethers Ethers are organic compounds with formula R-O-R, where R is not equal to H. They may be derived from alcohols by elimination of water, but the major method is catalytic hydration of olefins. They are volatile highly flammable compounds; when containing peroxides they can detonate on heating. The term ether is often used synonymously with ethyl ether.

Ethics Ethics is a branch of philosophy that deals with morality. It is concerned with distinguishing between right and wrong human actions, both at an individual and societal level. Ethics may also apply to the rules or standards that specify how particular members of an organisation should conduct themselves.

Eucarya The domain that contains organisms composed of eucaryotic cells with primarily glycerol fatty acyl diesters in their membranes and eucaryotic rRNA.

Eucaryotic cells Cells that have a membrane-delimited nucleus and differ in many other ways from procaryotic cells; protists, algae, fungi, plants, and animals are all eucaryotic.

Eugenics Deliberate manipulation of the genetic makeup of human populations, traditionally by selective birth control, infanticide, mass murder, genocide. Genetic engineering offers now opportunities for the eugenicist including genetic screening, in vitro fertilisation plus preimplantation screening, germ line genetic modification etc. Eugenic ideas can be traced to the ancient Greek philosopher Plato, but are more recently associated with Nazi Germany and Hitler.

Euglenoids A group of algae (the division Euglenophyta) or protozoa (order Euglenida) that normally have chloroplasts containing chlorophyll a and b. They usually have a stigma and one or two flagella emerging from an anterior gullet.

Eukaryote The major class of living things including all multicellular, higher organisms and some single-celled organisms that have a nucleus in their cells containing the, chromosomes.

Euler number Euler number (Eu) is a dimensionless quantity used in fluid mechanics, defined by

$$Eu = \frac{\Delta p}{\rho . v^2}$$

Where p is pressure, ρ is density, and v is velocity.

Eumycota A division of fungi in some classification systems. These are the true fungi consisting of the Zygomycetes, Ascomycetes, Basidiomycetes, and Chytridiomycetes.

Eutectic Eutectic is a solid solution consisting of two or more substances and having the lowest freezing point of any possible mixture of these components.

Eutectic point is the lowest temperature at which the eutectic mixture can exist in liquid phase. A liquid having the eutectic composition will freeze at a single temperature without change of composition.

Eutrophication The enrichment of an aquatic environment with nutrients.

Evaporation Process of more molecules leaving a liquid for the gaseous state than returning from the gas to the liquid. It can occur at any given temperature from the surface of a liquid. Evaporation takes place only from the surface of the liquid. Evaporation causes cooling. Evaporation is faster if the surface of the liquid is large, the temperature is higher and the surrounding atmosphere does not contain a large amount of vapour of the liquid.

Event What occurs when two particles collide or a single particle decays. Particle theories predict the probabilities of various possible events occurring when many similar collisions or decays are studied. They cannot predict the outcome for any single event.

Event horizon Surface surrounding a black hole outside of which internal measurements except mass, electric charge, and rotation velocity become immeasurable and matter, normally, can no longer escape from the black hole's gravitational field due to its high escape velocity

Evolution, theory of The theory of evolution as initially formulated by Charles Darwin in 1859 is the central theory of biology. All processes that enable life are the result of the process of evolution over a period estimated to be more than 3 billion years. The mechanism of evolution are mutation and natural selection. These two processes result in changes at the genetic (mutation) and physiological level.

Evolutionary distance A quantitative indication of the number of positions that differ between two aligned macromolecules, and presumably a measure of evolutionary similarity between molecules and organisms.

Excited state A greater-than-minimum energy state of any atom that is achieved when at least one of its electrons resides at a greater-than-normal distance from its parent nucleus.

Excluded volume The presence of one molecule reduces the volume available for other molecules; resulting reductions in their entropy are termed excluded volume effects.

Excystation The escape of one or more cells or organisms from a cyst.

Exergonic reaction A reaction that spontaneously goes to completion as written; the standard free energy change is negative, and the equilibrium constant is greater than one.

Exfoliative toxin or exfoliatin An exotoxin produced by Staphylococcus aureus that causes the separation of epidermal layers and the loss of skin surface layers. It produces the symptoms of the scaled skin syndrome.

Exit site (E site) The location on a ribosome to which an empty tRNA moves from the P site before it finally leaves the ribosome during protein synthesis.

Exoenzymes Enzymes that are secreted by cells.

Exoergic The opposite of endoergic; describes a transformation that releases energy.

Exogenote The piece of donor DNA that enters a bacterial cell during gene exchange and recombination.

Exon The region in a split or interrupted gene that codes for RNA which ends up in the final product.

Exothermic The opposite of endothermic; describes an exoergic transformation in which energy is released as heat. Exoergic reactions in solution are commonly exothermic.

Exotoxin A heat-labile, toxic protein produced by a bacterium as a result of its normal metabolism or because of the acquisition of a plasmid or prophage that redirects its metabolism. It is usually released into the bacterium's surroundings.

Exploratory engineering Design and analysis of systems that are theoretically possible but cannot be built yet, owing to limitations in available tools.

Exponential phase The phase of the growth curve during which the microbial population is growing at a constant and maximum rate, dividing and doubling at regular intervals.

Expressed sequence tag (EST) A partial gene sequence unique to a gene that can be used to identify and position the gene during genomic analysis.

Expression (of a gene) The central dogma of molecular biology says that genes (DNA) are transcribed into a message (RNA) which is translated into a polypeptide or protein, which in turn gives structural and functional features to a cell.

Expression vector A special cloning vector used to express recombinant genes in host cells; the recombinant gene is trans-cribed and its protein synthesized.

Exteins Polypeptide sequences of precursor self-splicing proteins that are joined together during formation of the final, functional protein. They are separated from one another by intein sequences, which they flank.

Extracutaneous sporotrichosis An infection by the fungus Sporothrix schenckii that spreads throughout the body.

Extreme barophilic bacteria Bacteria that require a high-pressure environment to function.

Extreme environment An environment in which physical factors such as temperature, ph, salinity, and pressure are outside of the normal range for growth of most microorganisms; these conditions allow unique organisms to survive and function.

Extremophiles Microorganisms that grow under harsh or extreme environmental conditions such as very high temperatures or low phs.

Extrinsic factor An environmental factor such as temperature that influences microbial growth in food.

F factor The fertility factor, a plasmid that carries the genes for bacterial conjugation and makes its E. Coli host cell the gene donor during conjugation.

F value The time in minutes at a specific temperature needed to kill a population of cells or spores.

F plasmid An F plasmid that carries some bacterial genes and transmits them to recipient cells when the F cell carries out conjugation; the transfer of bacterial genes in this way is often called sexduction.

F1 hybrid First generation after a hybrid has been formed.

F1 particle Particle on the inner mitochondrial membrane, which is the site of ATP synthesis by oxidative phosphorylation.

Facilitated diffusion Diffusion across the plasma membrane that is aided by a carrier.

Factor VII and IX Soluble blood proteins that forms part of the cascade of the 12 reactions of blood clotting. Factor VII deficiency is associated with haemophilia A while factor IX deficiency is associated with haemophilia B.

Facultative anaerobes Microorganisms that do not require oxygen for growth, but do grow better in its presence.

Facultative psychrophile *See* psychrotroph.

Fahrenheit scale Fahrenheit scale is the temperature scale in which 212 degrees is the boiling point of water and 32 degrees is the freezing point of water. The scale was invented in 1714 by a German physicist G.D. Fahrenheit (1686-1736).

32°F = 0°C

212°F = 100°C

1°F =(5/9)°C

$T(°C) = (5/9)[T(°F) - 32]$

$T(°F) = (9/5)T(°C) + 32$

Fahrenheit scale of temperature On the Fahrenheit scale, the ice point, the ice point (lower fixed point) is taken as 32°F and the steam point (upper fixed point) is taken as 212° F. The interval between these two points is divided into 180 equal divisions. Thus, unit division on the Fahrenheit scale is 1°F. The temperatures on the Celsius scale and the Fahrenheit scale are related by the relationship, C/100 = (F - 32) / 180. The temperature of a normal healthy person is 37°C or 98.6°F.

Fail-stop Describes a component or subsystem that, in the event of a failure, produces no output rather than producing a damaged or incorrect output.

Farad Farad (F) is the SI derived unit of electric capacitance. The farad is the capacitance of an electric capacitor between the two plates of which there appears a difference of electric potential of one volt when it is charged by a quantity of electricity equal to one coulomb.

Faraday constant Faraday constant (F) is the electric charge of 1 mol of singly charged positive ions.

$$F = N_A \times e = 96487 \text{ C mol}^{-1}$$

Where N_A is Avogadro's constant (6.022×10^{23} mol^{-1}) and e is the elementary charge (1.602×10^{-19} C).

Fas gene The gene that is active in target cells which are susceptible to killing by cells expressing the Fas ligand, a member of the TNF family of cytokines and cell surface molecules.

Fast breeder reactor (FBR) A fast neutron reactor (qv) configured to produce more fissile material than it consumes, using fertile material such as depleted uranium in a blanket around the core.

Fast neutron reactor A reactor with little or no moderator and hence utilising fast neutrons. It normally burns plutonium while producing fissile isotopes in fertile material such as depleted uranium.

Fatty acids Fatty acids are aliphatic monocarboxylic acids characterized by a terminal carboxyl group (R-COOH). Natural fatty acids commonly have a chain of 4 to 28 carbons (usually unbranched and even-numbered), which may be saturated or unsaturated. The most important of saturated fatty acids are butyric (C_4), lauric (C_{12}), palmitic (C_{16}), and stearic (C_{18}). The most common unsaturated acids are oleic, linoleic, and linolenic (all C_{18}).

The physical properties of fatty acids are determined by chain length, degree of unsaturation, and chain branching. Short-chain acids are pungent liquids, soluble in water. As chain length increases, melting points are raised and water-solubility decreases. Unsaturation and chain branching tend to lower melting points.

Fault-tolerant Describes a system that can suffer failure in a component or subsystem, yet continue to function correctly.

Fecal coliform Coliforms whose normal habitat is the intestinal tract and that can grow at 44.5°C.

Fecal enterococci Enterococci found in the intestine of humans and other warm-blooded animals. They are used as indicators of the fecal pollution of water.

Feedback inhibition A negative feedback mechanism in which a pathway end product inhibits the activity of an enzyme in the sequence leading to its formation; when the end product accumulates in excess, it inhibits its own synthesis.

Feral A term used to describe domestic or introduced animals living in wild conditions or plants that have become wild.

Fermentation An energy-yielding process in which an energy substrate is oxidized without an exogenous electron acceptor. Usually organic molecules serve as both electron donors and acceptors.

Fermi energy The average energy per particle when adding particles to a distribution but without changing the entropy or the volume. Chemists refer to this quantity as being the electrochemical potential.

Fermi level Fermi level is the highest energy of occupied states in a solid at zero temperature. The Fermi level in conductors lies in the conduction band, in insulators it lies in the valence band, and in semiconductors it falls in the gap between the conduction band and the valence band. It is named after the Italian physicst Enrico Fermi.

Fermilab Fermi National Accelerator Laboratory in Batavia, Illinois (near Chicago). Named after particle physics pioneer Enrico Fermi.

Fermion Any particle that has odd-half-integer (1/2, 3/2,) intrinsic angular momentum (spin), measured in units of h-bar. As a consequence of this peculiar angular momentum, fermions obey a rule called the Pauli Exclusion Principle, which states that no two fermions can exist in the same state at the same time. Many of the properties of ordinary matter arise because of this rule. Electrons, protons, and neutrons are all fermions, as are all the fundamental matter particles, both quarks and leptons.

Ferrites Ferrites are ceramic materials of nominal formula $MO.Fe_2O_3$, where M is a divalent metal (Co, Mn, NI, or Zn). The ferrites show either ferrimagnetism or ferromagnetism, but are not electrical conductors, and they are used in high-frequency circuits as magnetic cores, in rectifiers on memory and record tapes, and various related uses in radio, television, radar, computers, and automatic control systems.

Ferromagnetism Ferromagnetism is a type of magnetism in which the magnetic moments of atoms in a solid are aligned within domains which can in turn be aligned with each other by a weak magnetic field. The total magnetic moment of a sample of the substance is the vector sum of the magnetic moments of the component domains. In an unmagnetized piece of ferromagnetic material the magnetic moments of the domains themselves are not aligned; when an external field is applied those domains that are aligned with the field increase in size at the expense of the others. Ferromagnetic materials can retain their magnetization when the external field is removed, as long as the temperature is below a critical value, the Curie temperature. They are characterized by a large positive magnetic susceptibility.

Ferrous Ferrous ion. 1. the iron(II) ion, Fe^{2+}.
2. A compound that contains iron in the +2 oxidation state.

Fertile Capable of becoming fissile, by capturing neutrons, possibly followed by radioactive decay; e.g. U-238, Pu-240.

Fertilisation The union of male and female reproductive cells (gametes), during the process of sexual reproduction, to form a cell called a zygote.

Fever A complex physiological response to disease mediated by pyrogenic cytokines and characteri-zed by a rise in core body tempera-ture and activation of the immune system.

Fibroblast Common cell type found in connective tissue. Secretes an extracellular matrix rich in collagen and other extracellular matrix macromolecules. Migrates and proliferates readily in wounded tissue and in tissue culture.

Fick's law Fick's law is the statement that the flux J of a diffusing substance is proportional to the concentration gradient, i.e.,

$J = -D(dc/dx)$

Where D is called the diffusion coefficient.

Field A property of a point in space describing the forces that would be exerted on a particle if it was there.

Fimbria A fine, hairlike protein appendage on some gram-negative bacteria that helps attach them to surfaces.

Final host The host on/in which a parasitic organism either attains sexual maturity or reproduces.

First law of motion Every object remains at rest or in a state of uniform straight-line motion unless acted on by an unbalanced force.

First law of thermodynamics Energy can be neither created nor destroyed.

Fissile (of an isotope) Capable of capturing a slow (thermal) neutron and undergoing nuclear fission, e.g. U-235, U-233, Pu-239.

Fission The splitting of a heavy nucleus into two, accompanied by the release of a relatively large amount of energy and usually one or more neutrons. It may be spontaneous but usually is due to a nucleus absorbing a neutron and thus becoming unstable.

Fission products Daughter nuclei resulting either from the fission of heavy elements such as uranium, or the radioactive decay of those primary daughters. Usually highly radioactive.

Fissionable Capable of undergoing fission: If fissile, by slow neutrons; if fertile, by fast neutrons.

Fixation The process in which the internal and external structures of cells and organisms are preserved and fixed in position.

Fixative Chemical reagent such as formaldehyde or osmium tetro-xide used to preserve cells for microscropy. Samples treated with these reagents are said to be "fixed," and the process is called fixation.

Fixed target experiment An experiment in which the beam of particles from an accelerator is directed at a stationary (or nearly stationary) target. The target may be a solid, a tank containing liquid or gas, or a gas jet.

Flagellin The protein used to construct the filament of a bacterial flagellum.

Flagellum Long, whiplike protrusion whose undulations drive a cell through a fluid medium. Eucaryotic flagella are longer versions of cilia; bacterial flagella are completely different, being smaller and simpler in construction.

Flare Rapid release of energy from a localized region on the Sun in the form of electromagnetic radiation, energetic particles, and mass motions.

Flare star A member of a class of stars that show occasional, sudden, unpredicted increases in light. The total energy released in a flare on a Flare star can be much greater than the energy released in a solar flare.

Flash point Flash point is the lowest temperature at which a liquid or volatile solid gives off vapour sufficient to form an ignitable mixture with the air near the surface of the liquid or within the test vessel.

Flat or plane warts Small, smooth, slightly raised warts.

Flavin adenine dinucleotide An electron carrying cofactor often involved in energy production.

Flavour The name used for the different quarks types and for the different lepton types. For each charged lepton flavour there is a corresponding neutrino flavour. In other words, flavour is the quantum number that distinguishes the different quark/lepton types. Each flavour of quark and charged lepton has a different mass. For neutrinos we do not yet know if they have a mass or what the masses are.

Fluctuating noise Noise that varies continuously and to an appreciable extent over the period of observation. It can also include intermittent noise. As a guide, when the level varies noticeably by more than 5 dB over a period of less than one minute, the noise is considered to be fluctuating.

Fluid Matter that has the ability to flow or be poured; the individual molecules of a fluid are able to move, rolling over or by one another.

Fluid friction A friction force in which at least one of the object is as a fluid.

Fluid mosaic membrane The fluid mosaic model of cell membranes describes the structural and dynamical organization of biological membranes. It is composed of phospholipids that form large planar bilayers. In-between phospholipids exist membrane proteins and the alternating composition of phospholipids and proteins found in membranes has been compared to a mosaic structure. In addition, both components are not fixed in space but can freely move within the plane of the membrane. This 'fluidity' similar to the fluid or liquid state of water if it is not frozen is essential for the proper function of proteins in membranes.

Fluid mosaic model The currently accepted model of cell membranes in which the membrane is a lipid bilayer with integral proteins buried in the lipid, and peripheral proteins more loosely attached to the membrane surface.

Fluorescein Fluorescent dye that fluorescens green when illuminated with blue light or ultraviolet light.

Fluorescence microscope A microscope that exposes a specimen to light of a specific wavelength and then forms an image from the fluorescent light produced. Usually the specimen is stained with a fluorescent dye or fluorochrome.

Fluorescent dye Molecule that absorbs light at one wavelength and responds by emitting light at another wavelength; the emitted light is of longer wavelength (and hence of lower energy) than the light absorbed.

Fluorescent light The light emitted by a substance when it is irradiated with light of a shorter wavelength.

Flux The flow of fluid, particles, or energy through a given area within a certain time. In astronomy, this term is often used to describe the rate at which light flows. For example, the amount of light striking a single square centimeter of a detector in one second is its flux.

Foam Foams are dispersions of gases in liquids or solids. The gas globule may be of any size, from colloidal to macroscopic, as in soap bubbles. Bakers' bread and sponge rubber are examples of solid foams. Typical liquid foams are those used in fire-fighting, shaving creams, etc. Foams made by mechanical incorporation of air are widely used in the food industry. Foams can be stabilized by surfactants.

Focal contact Small region on the surface of a fibroblast or other cell that is anchored to the extracellular matrix. The attachment is mediated by transmembrane proteins such as integrins, which are linked, through other proteins, to actin filaments in the cytoplasm.

Focal length A property of a lens or mirror, equal to the distance from the lens or mirror to the image it forms of an object that is infinitely far away.

Fomite An object that is not in itself harmful but is able to harbour and transmit pathogenic organisms. Also called fomes.

Food chain The flow of energy and matter in living organisms through a producer-consumer sequence.

Food intoxication Food poisoning caused by microbial toxins produced in a food prior to consumption. The presence of living bacteria is not required.

Food poisoning A general term usually referring to a gastrointestinal disease caused by the ingestion of food contaminated by pathogens or their toxins.

Food web A network of many interlinked food chains, encompassing primary producers, consumers, decomposers, and detritivores.

Food-borne infection Gastrointestinal illness caused by ingestion of microorganisms, followed by their growth within the host. Symptoms arise from tissue invasion and/or toxin production.

Foot and mouth disease All species of cloven-hoofed animals are susceptible to FMD, including domestic livestock and wild ungulates such as buffalo, antelope and warthogs. Clinical signs are essentially similar in all species although the severity may vary considerably. The principal signs are pyrexia followed by vesicle formation in the mouth and feet resulting in salivation and lameness.

The disease is caused by a virus and is highly contagious but not dangerous to man.

Footpoint The intersection of magnetic loops with the photosphere.

Force Force is a push or pull which tends to change the state of rest or of uniform motion, the direction of motion, or the shape and size of a body. Force is a vector quantity. The SI unit of force is Newton, denoted by N. One N is the force which when acts on a body of mass 1 kg produces an acceleration of 1 m/s^2.

Force of gravitation The force with which two objects attract each other by virtue of their masses is called the force of gravitation. The force of attraction acts even if the two objects are not connected to each other. It is an action-at-a-distance force.

Formula unit Compare with empirical formula. One formula weight of a compound.

Formula weight. Formula mass. The formula weight is the sum of the atomic weights of the atoms in an empirical formula. Formula weights are usually written in atomic mass units (u).

Fossil fuel A fuel based on carbon presumed to be originally from living matter, e.g., coal, oil, gas. Burned with oxygen to yield energy.

Fractal A nested pattern that shows the same symmetry/geometry at any scale a pattern is looked at. It is an example of an infinite pattern in both larger and smaller dimensions. Fractals are geometrical abstractions and sometimes used to explain complexity in living organisms, also the comparison does not hold up on closer inspection. As abstractions, they are thought to continue into infinity, even the infinitely small, although physicists believe that there is a material limit to the what constitutes the smallest dimension. As for complex biological organisms, their structure is hierarchical with higher levels having emergent structures and properties not found at the lower levels. Thus it is not a true fractal.

Fracture strain An adjustment to stress in which materials crack or break as a result of the stress.

Fragmentation A type of asexual reproduction in which a thallus breaks into two or more parts, each of which forms a new thallus.

Frame of reference Distinct perspective of an event and its results based on an observer's motion.

Frameshift mutations Mutations arising from the loss or gain of a base or DNA segment, leading to a change in the codon reading frame and thus a change in the amino acids incorporated into protein.

Free electron An electron that has broken free of it's atomic bond and is therefore not bound to an atom.

Free energy change The total energy change in a system that is available to do useful work as the system goes from its initial state to its final state at constant temperature and pressure.

Free fall The motion of a body towards the earth when no other force except the force of gravity acts on it is called free fall. All freely falling bodies are weightless.

Free radical Free radical is a molecular fragment having one or more unpaired electrons, usually short-lived and highly reactive. They can be produced by photolysis or pyrolysis in which a bond is broken without forming ions. In formulas, a free radical is conventionally indicated by a dot (Cl·). Free radicals are known to be formed by ionising radiation and thus play a part in deleterious degradation effects that occur in irradiated tissue. They also act as initiators or intermediates in oxidation, combustion, photolysis, and polymerisation.

Freezing point The temperature at which a phase change of liquid to solid takes place; the same temperature as the melting point for a given substance.

Frequency Frequency is synonymous to pitch. Sounds have a pitch which is peculiar to the nature of the sound generator. For example, the sound of a tiny bell has a high pitch and the sound of a bass drum has a low pitch. Frequency or pitch can be measured on a scale in units of Hertz or Hz.

Friction The force that resists the motion of one surface relative to another with which it is in contact. The cause of friction is that surfaces, however smooth they may look to the eye, on the microscopic scale have many humps and crests. Thus the actual area of contact is very small indeed, and the consequent very high pressure leads to local pressure welding of the surface. In motion the welds are broken and remade continually.

Froude number Froude number (Fr) is a dimensionless quantity used in fluid mechanics, defined by

$$Fr = \frac{v}{(l \cdot g)^{\frac{1}{2}}}$$

Where v is velocity, l is length, and g is acceleration due to gravity.

Fruiting body A specialized structure that holds sexually or asexually produced spores; found in fungi and in some bacteria.

Frustule A silicified cell wall in the diatoms.

Fuel assembly Structured collection of fuel rods or elements, the unit of fuel in a reactor.

Fuel fabrication Making reactor fuel assemblies, usually from sintered UO_2 pellets which are inserted into zircalloy tubes, comprising the fuel rods or elements.

Fuel rod Long zirconium alloy tubes containing fissionable material for use in a nuclear reactor.

Fugacity Fugacity (f) is a thermodynamic function used in place of partial pressure in reactions involving real gases and mixtures. For a component of a mixture, it is defined by

$$D\mu = RT(\ln f)$$

Where μ is the chemical potential.

The fugacity of a gas is equal to the pressure if the gas is ideal. The fugacity of a liquid or solid is the fugacity of the vapour with which it is in equilibrium. The ratio of the fugacity to the fugacity in some standard state is the activity.

Fundamental charge Smallest common charge known; the magnitude of the charge of an electron and a proton, which is 1.60×10^{-19} coulomb.

Fundamental frequency The lowest frequency that can set up standing waves in an air column or on a string.

Fundamental interaction In the Standard Model the fundamental interactions are the electro-magne-tic, weak, strong and gravitational interactions. There is at least one more fundamental interaction in the theory that is responsible for funda-mental particle masses. Five interaction types are all that are needed to explain all observed physical phenomena.

Fundamental particle A particle with no internal substructure. In the Standard Model the quarks, leptons, photons, gluons, W+ and W- bosons, and the Z bosons are fundamental. All other objects are made from these.

Fundamental properties A property that cannot be defined in simpler terms other than to describe how it is measured; the fundamental properties are length, mass, time, and charge.

Fungicide An agent that kills fungi.

Fungistatic Inhibiting the growth and reproduction of fungi.

Fungus Achlorophyllous, hetero-trophic, spore-bearing eucaryotes with absorptive nutrition; usually, they have a walled thallus.

Fusion A nuclear process that releases energy when light atomic nuclei combine to form heavier nuclei. Fusion is the energy source for stars like our Sun.

G protein One of a large family of heterotrimeric GTP-binding proteins that are important intermediaries in cell-signaling pathways. Usually activated by the binding of a hormone or other signaling ligand to a seven-pass transmembrane receptor protein.

G0 phase State of withdrawal from the eucaroytic cell-division cycle by entry into a quiescent G1 phase; often seen in differentiated cells.

G1 phase Gap 1 phase of the eucaryotic cell-division cycle, between the end of cytokinesis and the start of DNA synthesis.

G2 phase Gap 2 phase of the eucaryotic cell-division cycle, between the end of DNA synthesis and the beginning of mitosis.

GAG Long, linear, highly charged polysaccharide composed of a repeating pair of sugars, one of which is always an amino sugar. Mainly found covalently linked to a protein core in extracellular matrix proteoglycans. Examples include chondroitin sulphate, hyaluronic acid, and heparin.

Gal Gal is a non-SI unit of acceleration, equal to 1 cm/s^2. Also called galileo.

Gallon Gallon (US) is a unit of volume equal to 3.785412 L.

Gallon is a unit of volume equal to 4.546090 L.

Gametangium A structure that contains gametes or in which gametes are formed.

Gamma radiation Gamma radiation is electromagnetic radiation of extremely short wavelength. Gamma radiation ranges in energy from about 10^{-15} to 10^{-10} J (10 keV to 10 MeV) (wavelength less than about 1 pm). Gamma rays are emitted by excited atomic nuclei during the process of passing to a lower excitation state.

Gamma rays are extremely penetrating and are absorbed by dense materials like lead and uranium. Exposure to gamma radiation may be lethal.

Gamma ray The highest energy quanta in the electromagnetic spectrum. Gamma rays are often defined to begin at 10 keV, although radiation from around 10 keV to several hundred keV is also referred to as hard x-rays.

Gamma-proteobacteria One of the five subgroups of proteobacteria, each with distinctive 16S rRNA sequences. This is the largest subgroup and is very diverse physiologically; many important genera are facultatively anaerobic chemoorganotrophs.

Ganglion Cluster of nerve cells and associated glial cells located outside the central nervous system.

Ganglioside Any glycolipid having one or more sialic acid residues in its structure. Found in the plasma membrane of eucaryotic cells and especially abundant in nerve cells.

Gap junction Communicating cell-cell junction that allows ions and small molecules to pass from the cyto-plasm of one cell to the cytoplasm of the next.

Gases A phase of matter composed of molecules that are relatively far apart moving freely in a constant, random motion and have weak cohesive forces acting between them, resulting in the characteristic indefinite shape and indefinite volume of a gas.

Gas gangrene A type of gangrene that arises from dirty, lacerated wounds infected by anaerobic bacteria, especially species of Clostridium. As the bacteria grow, they release toxins and ferment carbohydrates to produce carbon dioxide and hydrogen gas.

Gas vacuole A gas-filled vacuole found in cyanobacteria and some other aquatic bacteria that provides flotation. It is composed of gas vesicles, which are made of protein.

Gastritis Inflammation of the stomach.

Gastroenteritis An acute inflammation of the lining of the stomach and intestines, characterized by anorexia, nausea, diarrhea, abdominal pain, and weakness. It has various causes including food poisoning due to such organisms as E. Coli, S. Aureus, Campylobacter, and Salmonella species; consumption of irritating food or drink; or psychological factors such as anger, stress, and fear. Also called enterogastritis.

Gastrula Animal embryo at an early stage of development where cells are invaginating to form the rudiment of a gut cavity.

Gate In digital logic, a component that can switch the state of an output dependent on the states of one or more inputs.

Gauss Gauss (G) is a non-SI unit of magnetic flux density (B). $1\ G = 10^{-4}\ T$.

Gaussian system of units Gaussian system of units is a hybrid system used in electromagnetic theory, which combines features of both the electrostatic CGS subsystem (esu) and electromagnetic CGS subsystem (emu). With three base units, it uses em units in magnetism and es units in electrostatics. This involves using the constant c (the velocity of light in vacuum) to interrelate these sets of units.

Gel Gels are colloids in which both dispersed and continuous phases have a three-dimensional network throughout the material, so that it forms a jelly-like mass. One component may sometimes be removed to leave a rigid gel.

Gene A gene is an hereditary unit of an organism that cannot be partitioned any further into smaller units; it is made of DNA. Functionally, a gene consists of regulatory and coding sequences. The regulatory sequences allow a cell to control when and how a gene is expressed its gene product (= RNA or protein) encoded by the coding sequence is synthesized. Often, gene products are only functional as groups (protein complexes) that require the expression of more than one gene (heteromeric complexes) or of a single gene in high copy numbers (homomeric complexes).

Gene amplification The process whereby genes or a sequence of DNA in the genome is greatly increased in number of copies.

Gene bank A collection of cells or artificial chromosomes containing known genetic information.

Gene cloning The technique of making many copies of a gene.

Gene expression The process by which the information coded within a gene is converted into proteins that ultimately control all the operations in a cell.

Gene gun A device that uses high-pressure gas or another propellant to shoot a spray of DNA-coated microprojectiles into cells and transform them. Sometimes it is called a biolistic device.

Gene mapping The process of determining where genes are located on individual chromosomes, their position in relation to other genes and the distance between them.

Gene pair Corresponding genes in each of a pair of matching chromosomes.

Gene pool A term used to describe all the genes at a given locus in the population. The size of the pool is related to the genetic diversity in the population.

Gene silencing The process(es) whereby certain genes in the genome are prevented from being expressed by chemical modifications and other means.

Gene splicing A technique used to join segments of DNA to form a new genetic combination.

Gene stacking Accumulation of several advantageous traits in an organism, usually considered in the context of herbicide tolerance genes in plants (weeds).

Gene technology The technology to take a single gene from a plant or animal cell and insert it into another plant or animal cell of a different species.

Gene testing Methods that identify the presence, absence or mutation of a particular gene in an individual.

Gene therapy Correcting the genetic make-up of a patient by adding the correct genes in a form which will be expressed, either to the somatic tissues which are affected or to the germ line cells.

General recombination Recombination involving a reciprocal exchange of a pair of homologous DNA sequences; it can occur at any place on the chromosome.

General relativity Theory that explains the relations of spacetime and gravity.

Generalized transduction The transfer of any part of a bacterial genome when the DNA fragment is packaged within a phage capsid by mistake.

Generation A set of one of each charge type of quark and lepton, grouped by mass. The first generation contains the up and down quarks, the electron and the electron neutrino.

Generation time The time required for a microbial population to double in number.

Genetic code The code establishing the correspondence between the sequence of bases in nucleic acids (DNA and the complementary RNA) and the sequence of amino acids in proteins.

Figure Genetic code

Genetic counselling The counselling of individuals and prospective parents who are at risk of a particular genetic disease, either themselves or their potential child. It provides them and their families with education and information about genetic-related conditions such as the probabilities, dangers, diagnosis and treatment, and helps them make informed decisions.

Genetic determinism Determinism is the doctrine that all acts, choices and events are the inevitable consequence of antecedent sufficient causes. Genetic determinism is the doctrine that the organism is the inevitable consequence of its genetic makeup, or the sum of its genes.

Genetic disorder A hereditary condition that results from a defective gene or chromosome.

Genetic engineering The manipulating of genetic material in the laboratory. It includes isolating, copying and multiplying genes, recombining genes or DNA from different species, and transferring genes from one species to another, bypassing the reproductive process.

Genetic fingerprinting A technique which enables genetic relationships between close relatives, or the identity of individuals to be established - usually beyond reasonable doubt.

Genetic information Refers to the information content of genes or genomes and is organized in sequences of nucleotides, structures of genes, and arrangement of genes within genomes. Genetic informa-tion is the information that is inherited from generation to generation and can be accessed by the cellular machinery with the help of proteins to synthesize all necessary components for the growth maintenance of an organism.

Genetic inheritance The transfer of genetic instructions for different characteristics, such as the colour and size of the cell or organism, to successive generations, via reproduction.

Genetic map The body of informa-tion on the relative positions of genes on chromosomes. Much of the effort of the Human Genome Project is directed to mapping chromosomes.

Genetic marker A harmless variable inherited change in DNA or protein that can be used to locate a diseased gene on a particular chromosome. Any segment of DNA that can be identified, or whose chromosomal location is known, so that it can be used as a reference point to map or locate other genes. Any gene which has an identifiable phenotype that can be used to track the presence or absence of other genes on the same piece of DNA transferred into a cell.

Genetic modification A technique where individual genes can be copied and transferred to another living organism to alter its genetic make up and thus incorporate or delete specific characteristics into or from the organism. The technology is also referred to as genetic engineering, genetic manipulation and gene technology.

Genetic mutation Sudden change in the chromosomal DNA of an individual gene. It may produce inherited changes in descendants. Mutation in some organisms can be made more frequent by irradiation.

Genital herpes A sexually transmitted disease caused by the herpes simplex virus type 2.

Genome The genome denotes the full set of genes or genetic information of an organism. It included both coding and non-coding sequences and is physically partitioned into chromosomes. The importance of coding sequences is for protein synthesis and RNA synthesis, while non-coding sequences contain regulatory sequences, sequences of old, inactive genes, repeat sequences that allow recombination of genetic information from different chromosomes, locations, or even foreign DNA that is introduces by microbial or viral infection. Many non-coding sequences are transposable elements meaning that they can copy and insert themselves at many different sites within chromosomes. These rearrangement of physical location of DNA strands affects number, location, and sequence of genes coding for proteins and RNA and thus are vital for generating mutations important for evolutionary fitness of an organism. The human genome has been found to contain only 5%

coding sequences, while half of all non-coding portions are made of transposable elements reminiscent of viral DNA. This similarity between human and viral DNA indicates that human evolution cannot be thought of as independent but is closely related to the evolution of viruses. The modern existence of pathogenic viruses is an indication of the importance of this co-evolution that likely has helped humans to maintain a heterogeneous genepool important for rapid adaptation to environmental changes.

Genomics 1. The study of the DNA sequence in the chromosomes of an organism. This includes the genes that code for proteins, the regulatory sequences that control the genes and the non-coding DNA segments.

2. The study of the molecular organization of genomes, their information content, and the gene products they encode.

Genotype The genetic description of an organism; often only one or two genes out of thousands are of interest in a genetic comparison between individuals or the analysis of genealogical traits, family history etc. The genotype is the genetic information underlying a phenotype, the exterior expression of characteristics or traits. Most phenotypes that are really physical or functional attributes of an organism are multifactorial, meaning that several genes contribute to its expression. Even at the level of cellular mechanism and metabolism, pheno-types are multifactorial because of the particular composition of enzymes as protein complexes, where individual proteins are coded for by different genes. Photosyn-thesis, for example, is the concerted action of dozens of proteins (genes) with copy numbers in the hundreds to enable a simple chemical equation carbon dioxide + water = sugar. In fact this simple overall equation is really performed in many different subsets of reactions.

Genus A well-defined group of one or more species that is clearly separate from other genera.

Geographic information system (GIS) A data management system that organizes and displays digital map data from remote sensing and aids in the analysis of relationships between mapped features.

Geomagnetic storm A worldwide disturbance of the Earth's magnetic field, associated with solar activity.

Geosynchronous orbit The orbit of a satellite that travels above the Earth's equator from west to east so that it has a speed matching that of the Earth's rotation and remains stationary in relation to the Earth (also called geostationary). Such an orbit has an altitude of about 35,900 km (22,300 miles).

Germ cells The gametes or reproductive cells which are ovum and sperm, or one of the precursor cells that will develop into ovum or sperm.

Germ line Sperm and egg cells (ova) and their precursors.

Germ line gene therapy Used to describe genetic modification or 'therapy' of the sex cells (sperm, ova & their precursors).

Germicide An agent that kills pathogens and many nonpathogens but not necessarily bacterial endospores.

Germination The stage following bacterial endospore activation in which the endospore breaks its dormant state. Germination is followed by outgrowth.

Ghon complex (gon) The initial focus of parenchymal infection in primary pulmonary tuberculosis.

Giardiasis A common intestinal disease caused by the parasitic protozoan Giardia lamblia.

Gibbs free energy Gibbs free energy (G) is an important function in chemical thermodynamics, defined by

$$G = H - TS$$

Where H is the enthalpy, S the entropy, and T the thermodynamic temperature. Gibbs free energy is the energy liberated or absorbed in a reversible process at constant pressure and constant temperature. Sometimes called Gibbs energy and, in older literature, simply "free energy".

Changes in Gibbs free energy, ΔG, are useful in indicating the conditions under which a chemical reaction will occur. If ΔG is negative the reaction will proceed spontaneo-usly to equilibrium. In equilibrium position $\Delta G = 0$.

Gibbs phase rule Gibbs phase rule is the relationship used to determine the number of state variables, usually chosen from among temperature, pressure, and species composition in each phase, which must be specified to fix the thermodynamic state of a system in equilibrium:

$$F = C - P + 2$$

Where C is the number of components in a mixture, P is the number of phases, and F is the degrees of freedom, i.e., the number of intensive variables that can be changed independently without affecting the number of phases.

Giga One billion units.

Gingivitis Inflammation of the gingival tissue.

Gingivostomatitis Inflammation of the gingiva and other oral mucous membranes.

Glass transition temperature Glass transition temperature is the temperature at which an amorphous polymer is transformed, in a reversible way, from a viscous or rubbery condition to a hard and relatively brittle one.

Glauber's salt Glauber's salt is sodium sulphate decahydrate ($Na_2SO_4 \times 10H_2O$). Loses water of hydration at 100°C. Energy storage capacity is more than seven times that of water.

Gliding motility A type of motility in which a microbial cell glides along when in contact with a solid surface.

Global regulatory systems Regulatory systems that simultaneously affect many genes and pathways.

Glomerulonephritis An inflammatory disease of the renal glomeruli.

Glucans Polysaccharides composed of glucose units held together by glycosidic linkages. Some types of glucans have a(1_3) and a(1_6) linkages and bind bacterial cells together on teeth forming a plaque ecosystem.

Gluconeogenesis The synthesis of glucose from noncarbohydrate precursors such as lactate and amino acids.

Gluon (g) The carrier particle of the strong interactions.

Glycerides Glycerides are esters of glycerol (propane-1,2,3-triol) with fatty acids, widely distributed in nature. They are by long-established custom subdivided into trigly-cerides, 1,2- or 1,3-diglycerides, and 1- or 2-monoglycerides, according to the number and positions of acyl groups.

Glycocalyx A network of polysac-charides extending from the surface of bacteria and other cells.

Glycogen The major complex carbohydrate in animal cells made of glucose. Glycogen is for animals what starch is for plants. Although glycogen is an important long term storage of energy in muscle and liver cells, it is of little nutritional significance, because most glycogen in muscle spontaneously degrades during slaughtering. Thus meats, except liver, have little or no carbohy-drate content.

Glycolysis A metabolic pathway found in all organisms. This pathway consists of ten chemical reactions catalyzed by proteins (enzymes) and is responsible for the degradation and synthesis of carbohydrates. Glycolysis does not depend on the presence of oxygen and is able to provide the cell with the universal energy currency called ATP, short for adenosine triophosphate. This pathway can degrade glucose only partially and will produce waste products such as lactate (in mammalian muscle causing sour muscle under anaerobic exercise conditions) or ethanol in microorganisms (used for fermentation of wine or beer). In the presence of oxygen, no waste products are formed and instead further degraded to carbon dioxide and water. The latter processes are known as Krebs cycle and oxidative phosphorylation.

Glycolytic pathway See Embden-Meyerhof pathway.

Glyoxylate cycle A modified tricarbo-xylic acid cycle in which the decarboxylation reactions are bypassed by the enzymes isocitrate lyase and malate synthase; it is used to convert acetyl-coa to succinate and other metabolites.

Gnotobiotic Animals that are germfree (microorganism free) or live in association with one or more known microorganisms.

Golgi apparatus A membranous eucaryotic organelle composed of stacks of flattened sacs (cisternae), which is involved in packaging and modifying materials for secretion and many other processes.

Gonococci Bacteria of the species *Neisseria gonorrhoeae*-the organism causing gonorrhea.

Gonorrhea An acute infectious sexually transmitted disease of the mucous membranes of the genitourinary tract, eye, rectum, and throat. It is caused by Neisseria gonorrhoeae.

Graft-versus-host disease A disease that results when mature post-thymic T cells in donor grafts recognize the host as foreign and attack it.

Grain Grain (gr) is a non-SI unit of mass, equal to 64.79891 mg.

Gram stain A differential staining procedure that divides bacteria into gram-positive and gram-negative groups based on their ability to retain crystal violet when decolourized with an organic solvent such as ethanol.

Gram-formula weight The mass in grams of one mole of a compound that is numerically equal to its formula weight.

Grana A stack of thylakoids in the chloroplast stroma.

Grand unified theory A yet-unknown explanation of the Universe's basic particles so that the four forces are expressed as a single force, thought to be very simple and self-explanatory in the Universe during Planck time.

Granuloma Term applied to nodular inflammatory lesions containing phagocytic cells.

Graphite Crystalline carbon used in very pure form as a moderator, principally in gas-cooled reactors, but also in Soviet-designed RBMK reactors.

Grashof number Grashof number (Gr) is a dimensionless quantity used in fluid mechanics, defined by

$$Gr = l^3 g \alpha \delta t \rho^2 / \eta^2$$

Where T is temperature, ρ is density, l is length, η is viscosity, α is cubic expansion coefficient, and g is acceleration of gravity.

Gravimetry Gravimetry is the quantitative measurement of an analyte by weighing a pure, solid form of the analyte. Since gravimetric analysis is an absolute measurement, it is the principal method for analyzing and preparing primary standards.

A typical experimental procedure to determine an unknown concentra-tion of an analyte in solution is as follows:

- quantitatively precipitate the analyte from solution

- collect the precipitate by filtering and wash it to remove impurities

- dry the solid in an oven to remove solvent

- weigh the solid on an analytical balance

- calculate the analyte concentration in the original solution based on the weight of the precipitate.

Gravitational constant G The constant G which appears in the equation for Newton's law of gravitation is called the universal constant of gravitation or the gravitational constant. Numerically it is equal to the force of gravitation, which acts between two bodies of mass 1kg each separated by a distance of 1m. The value of G is 6.67×10^{-11} Nm²/kg².

Gravitational field The force per unit mass exerted on a test mass at a given point in space.

Gravitational instability A condition that occurs when an object's inward-pulling gravitational forces exceed the outward-pushing pressure forces, thus causing the object to collapse on itself. For example, when the pressure forces within an interstellar gas cloud cannot resist the gravitational forces that act to compress the cloud, then the cloud collapses upon itself to form a star.

Gravitational interaction The interaction of particles due to their mass/energy.

Graviton The carrier particle of the gravitational interactions; not yet directly observed.

Gravity (Gravitational Force) The attractive force between all masses in the universe. All objects that have mass possess a gravitational force that attracts all other masses. The more massive the object, the stronger the gravitational force. The closer objects are to each other, the stronger the gravitational attraction.

Gray Gray (Gy) is the SI derived unit of absorbed dose of radiation. The gray is the absorbed dose when the energy per unit mass imparted to matter by ionizing radiation is one joule per kilogram (Gy = J/kg). The unit is named after the British scientist Louis Harold Gray (1905-1965).

Greenhouse effect The process of increasing the temperature of the lower parts of the atmosphere through redirecting energy back toward the surface; the absorption and reemission of infrared radiation by carbon dioxide, water vapour, and a few other gases in the atmosphere.

Greenhouse gases Gases released from the earth's surface through chemical and biological processes that interact with the chemicals in the stratosphere to decrease the release of radiation from the earth. It is believed that this leads to global warming.

Grignard reagents Grignard reagents are organomagnesium halides, RMgX, having a carbon-magnesium bond (or their equilibrium mixtures in solution with $R_2Mg + MgX_2$).

Griseofulvin An antibiotic from *Penicillium griseofulvum* given orally to treat chronic dermatophytic infections of skin and nails.

Ground state The minimum energy state of an atom that is achieved when all of its electrons have the lowest possible energy and therefore are as close to the nucleus as possible.

Group 1. A substructure that imparts characteristic chemical behaviors to a molecule, for example, a carboxylic acid group. (also: functional group).

2. A vertical column on the periodic table, for example, the halogens. Elements that belong to the same group usually show chemical similarities, although the element at the top of the group is usually atypical.

Group translocation A transport process in which a molecule is moved across a membrane by carrier proteins while being chemically altered at the same time.

Growth factors Organic compounds that must be supplied in the diet for growth because they are essential cell components or precursors of such components and cannot be synthesized by the organism.

Growth hormone A protein, produced by the pituitary gland that promotes growth of the whole body.

Guanine A purine derivative, 2-amino-6-oxypurine, found in nucleosides, nucleotides, and nucleic acids.

Guillain-Barr syndrome A relatively rare disease affecting the peripheral nervous system, especially the spinal nerves, but also the cranial nerves. The cause is unknown, but it most often occurs after an influenza infection or flu vaccination. Also called French Polio.

Gumma A soft, gummy tumor occurring in tertiary syphilis.

Gut-associated lymphoid tissue (GALT) The defensive lymphoid tissue present in the intestines.

Hadron A particle made of strongly-interacting constituents. These include the mesons and baryons. Such particles participate in residual strong interactions.

Haematopoietic stem cells Stem cells that make all the blood cells in the body. They are found in the bone marrow - the tissue that fills most bone cavities.

Haemoglobin The red oxygen carrying pigment of the blood. Haemoglobin incorporates two pairs of polypeptides called globins. Various gene mutations which affect the kinds of globins made, or their amounts, can result in diseases called the haemoglobinopathies, notably thalassaemias and sickle cell disease.

Haemophilia A single gene disorder, which affects about 1 in 1000 males, in which there is defective production of a protein that is necessary for blood clotting and thereby prevents excessive bleeding. Its inheritance is X-linked, i.e. the gene is on the X chromosome.

Hair cell Specialized sensory epithelial cell in the ear with bundles of giant microvilli (stereocilia) protruding from its apical surface. Sound vibrations tilt the stereocilia, evoking an electrical change in the hair cell, which thus acts as a sound detector.

Half-life For a given reaction the half life $t_{1/2}$ of a reactant is the time required for its concentration to reach a value that is the arithmetic mean of its initial and final (equilibrium) value.

In nuclear chemistry, (radioactive) half life is defined, for a simple radioactive decay process, as the time required for the activity to decrease to half its value by that process.

$$N = N_0/2$$

Halide Halide ion. A compound or ion containing fluorine, chlorine, bromine, iodine, or astatine.

Halobacteria or extreme halophiles A group of archaea that have an absolute dependence on high NaCl concentrations for growth and will not survive at a concentration below about 1.5 M NaCl.

Halocarbon Halocarbon is a compound containing no elements other than carbon, one or more halogens, and sometimes hydrogen. The simplest are compounds such as tetrachloro-methane (CCl_4), tetrabromo-methane (CBr_4), etc. The lower members of the various homologous series are used as refrigerants, propellant gases, fire-extinguishing agents, and blowing agents for urethane foams. When polymerized, they yield plastics characterized by extreme chemical resistance, high electrical resistivity, and good heat resistance.

Halogens The halogens are the elements fluorine (F) chlorine (Cl), bromine (Br), iodine (I), and astatine (At). They are non-metals, and make up part of the 17 group in the periodic table. Compounds of these elements are called halogenides or halides.

The halogens all have a strong unpleasant odour and will burn flesh. They do not dissolve well in water. The five elements are strongly electronegative. They are oxidizing agents, with fluorine being the strongest and astatine being the weakest. They react with most metals and many non-metals.

Halogens form molecules which consists of atoms covalently bonded. With increasing atomic weight there is a gradation in physical properties. For example: Fluorine is a pale green gas of low density. Chlorine is a greenish-yellow gas 1.892 times as dense as fluorine. Bromine is a deep reddish-brown liquid which is three times as dense as water. Iodine is a grayish-black crystalline solid with a metallic appearance. And astatine is a solid with properties which indicate that it is somewhat metallic in character.

Halophile A microorganism that requires high levels of sodium chloride for growth.

Hantavirus pulmonary syndrome The disease in humans caused by the pulmonary syndrome hantavirus. Deer mice shed the virus in their feces, humans inhale the virus and first develop ordinary flulike aches and pains. Within a few days the hantavirus causes lung damage and capillary leakage. After about a week the infected person enters a crisis phase and may die.

Haploid Used to describe a cell having half the usual number of chromosomes, e.g. sperm and ova.

Hapten A molecule not immunogenic by itself but that, when coupled to a macromolecular carrier, can elicit antibodies directed against itself.

Harborage transmission The mode of transmission in which an infectious organism does not undergo morphological or physiological changes within the vector.

Hardness Hardness is the resistance of a material to deformation of an indenter of specific size and shape under known load. This definition applies to all types of hardness scales except Mohs scale, which is based on the concept of scratch hardness and is used chiefly for minerals. The most generally used hardness scales are Brinell (for cast iron), Rockwell (for sheet metal and heat-treated steel), Knoop (for metals).

Harmonic oscillator A system in which a mass is subject to a linear restoring force, like an ideal spring. A harmonic oscillator vibrates at a fixed frequency, independent of amplitude.

Hay fever Allergic rhinitis; a type of atopic allergy involving the upper respiratory tract.

Health (helth) A state of optimal physical, mental, and social wellbeing, and not merely the absence of disease and infirmity.

Healthy carrier An individual who harbours a pathogen, but is not ill.

Heat Heat is a form of energy associated with and proportional to molecular motion. It can be transferred from one body to another by radiation, conduction, or convection.

Heat of atomization is the energy required to dissociate one mole of a given substance into atoms.

Heat of combustion is the heat evolved when a definite quantity of a substance is completely oxidized (burned).

Heat of crystallization is the heat evolved or absorbed when one mole of given substance crystallizes from a saturated solution of the same substance.

Heat of formation is the heat evolved or absorbed when one mole of a compound is formed in their standard state from its constituent elements.

Heat of fusion is the heat required to convert a substance from the solid to the liquid state with no temperature change (also called latent heat of fusion or melting).

Heat of hydration is the heat evolved or absorbed when a hydrate of a compound is formed.

Heat of reaction is the heat evolved or absorbed as a result of the complete chemical reaction of molar amounts of the reactants.

Heat of sublimation is the energy required to convert one mole of a substance from the solid to the gas state without the appearance of the liquid state.

Heat of vaporization is the heat required to convert a substance from the liquid to the gaseous state with no temperature change.

As defined in thermodynamics, heat is the energy that flows between two systems as a result of temperature differences (a system contains neither heat nor work, but can produce heat or do work). Heat thus differs from thermal energy.

Heat capacity Heat capacity is defined in general as dq/dt, where dq is the amount of heat that must be added to a system to increase its temperature by a small amount dt. The heat capacity at constant pressure is $C_p = (H/T)_p$; that at constant volume is $C_V = (E/?)_V$, where H is enthalpy, E is internal energy, p is pressure, V is volume, and T is temperature. An upper case C normally indicates the molar heat capacity, while a lower case c is used for the specific heat capacity.

Heat death of the Universe Time at which no work will be able to be done because all heat energy in the Universe will be evenly distributed

(so that no further increase in entropy is possible)

Heat-shock proteins Proteins produced when cells are exposed to high temperatures or other stressful conditions. They protect the cells from damage and often aid in the proper folding of proteins.

Heavy vehicle Heavy vehicles are assumed to be buses, rigid trucks and semi trailer trucks with a tare weight greater than 3 tonnes. Also heavy vehicles can be defined in terms of length as buses, or trucks with a length exceeding 5.25 metres.

Heavy water Water containing an elevated concentration of molecules with deuterium ("heavy hydrogen") atoms.

Heavy water reactor (HWR) A reactor which uses heavy water as its moderator, e.g. Canadian CANDU.

Hectare Hectare (ha) is a unit of area equal to 10^4 m². The unit is still used in agriculture.

Heisenberg uncertainty principle Heisenberg uncertainty principle is the principle that it is not possible to know with unlimited accuracy both the position and momentum of a particle. German physicist Werner Heisenberg (1901-1976) discovers this principle in 1927.

Helical In virology this refers to a virus with a helical capsid surrounding its nucleic acid.

Helicases Enzymes that use ATP energy to unwind DNA ahead of the replication fork.

Helmholz free energy Helmholz free energy (A) is a thermodynamic function defined by $A = U - TS$, where U is the internal energy, S the entropy, and T the thermodynamic temperature. For a reversible isothermal process ΔA represents the useful work available.

Hemadsorption The adherence of red blood cells to the surface of something, such as another cell or a virus.

Hemagglutination The agglutination of red blood cells by antibodies.

Hemagglutinin The antibody responsible for a hemagglutination reaction.

Heme Cyclic organic molecule containing an iron atom that carries oxygen in hemoglobin and carries an electron in cytochromes.

Hemi-cellulose A type of dietary fiber made up glucose and many other types of sugars and differs from cellulose, which only contains glucose.

Hemidesmosome Specialized cell junction between an epithelial cell and the underlying basal lamina.

Hemoflagellate A flagellated protozoan parasite that is found in the bloodstream.

Hemolysin A substance that causes hemolysis (the lysis of red blood cells). At least some hemolysins are enzymes that destroy the phospholipids in erythrocyte plasma membranes.

Hemolysis The disruption of red blood cells and release of their hemoglobin. There are several types of hemolysis when bacteria such as *streptococci* and *staphylococci* grow on blood agar. In a-hemolysis, a narrow greenish zone of incomplete hemolysis forms around the colony. A clear zone of complete hemolysis without any obvious colour change is formed during b-hemolysis.

Hemolytic uremic syndrome A kidney disease characterized by blood in the urine and often by kidney failure. It is caused by enterohemorrhagic strains of *Escherichia coli* O157:H7 that produce a Shiga-like toxin, which attacks the kidneys.

Hemorrhagic fever A fever usually caused by a specific virus that may lead to hemorrhage, shock, and sometimes death.

Henry Henry (H) is the SI derived unit of inductance equal to the inductance of a closed circuit in which an e.m.f. of one volt is produced when the electric current in the circuit varies uniformly at the rate of one ampere per second (H = V·s/A). The unit is named after the US physicist Joseph Henry.

Henry's law Henry's law is discovered in 1801 by the British chemist William Henry (1775-1836). At a constant temperature the mass of gas dissolved in a liquid at equilibrium is proportional to the partial pressure of the gas. It applies only to gases that not react with the solvent.

$$X_i = K_x \cdot p_i$$

Where p_i is the partial pressure of component i above the solution, x_i is its mole fraction in the solution, and K_x is the Henry's law constant.

Hepatitis Liver inflammation usually caused by a virus.

Hepatitis A A type of hepatitis that is transmitted by fecal-oral contamination; it primarily affects children and young adults, especially in environments where there is poor sanitation and overcrowding. It is caused by the hepatitis A virus, a single-stranded RNA virus.

Hepatitis B This form of hepatitis is caused by a double-stranded DNA virus (HBV) formerly called the "Dane particle." The virus is transmitted by body fluids.

Hepatitis C About 90% of all cases of viral hepatitis can be traced to either HAV or HBV. The remaining 10% is believed to be caused by one and possibly several other types of viruses. At least one of these is hepatitis C (formerly non-A, non-B).

Hepatitis D The liver diseases caused by the hepatitis D virus in those individuals already infected with the hepatitis B virus.

Hepatitis E The liver disease caused by the hepatitis E virus. Usually, a subclinical, acute infection results; however, there is a high mortality in women in their last trimester of pregnancy.

Herbicide A substance that kills plants. Herbicides are used in agriculture, horticulture and gardening to control unwanted plants. Herbicides can be selective, and kill selected species, or non-selective (broad spectrum), and kill all plants.

Herd immunity The resistance of a population to infection and spread of an infectious organism due to the immunity of a high percentage of the population.

Hereditary disorders A pathological condition due to changes in individual genes, or groups of genes or in sections of chromosomes or whole chromosomes. These changes may be passed from parents to offspring.

Herman the bull A Dutch bull engineered to contain the human lactoferrin gene which codes for the protein lactoferrin used in the treatment of sepsis. Human lactoferrin is produced in the milk of cows bred from this bull. (Said to be named after Herman de Boer the managing director of Gene Pharming, Holland)

Herpetic keratitis An inflammation of the cornea and conjunctiva of the eye resulting from a herpes simplex virus infection.

Hertz Hertz (Hz) is the SI derived unit, with a special name, for frequency. The hertz is the frequency of a periodic phenomenon of which the period is one second (Hz = 1 s^{-1}). It is named after the German scientist Heinrich Hertza (1857 - 1894).

Heterocaryon Cell with two or more nuclei produced by the fusion of two or more different cells.

Heterochromatin Region of a chromosome that remains unusually condensed and transcriptionally inactive during interphase.

Heterocyclic compounds Heterocyclic compounds are cyclic compounds having as ring members atoms of at least two different elements, e.g., quinoline, 1,2-thiazole.

Heterocysts Specialized cells produced by cyanobacteria that are the sites of nitrogen fixation.

Heteroduplex DNA A double-stranded stretch of DNA formed by two slightly different strands that are not completely complementary.

Heterogeneous nuclear RNA (hnRNA) The RNA transcript of DNA made by RNA polymerase II; it is then processed to form mRNA.

Heterolactic fermenters Micro-organisms that ferment sugars to form lactate, and also other products such as ethanol and CO_2.

Heterotroph An organism that uses reduced, preformed organic molecules as its principal carbon source.

Heterotrophic nitrification Nitrification carried out by chemoheterotrophic micro-organisms.

Heterozygote Diploid cell or individual having two different alleles of a specified gene.

Heterozygous Identifies the two alleles of a diploid organism as being different from each other. If both alleles are genetically identical, the cell or organism is homozygous. Often, one of the two alleles is the dominant, the other the recessive allele. If a dominant allele is present, one copy is enough to establish the corresponding phenotype. The recessive allele for light eye colour cannot be expressed, until two copies of the allele are present.

Heusler alloys Heusler alloys are alloys of manganese, copper, aluminum, nickel, and sometimes other metals which find important uses as permanent magnets.

Hexon or hexamer A capsomer composed of six protomers.

Hexose monophosphate pathway See pentose phosphate pathway.

Hfr strain A bacterial strain that donates its genes with high frequency to a recipient cell during conjugation because the F factor is integrated into the bacterial chromosome.

High oxygen diffusion environment A microbial environment in close contact with air and through which oxygen can move at a rapid rate.

High-energy molecule A molecule whose hydrolysis under standard conditions makes available a large amount of free energy (the standard free energy change is more negative than about 27 kcal/mole); a high-energy molecule readily decomposes and transfers groups such as phosphate to acceptors.

High-level wastes Extremely radioactive fission products and transuranic elements (usually other than plutonium) in spent nuclear fuel. They may be separated by reprocessing the spent fuel, or the spent fuel containing them may be regarded as high-level waste.

Highly (or High)-enriched uranium (HEU) Uranium enriched to at least 20% U-235. (That in weapons is about 90% U-235.)

Histone A small basic protein with large amounts of lysine and arginine that is associated with eucaryotic DNA in chromatin.

Histoplasmosis A systemic fungal infection caused by Histoplasma capsulatum var capsulatum.

Hives An eruption of the skin.

Holdfast A structure produced by some bacteria and algae that attaches the cell to a solid object.

Hole Particle associated with an empty electron level in an almost filled band.

Holoenzyme A complete enzyme consisting of the apoenzyme plus a cofactor.

Holography Holography is a technique for creating a three-dimensional image of an object by recording the interference pattern between a light beam diffracted from the object and a reference beam. The image can be reconstructed from this pattern by a suitable optical system.

Holozoic nutrition In this type of nutrition, nutrients are acquired by phagocytosis and the subsequent formation of a food vacuole or phagosome.

Homeostasis In biology used to describe a condition where an organism maintains a stable structure where in fact a constant flux of molecules occurs. Although many organisms can live for years, all cellular components like proteins, membranes, sugars, and nucleic acids are constantly recycled while never compromising the integrity of the organism as a whole. This turnover processes can be characterized by specific half-life values that for most proteins, membranes, and RNA (but not DNA structures) are measured in hours. In a more narrow sense homeostasis refers to the maintenance of water and salt concentration in cells.

Homolactic fermenters Organisms that ferment sugars almost completely to lactic acid.

Hooke's law When a load is applied to any elastic body is deformed or strained, then the resulting stress is proportional to the strain. Stress is measured in units of force per unit area, strain is the extent of the deformation.

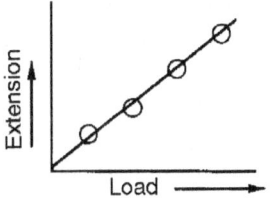

Figure Graph depicting Hooke's law

Horizontal gene transfer The process in which genes are transferred from one mature, independent organism to another.

Hormogonia Small motile fragments produced by fragmentation of filamentous cyanobacteria; used for asexual reproduction and dispersal.

Horse power Horse power is obsolete non-SI of power introduced by James Watt in 1782 to allow to describe the power of steam machinery. It was equal to the work effort of a horse needed to raise vertically 528 cubic feet of water to one metre in one minute (HP = 735.498750 W).

Host The body of an organism that harbors another organism. It can be viewed as a microenvironment that shelters and supports the growth and multiplication of a parasitic organism.

Host restriction The degradation of foreign genetic material by nucleases after the genetic material enters a host cell.

HPLC HPLC is abbreviation for high-performance liquid chromatography. HPLC is a variation of liquid chromato-graphy that utilizes high-pressure pumps to increase the efficiency of the separation.

Human herpesvirus 6 HHV-6 was discovered in 1986 and was initially called the human B-lymphotropic virus. The virus was later shown to have a marked tropism for CD41 T cells and was renamed HHV-6. HHV-6 is genetically similar to cytomegalo-virus. HHV-6 causes exanthem subitum (roseola infantum or sixth disease) in infants and has been suspected of involvement in many conditions, including opportunistic infections in immunocompromised patients, hepatitis, lymphoproliferative diseases, synergistic interactions with HIV, lymphadenitis, and chronic fatigue syndrome.

Human immunodeficiency virus (HIV) A lentivirus of the family Retroviridae that is associated with the onset of AIDS.

Human leukocyte antigen complex (HLA) An antigen on the surface of cells of human tissues and organs that is recognized by the immune system cells and therefore is important in graft rejection and regulation of the immune response. This is the same as MHC class II.

Humoral The type of immunity that results from the presence of soluble antibodies in blood and lymph; also known as antibody-mediated immunity.

Hybridoma A fast-growing cell line produced by fusing a cancer cell (myeloma) to another cell, such as an antibody-producing cell.

Hydrate A hydrate is an addition compound that contains water in weak chemical combination with another compound. For example, crystals of $CuSO_4.5H_2O$ (copper sulphate pentahydrate) are made of regularly repeating units, each containing 5 molecules of water weakly bound to a copper (II) ion and a sulphate ion.

Hydration Hydration is addition of water or the elements of water to a molecular entity. The term is also used in a more restricted sense for the process:

$$A^+B^- \rightleftharpoons A^+(aq) + B^-(aq)$$

Hydrazine (NH_2NH_2) A colourless, fuming, corrosive liquid that is a powerful reducing agent. NH_2NH_2 is used in jet and rocket fuels, and as an intermediate in the manufacture of agricultural, textile, photographic, and industrial chemicals.

Hydrocarbon Compare with alkane, alkene, alkyne, and organic.

Hydrocarbons are organic compounds that contain only hydrogen and carbon. The simplest hydrocarbons are the alkanes.

Hydrogenosome A microbody like organelle that contains a unique electron transfer pathway in which hydrogenase transfers electrons to protons and molecular hydrogen is formed.

Hydrolysis Hydrolysis is a chemical reaction in which water reacts with another substance to form two or more new substances. This involves ionization of the water molecule as well as splitting of the compound hydrolyzed, e.g.

$$CH_3COOC_2H_5 + H_2O \rightleftharpoons CH_3COOH + C_2H_5OH$$

Examples are conversion of starch to glucose by water in presence of suitable catalysts and reaction of the ions of a dissolved salt to form various products, such as acids, complex ions, etc.

Hydromagnetic wave A wave in which both the plasma and magnetic field oscillate.

Hydronium ion (H_3O^+) Hydronium. The H_3O^+ ion, formed by capture of a hydrogen ion by a water molecule. A strong covalent bond is formed between the hydrogen ion and water oxygen; all hydrogen ions in aqueous solution are bound inside hydronium ions.

Hydrophilic Hydrophilic is having a strong tendency to bind or absorb water, which results in swelling and formation of reversible gels. This property is characteristic of carbohydrate.

Hydrophobic Hydrophobic is antagonistic to water, incapable of dissolving in vater. This property is characteristic of oil, fats, waxes, and many resins.

Hydrophobic interaction Hydrophobic interaction is the tendency of hydrocarbons to form intermolecular aggregates in an aqueous medium, and analogous intramolecular interactions. The name arises from the attribution of the phenomenon to the apparent repulsion between water and hydrocarbons. Use of the misleading alternative term hydrophobic bond is discouraged.

Hydroxide (OH^-) Hydroxide ion. 1. The OH^- ion.

2. Compounds containing the OH^- ion.

Hygroscopic Able to absorb moisture from air. For example, sodium hydroxide pellets are so hygroscopic that they dissolve in the water they absorb from the air.

Hygroscopicity The ability of a substance to absorb moisture from air.

Hyperendemic disease A disease that has a gradual increase in occurrence beyond the endemic level, but not at the epidemic level, in a given population; also may refer to a disease that is equally endemic in all age groups.

Hypermutation A rapid production of multiple mutations in a gene or genes through the activation of special mutator genes. The process may be deliberately used to maximize the possibility of creating desirable mutants.

Hyperpolarization A mechanism by which a membrane potential is made more negative inside with respect to the outside of the cell. Hyperpolarization causes neurons and muscle cells to be electrically silent and stabilize at a resting potential. Hyperpolarization is the result of moving positive charges from in to out of a cell which is usually the result of K^+ ions moving out, but can also be achieved by moving Cl^- ions into the cell.

Hypersensitivity A condition of increased immune sensitivity in which the body reacts to an antigen with an exaggerated immune response that usually harms the individual. Also termed an allergy.

Hypertext markup language Used to format information for the World Wide Web.

Hyperthermophile A bacterium that has its growth optimum between 80 degrees C and about 113 degrees C. Hyperthermophiles usually do not grow well below 55 degrees C.

Hypha The unit of structure of most fungi and some bacteria; a tubular filament.

Hypoferremia Deficiency of iron in the blood.

Hypotheca The smaller half of a diatom frustule.

Hypothesis A testable scientific idea that can be proved right or wrong with experiments. A hypothesis is a formulation of a question that lends itself to a prediction. This prediction can be verified or falsified. A question can only be used as scientific hypothesis, if their is an experimen-tal approach or observational study that can be designed to check the outcome of a prediction.

Hypoxic Having a low oxygen level.

Iatrogenic Created by a medical doctor.

Ice-point It is the melting point of pure melting ice under 1 atm pressure. The ice point is taken as the lower fixed point for temperature scales.

Icosahedral In virology this term refers to a virus with an icosahedral capsid, which has the shape of a regular polyhedron having 20 equilateral triangular faces and 12 corners.

Ideal gas Ideal gas is a gas in which there is complete absence of cohesive forces between the component molecules; the behavior of such a gas can be predicted accurately by the ideal gas equation through all ranges of temperature and pressure. The concept is theoretical, since no actual gas meets the ideal requirement.

Ideal gas law The generalized ideal gas law is derived from a combination of the laws of Boyle and Charles. Ideal gas law is the equation of state

$$Pv = RT$$

Which defines an ideal gas, where p is pressure, V molar volume, T temperature, and R the molar gas constant (8.314 $JK^{-1}mol^{-1}$).

Ideal solution Ideal solution is a solution in which solvent-solvent and solvent-solute interactions are identical, so that properties such as volume and enthalpy are exactly additive. Ideal solutions follow Raoult's law, which states that the vapour pressure p_i of component i is $p_i = x_i \, p_i*$, where x_i is the mole fraction of component i and p_i* the vapour pressure of the pure substance i.

Identification The process of determining that a particular isolate or organism belongs to a recognized taxon.

Idiotype A set of one or more unique epitopes in the variable region of an immunoglobulin that distinguishes it from immunoglobulins produced by different plasma cells.

IgA Immunoglobulin A; the class of immunoglobulins that is present in dimeric form in many body secretions and protects body surfaces. IgA is also present in serum.

IgD Immunoglobulin D; the class of immunoglobulins found on the surface of many B lymphocytes; though to serve as an antigen receptor in the stimulation of antibody synthesis.

IgE Immunoglobulin E; the immunoglobulin class that binds to mast cells and basophils, and is responsible for type I or anaphylactic hypersensitivity reactions such as hay fever and asthma. IgE is also involved in resistance to helminth parasites.

IgG Immunoglobulin G; the predomi-nant immunoglobulin class in serum. Has functions such as neutralizing toxins, opsonizing bacteria, activating complement, and crossing the placenta to protect the fetus and neonate.

IgM Immunoglobulin M; the class of serum antibody first produced during an infection. It is a large, pentameric molecule that is active in agglutinating pathogens and activating complement. The monomeric form is present on the surface of some B lymphocytes.

Image A place where an object appears to be, because the rays diffusely reflected from any given point on the object have been bent so that they come back together and then spread out again from the image point, or spread apart as if they had originated from the image.

Immobilization The incorporation of a simple, soluble substance into the body of an organism, making it unavailable for use by other organisms.

Immune complex The product of an antigen-antibody reaction, which may also contain components of the complement system.

Immune machines Medical nanoma-chines designed for internal use, especially in the bloodstream and digestive tract, able to identify and disable intruders such as bacteria and viruses.

Immune response Response made by the immune system of a vertebrate when a foreign substance or microorganism enters its body.

Immune surveillance The still somewhat hypothetical process in which lymphocytes such as natural killer (NK) cells recognize and destroy tumor cells; other cells with abnormal surface antigens also may be destroyed.

Immune system The defensive system in a host consisting of the nonspecific and specific immune responses. It is composed of widely distributed cells, tissues, and organs that recognize foreign substances and microorganisms and acts to neutralize or destroy them.

Immunity Refers to the overall general ability of a host to resist a particular disease; the condition of being immune.

Immunoblotting The electrophoretic transfer of proteins from polyacry-lamide gels to nitrocellulose sheets to demonstrate the presence of specific proteins through reaction with labeled antibodies.

Immunocontraception A method of reducing fertility of a pest species by controlling or preventing conception and pregnancy. Used in rabbits, it depends on the insertion of genes using the myxoma virus.

Immunodeficiency The inability to produce a normal complement of

Immunotoxin

antibodies or immunologically sensitized T cells in response to specific antigens.

Immunodiffusion A technique involving the diffusion of antigen and/or antibody within a semisolid gel to produce a precipitin reaction where they meet in proper proportions. Often both the antibody and antigen diffuse through the gel; sometimes an antigen diffuses through a gel containing antibody.

Immunoelectrophoresis The electrophoretic separation of protein antigens followed by diffusion and precipitation in gels using antibodies against the separated proteins.

Immunofluorescence A technique used to identify particular antigens microscopically in cells or tissues by the binding of a fluorescent antibody conjugate.

Immunoglobulin (IG) An antibody molecule. Higher vertebrates have five classes of immunoglobulin - IgA, IgD, IgE, IgG, and IgM - each with a different role in the immune response.

Immunoglobulin like (Ig like) domain Characteristic protein domain of about 100 amino acids that is found in antibody molecules and in many other proteins that form the Ig superfamily.

Immunology Immunology is the science of molecular self-defense of organisms against infections. It deals with the immune system, a complex organ that produces both cells and proteins involved in detecting and destroying foreign molecules and microorganisms. It is most elaborate in mammals. The immune cells are white blood cells, originate from the bone marrow and mature in the lymph system. Some of these cells produce antibodies that circulate in the blood as a result of a detected infection. These antibodies can be produced for a very long time after the initial infection and are the basis of immunity against further infection by the same microorganism. If the microorganism mutates, as if often the case, immunity is no longer given and a new response must be provided by the immune system. In order to avoid costly development of antibodies, the innate immune system provides a broad and less specific protection against a large class of pathogens. Sometimes, the immune system overreacts and destroys cells of the body. The result is an autoimmune disease. Common autoimmune diseases are arthritis, lupus, and type I or juvenile diabetes. There are no known cures for autoimmune disease except for immune system suppressant and pain relievers.

Immunopathology The study of diseases or conditions resulting from immune reactions.

Immunoprecipitation A reaction involving soluble antigens reacting with antibodies to form a large aggregate that precipitates out of solution.

Immunotoxin A monoclonal antibody that has been attached to a specific toxin or toxic agent (antibody 1 toxin 5 immunotoxin) and can kill specific target cells.

Impetigo This superficial cutaneous disease, most commonly seen in children, is characterized by crusty lesions, usually located on the face; the lesions typically have vesicles surrounded by a red border. It is the most frequently diagnosed skin infection caused by *S. pyogenes*.

Imprinting This is when genes are suppressed or silenced depending on which parent they were received from. When DNA is passed to daughter cells after fertilization of an egg by a sperm, certain alleles can become active only if they were received from the mother, others only if they came from the father. If a gene is suppressed through imprinting from one parent, and the allele from the other parent is not expressed because of mutation, neither can act and the child will be deficient. A healthy child cannot be produced when both sets of chromosomes come from the same parent. Imprinting of the same areas will occur and all these genes will be suppressed.

Impulse The impulse acting on a body is equal to the product of the force acting on the body and the time for which it acts. If the force is variable, the impulse is the integral of Fdt from t0 to t1. The impulse of a force acting for a given time interval is equal to change in momentum produced over that interval. $J=m(v-u)$, assuming that the mass m remains constant while the velocity changes from v to u. The SI units of impulse are kg m/s.

Impulsive force The force which acts on a body for a very short time but produces a large change in the momentum of the body is called an impulsive force.

Impulsive noise Having a high peak of short duration or a sequence of such peaks. A sequence of impulses in rapid succession is termed repetitive impulsive noise.

Impurity A foreign atom in a crystal.

***In situ* leaching (ISL)** The recovery by chemical leaching of minerals from porous orebodies without physical excavation. Also known as solution mining.

Incandescent Matter emitting visible light as a result of high temperature for example, a light bulb, a flame from any burning source, and the sun are all incandescent sources because of high temperature.

Inclusion bodies Granules of organic or inorganic material lying in the cytoplasmic matrix of bacteria.

Inclusion conjunctivitis An acute infectious disease that occurs throughout the world. It is caused by *Chlamydia trachomatis* that infects the eye and causes inflammation and the occurrence of large inclusion bodies.

Incubation period The period after pathogen entry into a host and before signs and symptoms appear.

Incubatory carrier An individual who is incubating a pathogen in large numbers but is not yet ill.

Independence The lack of any relationship between two random events.

Index case The first disease case in an epidemic within a given population.

Index of refraction For a non-absorbing medium, index of refraction (n) is the ratio of the velocity of electromagnetic radiation *in vacuo* to the phase velocity of radiation of a specified frequency in the medium.

Indicator Indicator is a substance used to show the presence of a chemical substance or ion by its colour. Acid-base indicators are compounds, such as phenolphtaleine and methyl orange, that change colour reversibly, depending on whether the solution is acidic or basic. Oxidation-reduction indicators are substances that show a reversible colour change between oxidized and reduced forms.

Inducer A small molecule that stimulates the synthesis of an inducible enzyme.

Inducible enzyme An enzyme whose level rises in the presence of a small molecule that stimulates its synthesis.

Induction The production of an electric field by a changing magnetic field, or vice-versa.

Industrial ecology The study of the ecology of industrial societies with a major focus on material cycling, energy flow, and the ecological impacts of such societies.

Inertia The property of matter that causes it to resist any change in its state of rest or of uniform motion. There are three kinds of inertia- inertia of rest, inertia of motion and inertia of direction. The mass of a body is a measure of its inertia.

Inertial frame A frame of reference that is not accelerating, one in which Newton's first law is true.

Infantile paralysis See poliomyelitis.

Infection The invasion of a host by a microorganism with subsequent establishment and multiplication of the agent. An infection may or may not lead to overt disease.

Infection thread A tubular structure formed during the infection of a root by nitrogen-fixing bacteria. The bacteria enter the root by way of the infection thread and stimulate the formation of the root nodule.

Infectious disease Any change from a state of health in which part or all of the host's body cannot carry on its normal functions because of the presence of an infectious agent or its products.

Infectious disease cycle The chain or cycle of events that describes how an infectious organism grows, reproduces, and is disseminated.

Infectious dose 50 Refers to the dose or number of organisms that will infect 50% of an experimental group of hosts within a specified time period.

Infectious mononucleosis An acute, self-limited infectious disease of the lymphatic system caused by the Epstein-Barr virus and characterized by fever, sore throat, lymph node and spleen swelling, and the proliferation of monocytes and abnormal lymphocytes.

Infectivity Infectiousness; the state or quality of being infectious or communicable.

Infertile Incapable of initiating, sustaining, or supporting reproduction, alternatively: not fertilised and therefore incapable of growing and developing.

Inflammation A localized protective response to tissue injury or destruction. Acute inflammation is characterized by pain, heat, swelling, and redness in the injured area.

Inflammatory response Local response of a tissue to injury or infection. Caused by invasion of white blood cells, which release various local mediators such as histamine.

Influenza or flu An acute viral infection of the respiratory tract, occurring in isolated cases, epidemics, and pandemics. Influenza is caused by three strains of influenza virus, labeled types A, B, and C, based on the antigens of their protein coats.

Informed consent A term used to describe the responsibility of doctors or researchers to ensure that patients or people being researched have an understanding of the relevant facts regarding their care or participation in research. We can also say that consumers of have a right to practice informed consent when they buy particular foods. Informed consent relies on our having access to reliable, truthful, and complete information.

Infrasonic Sound waves having too low a frequency to be heard by the human ear; sound having a frequency of less than 20 Hz.

Ingoldian fungi Aquatic hyphomycetes that often have a characteristic tetraradiate hyphal development form and which sporulate under water. Discovered by the British mycologist, C. T. Ingold, in the 1940s.

Inherited Traits or characteristics that come from one's ancestors and are transmitted from parents to offspring through genes. The traits will therefore be present at birth.

Inner cell mass Within a blastocyst - the hollow ball of cells that forms soon after an egg is fertilised - there is a mass of cells on one side which will form the body of the embryo. This is referred to as the inner cell mass. This is where embryonic stem cells are taken from.

Inorganic compound Inorganic. A compound that does not contain carbon chemically bound to hydrogen. Carbonates, bicarbonates, carbides, and carbon oxides are considered inorganic compounds, even though they contain carbon.

Inorganic This term has several meanings, including:

Chemicals which are not organic, that is, not manufactured within living organisms.

Any chemical compound which is not based on carbon chains or rings.

Input traits Traits introduced into crop plants with the aim of lowering the cost of production and improving the performance of the crop in the field. For example: pesticide resistance, herbicide tolerance and disease resistance. This is in comparison to traits introduced into the crop to produce products with enhanced value. These are referred to as output traits.

Insertion sequence A simple transposon that contains genes only for those enzymes, such as the transposase, that are required for transposition.

Insulator Insulator is a material in which the highest occupied energy band (valence band) is completely filled with electrons, while the next higher band is empty. Solids with an energy gap of 5 ev or more are generally considered as insulators at room temperature. Their conductivity is less than 10^{-6} S/m and increases with temperature.

Integration The incorporation of one DNA segment into a second DNA molecule to form a new hybrid DNA. Integration occurs during such processes as genetic recombination, episome incorpora-tion into host DNA, and prophage insertion into the bacterial chromosome.

Integrins A large and broadly distributed family of a/b heterodimers. Integrins are cellular adhesion receptors that mediate cell-cell and cell-substratum interactions. Integrins usually recognize linear amino acid sequences on protein ligands.

Inteins Internal intervening sequences of precursor self-splicing proteins that separate exteins and are removed during formation of the final protein.

Intensity The amount, degree, or quantity of energy passing through a point per unit time. For example, the intensity of light that Earth receives from the Sun is far greater than that from any other star because the Sun is the closest star to us.

Intensity map A colour-coded map of radiation intensity as a function of position. Different colours or shades represent different intensities of observed radiation.

Interaction A process in which a particle decays or it responds to a force due to the presence of another particle. Also used to mean the underlying property of the theory that causes such effects.

Intercalating agents Molecules that can be inserted between the stacked bases of a DNA double helix, thereby distorting the DNA and inducing insertion and deletion mutations.

Interdigitating dendritic cell Special dendritic cells in the lymph nodes that function as potent antigen-presenting cells and develop from Langerhans cells.

Interference Phenomenon of light where the relative phase difference between two light waves produces light or dark spots, a result of light's wavelike nature.

Interferon A glycoprotein that has nonspecific antiviral activity by stimulating cells to produce antiviral proteins, which inhibit the synthesis of viral RNA and proteins. Interferons also regulate the growth, differentiation, and/or function of a variety of immune system cells. Their production may be stimulated by virus infections, intracellular pathogens, protozoan parasites, endotoxins, and other agents.

Interleukin A glycoprotein produced by macrophages and T cells that regulates growth and differentiation, particularly of lymphocytes. Interleukins promote cellular and humoral immune responses.

Intermediate filaments Small protein filaments, about 8 to 10 nm in diameter, in the cytoplasmic matrix of eucaryotic cells that are important in cell structure.

Intermediate host The host that serves as a temporary but essential environment for development of a parasite and completion of its life cycle.

Intermittent noise The level suddenly drops to that of the background noise several times during the period of observation. The time during which the noise remains at levels different from that of the ambient is one second or more.

Intermolecular forces Forces of interaction between molecules.

Internal energy Sum of all the potential energy and all the kinetic energy of all the molecules of an object.

International system of units International System of Units (SI) is the unit system adopted by the General Conference on Weights and Measures in 1960 and recommended for use in all scientific and technical fields. It consists of seven base units (metre, kilogram, second, ampere, kelvin, mole, candela), plus derived units and prefixes.

Interrupted genes Genes whose coding sequence is interrupted at intervals by long stretches of non-coding sequences. The coding regions came to be known as exons and the non-coding regions as introns. This structure is now found to be characteristic of most eukaryotic genes. The number and size of introns vary greatly, and they are often much longer than the coding sequences. After transcrip-tion, the intron regions are removed, or spliced out form the RNA transcript before it is translated into protein.

Interspecies hydrogen transfer The linkage of hydrogen production from organic matter by anaerobic heterotrophic microorganisms to the use of hydrogen by other anaerobes in the reduction of carbon dioxide to methane. This avoids possible hydrogen toxicity.

Intertriginous candidiasis A skin infection caused by *Candida* species. Involves those areas of the body, usually opposed skin surfaces, that are warm and moist (axillae, groin, skin folds).

Intoxication A disease that results from the entrance of a specific toxin into the body of a host. The toxin can induce the disease in the absence of the toxin-producing organism.

Intraepidermal lymphocytes T cells found in the epidermis of the skin that express the gd T-cell receptor.

Intramolecular Describes an interaction within a single molecule. Intramolecular interactions between widely separated parts of a molecule resemble intermolecular interactions in most respects.

Intranuclear inclusion body A structure found within cells infected with the cytomegalovirus.

Intrinsic carrier density The density of electrons and holes in an intrinsic semiconductor.

Intrinsic factors Food-related factors such as moisture, pH, and available nutrients that influence microbial growth.

Intrinsic semiconductor A semiconductors free of defects or impurities.

Intron A noncoding intervening sequence in a split or interrupted gene, which codes for RNA that is missing from the final RNA product.

Invariant A quantity that does not change when transformed.

Invasiveness The ability of a microorganism to enter a host, grow and reproduce within the host, and spread throughout its body.

Inverse proportion The relationship in which the value of one variable increases while the value of the second variable decreases at the same rate (in the same ratio).

Inverse square law A law that describes any quantity, such as gravitational force, that decreases with the square of the distance between two objects. For example, if the distance between two objects is doubled, then the gravitational force exerted between them is one-fourth as strong. Likewise, if the distance to a star is doubled, then its apparent brightness is only one-fourth as great.

Ion An atom or molecule that has acquired a charge by either gaining or losing electrons. An atom or molecule with missing electrons has a net positive charge and is called a cation; one with extra electrons has a net negative charge and is called an anion.

Ion exchanger Ion-exchanger is a solid or liquid material containing ions that are exchangeable with other ions with a like charge that are present in a solution in which the material is insoluble. Ion-exchange resins consist of various copolymers having a cross-linked three-dimensional structure to which ionic groups have been attached.

Ionic bond Ionically bound; ionic bonding. An attraction between ions of opposite charge. Potassium bromide consists of potassium ions (K^+) ionically bound to bromide ions (Br^-). Unlike covalent bonds, ionic bond formation involves transfer of electrons, and ionic bonding is not directional.

Ionic compound Salt. A compound made of distinguishable cations and anions, held together by electrostatic forces.

Ionic strength Ionic strength (μ or I) is a measure of the total concentration of ions in a solution, defined by

$$\mu = \frac{1}{2}\sum c_i z_i^2$$

Where z_i is the charge of ionic species i and c_i is its concentration.

Ionising radiation Radiation capable of breaking chemical bonds, thus causing ionisation of the matter through which it passes and damage to living tissue.

Ionization energy Ionization energy is the minimum energy required to remove an electron from an isolated atom or molecule in the gaseous phase.

Ionization The process by which ions are produced, typically by collisions with other atoms or electrons, or by absorption of electromagnetic radiation.

Ionized An atom or a particle that has a net charge because it has gained or lost electrons.

Ionizing radiation Radiation of very short wavelength or high energy that causes atoms to lose electrons or ionize.

Ionosphere The region of the Earth's upper atmosphere containing a small percentage of free electrons and ions produced by photoionization of the constituents of the atmosphere by solar ultraviolet radiation. The ionosphere significantly influences radiowave propagation of frequencies less than about 30 MHz.

Irradiate Subject material to ionising radiation. Irradiated reactor fuel and components have been subject to neutron irradiation and hence become radioactive themselves.

Isobar Isobar is a line connecting points of equal pressure on a graphical representation of a physical system.

Isochore Isochore is a line or surface of constant volume on a graphical representation of a physical system.

Isoelectric point Isoelectric point is the pH of a solution or dispersion at which the net charge on the macro-molecules or colloidal particles is zero. In electrophoresis there is no motion of the particles in an electric field at the isoelectric point.

Isoelectronic Two molecules are described as isoelectronic if they have the same number of valence electrons in similar orbitals, although they may differ in their distribution of nuclear charges (e.g., H-C N and H-N$^+$ C$^-$.

Kinetic- Pertaining to the rates of chemical reactions. A fast reaction is said to have fast kinetics; if the balance of products in a reaction is controlled by reaction rates rather than by thermodynamic equilibria, the reaction is said to be kinetically controlled.

Isomers Isomers are compounds that have identical molecular formulae but differ in the nature or sequence of bonding of their atoms or in the arrangement of their atoms in space.

Isomorphism Isomorphism is the existence of two or more substances that have the same crystal structure, so that they form solid solutions.

Isostasy A balance or equilibrium between adjacent blocks of crust.

Isotherm Isotherm is a line connecting points of equal temperature on a graphical representation of a physical system.

Isothermal process Isothermal process is a thermodynamic process in which the temperature of the system does not change.

Isotones Isotones are nuclides having the same neutron number N but different atomic number Z.

Isotope An atomic form of an element having a particular number of neutrons. Different isotopes of an element have the same number of protons but different numbers of neutrons and hence different atomic mass, e.g. U-235, U-238. Some isotopes are unstable and decay (qv) to form isotopes of other elements.

Isotopic abundance Compare with natural abundance.

The fraction of atoms of a given isotope in a sample of an element.

Isotopic mass Isotopic masses. The mass of a single atom of a given isotope, usually given in daltons.

Isotropy Isotropy is the property of molecules and materials of having identical physical properties in all directions.

Isotype A variant form of an immunoglobulin that occurs in every normal individual of a particular species. Usually the characteristic antigenic determinant is in the constant region of H and L chains.

IUPAC International Union of Pure and Applied Chemistry (IUPAC) is a voluntary nonprofit association of national organizations representing chemist in 45 member countries. It was formed in 1919 with the object of facilitating international agreement and uniform practice in both academic and industrial aspects of chemistry.

J chain A polypeptide present in polymeric IgM and IgA that links the subunits together.

Jaccard coefficient (SJ) An association coefficient used in numerical taxonomy; it is the proportion of characters that match, excluding those that both organisms lack.

Joule Joule (J) is the SI derived unit of energy, work, and heat. The joule is the work done when the point of application of a force of one newton is displaced a distance of one metre in the direction of the force (J = N m). The unit is named after the British scientist James Prescott Joule (1818-1889).

Joule-Thomson coefficient Joule-Thomson coefficient (μ) is a parameter which describes the temperature change when a gas expands adiabatically through a nozzle from a high pressure to a low pressure region. It is defined by

$$\mu = \left(\frac{\partial T}{\partial p}\right)_H$$

Where H is enthalpy.

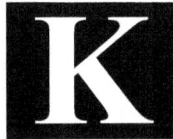

Kaon (K) A meson containing a strange quark and an anti-up quark, or an anti-strange quark and an up (or down) quark.

Karyotype The number and ordering of eukaryotic chromosomes according to size and appearance. The karyotype of an organism is a conserved feature and any changes in number and size of chromosomes are mutations that cause severe diseases and birth defects and are commonly lethal. The importance of chromosome structure is found in the spatial organization of genes on chromosomes, which has been found to be influencing when genes can be expressed, i.e., used to make a protein or functional RNA.

Kelp (kelp) A common name for any of the larger members of the order Laminariales of the brown algae.

Kelvin Kelvin (K) is the SI base unit of thermodynamic temperature. The kelvin, unit of thermodynamic temperature, is the fraction 1/273.16 of the thermodynamic temperature of the triple point of water. The unit is named after the British scientist Sir. W. Thompson, Lord Kelvin (1824-1907).

Kelvin scale of temperature On this scale, the ice-point is taken as 273.15K and the boiling point is taken as 373.15K. The interval between these two points is divided into 100 equal parts. Each division is equal to 1K.

Kepler's first law Relationship in planetary motion that each planet moves in an elliptical orbit, with the sun located at one focus.

Kepler's second law Relationship in planetary motion that an imaginary line between the sun and a planet moves over equal areas of the ellipse during equal time intervals.

Kepler's third law Relationship in planetary motion that the square of the period of an orbit is directly proportional to the cube of the radius of the major axis of the orbit.

Keratin (cytokeratin) Member of the family of proteins that form keratin intermediate filaments, mainly in epithelial cells. Some specialized keratins are found in hair, nails, and feathers.

Keratinocyte Cell found in skin-associated lymphoid tissue; secretes cytokines that may induce an inflammatory response.

Keratitis Inflammation of the cornea of the eye.

Ketones Ketones are compounds in which a carbonyl group is bonded to two carbon atoms: $R_1R_2C=O$ (neither R may be H). They are derived by oxidation of secondary alcohols. The simplest member of the series is acetone, $(CH_3)_2CO$.

Kilocalorie The amount of energy required to increase the temperature of one kilogram of water one degree Celsius: equivalent to 1,000 calories.

Kilogram Kilogram (kg) is the SI base unit of mass; it is equal to the mass of the international prototype of the kilogram.

The prototype of the standard is a cylinder of platinum-iridium alloy, 39 mm in diameter and 39 mm high. Prototype of the kilogram kept by the Bureau International des Poids et Mesures at Souvres, near Paris.

Kilometre (km) A measure of distance in the metric system equal to 1000 metres or about 0.6 of a mile.

Kinetic energy Energy possessed by a body by the virtue of its motion is called kinetic energy. Kinetic energy = $1/2\ m\ v^2$.

Kinetic friction A friction force between surfaces that are slipping past each other.

Kinetoplast A special structure in the mitochondrion of kinetoplastid protozoa. It contains the mitochondrial DNA.

Kirby Bauer method A disk diffusion test to determine the susceptibility of a microorganism to chemotherapeutic agents.

Kjeldhal flask Kjeldhal flask is a round bottom flask with a long wide neck that is used in the determination of nitrogen by Kjeldhal's method.

Kjeldhal's method Kjeldhal's method is an analytical method for determination of nitrogen in certain organic compounds. The method was developed by the Danish chemist Johan Kjeldahl (1849-1900).

It involves addition of a small amount of anhydrous potassium sulphate to the test compound, followed by heating mixture with concentrated sulphuric acid, often with a catalyst such as copper sulphate. As a result ammonia is formed. After alkalyzing the mixture with sodium hydroxide, the ammonia is separated by distillation, collected in standard acid, and the nitrogen determined by back-titration.

Knudsen number Knudsen number (Kn) is a dimensionless quantity used in fluid mechanics, defined by

$Kn = \lambda/l$

Where λ is mean free path and l is length.

Koch's postulates A set of rules for proving that a microorganism causes a particular disease.

Koplik's spots Lesions of the oral cavity caused by the measles (rubeola) virus that are characterized by a bluish white speck in the center of each.

Korean hemorrhagic fever An acute infection caused by a virus that produces varying degrees of hemorrhage, shock, and sometimes death.

Krebs cycle See Tricarboxylic acid (TCA) cycle.

L1 The sound pressure level that is exceeded for 1% of the time for which the given sound is measured.

L10 The sound pressure level that is exceeded for 10% of the time for which the given sound is measured.

L10(1hr) The L10 level measured over a 1 hour period.

L10(18hr) The arithmetic average of the L10(1hr) levels for the 18 hour period between 6am and 12 midnight on a normal working day. It was a common traffic noise descriptor. For traffic noise it is usually about 3dB(A) higher than Leq (24 hours).

L90 The level of noise exceeded for 90% of the time. The bottom 10% of the sample is the L90 noise level expressed in units of dB(A).

Label Chemical group or radioactive atom added to a molecule in order to follow its progress through a biochemical reaction or to locate it spatially. Also, as a verb, to add such a group or atom to a cell or molecule.

Lactic acid fermentation A fermentation that produces lactic acid as the sole or primary product.

Lag phase A period following the introduction of microorganisms into fresh culture medium when there is no increase in cell numbers or mass during batch culture.

Lager Pertaining to the process of aging beers to allow flavour development.

Lagging strand One of the two newly made strands of DNA found at a replication fork. The lagging strand is made in discontinuous lengths that are later joined covalently.

Laminar flow Laminar flow is smooth, uniform, non-turbulent flow of a gas or liquid in parallel layers, with little mixing between layers. It is characterized by small values of the Reynolds number.

Laminarin One of the principal storage products of the golden-brown algae; a polymer of glucose.

Lancefield system One of the serologically distinguishable groups (as group A, group B) into which streptococci can be divided.

Land farming The addition of waste material, such as a hydrocarbon waste, to the soil surface so that it will be degraded. The soil may be moistened or mixed to stimulate the desired degradation process.

Langerhans cell Cell found in the skin that internalizes antigen and moves in the lymph to lymph nodes where it differentiates into a dendritic cell.

Lanthanides Lanthanides (lanthanons, lanthanoids or rare-earth elements) are a series of fourteen elements in the periodic table, generally considered to range in proton number from cerium to lutetium inclusive. It was convenient to divide these elements into the cerium group or light earth: cerium (Ce), praseodymium (Pr), neodymium (Nd), promethium (Pm), sama-rium (Sm), europium (Eu); and the yttrium group or heavy earths: gadolinium (Gd), terbium (Tb), dysprosium (Dy), holmium (Ho), erbium (Er), thulium (Tm), ytterbium (Yb), lutetium (Lu). The position of lanthanum is somewhat equivocal and, although not itself a lanthanides, it is often included with them for comparative purpose. The lanthanides are sometimes simply called the rare earths. Apart from unstable Pm the lanthanides are actually not rare. Cerium is the 26. Most abundant of all elements, 5 times as abundant as Pb. All are silvery very reactive metals.

Laser Laser is a light amplifier usually used to produce monochromatic coherent radiation in the infrared, visible, and ultraviolet regions of the electromagnetic spectrum.

Late mRNA Messenger RNA produced later in a virus infection, which codes for proteins needed in capsid construction and virus release.

Latent heat Latent Heat (L) is the quantity of heat absorbed or released when a substance changes its physical phase at constant temperature.

Latent heat of fusion The quantity of heat required to convert one unit mass of a substance from solid to the liquid state at its melting point is called its latent heat of fusion (L). The SI unit of latent heat of fusion is J kg^{-1}.

Latent heat of vaporization The heat absorbed when one gram of a substance changes from the liquid phase to the gaseous phase, or the heat released when one gram of gas changes from the gaseous phase to the liquid phase.

Latent period The initial phase in the one-step growth experiment in which no phages are released.

Latent virus infections Virus infections in which the virus quits reproducing and remains dormant for a period before becoming active again.

Lattice constants Lattice constants are parameters specifying the dimen-sions of a unit cell in a crystal lattice, specifically the lengths of the cell edges and the angles between them.

Lattice energy Lattice energy is the energy per ion pair required to separate completely the ions in a crystal lattice at a temperature of absolute zero.

Law of conservation of energy The change of one form of energy into another is called transformation of energy. For example, when a body

Length contraction

falls its potential energy is converted to kinetic energy.

Law of conservation of mass There is no change in total mass during a chemical change. The demonstration of conservation of mass by Antoine Lavoisier in the late 18th century was a milestone in the development of modern chemistry.

Law of conservation of matter Matter is neither created nor destroyed in a chemical reaction.

Law of conservation of momentum The total momentum of a group of interacting objects remains constant in the absence of external forces.

Law of multiple proportions When one element can combine with another to form more than one compound, the mass ratios of the elements in the compounds are simple whole-number ratios of each other. For example, in CO and in CO_2, the oxygen-to-carbon ratios are 16:12 and 32:12, respectively. Note that the second ratio is exactly twice the first, because there are exactly twice as many oxygens in CO_2 per carbon as there are in CO.

Le Chatelier's principle The idea that a system at equilibrium will respond to a stress placed upon it in such a manner as to partially offset that stress. The principle was first stated in 1888 by French physical chemist Henri Le Chatelier (1850-1936).

Leader sequence A nontranslated sequence at the 5_ end of mRNA that lies between the operator and the initiation codon; it aids in the initiation and regulation of transcription.

Leading strand One of the two newly made strands of DNA found at a replication fork. The leading strand is made by continuous synthesis in the 5´-to-3´ direction.

Lecithin A major component of cell membranes containing equal amounts of saturated and monounsaturated fatty acids, phosphate, and choline. Lecithin is a member of the lipid group called phospholipids. Its biochemical name is phosphatidylcholine (PC).

Lectin Protein that binds tightly to a specific sugar. Abundant lectins derived from plant seeds are often used as affinity reagents to purify glycoproteins or to detect them on the surface of cells.

Lectin complement pathway The lectin pathway for complement activation is triggered by the binding of a serum lectin (mannan-binding lectin; MBL) to mannose-containing proteins or to carbohydrates on viruses or bacteria.

Legionellosis See Legionnaires' disease.

Legionnaires' disease (legionellosis) A pulmonary form of legionellosis, resulting from infection with Legionella pneumophila.

Leishmanias Zooflagellates, members of the genus Leishmania, that cause the disease leishmaniasis.

Length contraction Relativistic distortion of observed length due to differently accelerated reference frames.

LEP The Large Electron Positron Collider at the CERN laboratory in Geneva, Switzerland.

Lepromatous A relentless, progressive form of leprosy in which large numbers of Mycobac-terium leprae develop in skin cells, killing the skin cells and resulting in the loss of features. Disfiguring nodules form all over the body.

Leprosy or Hansen's disease A severe disfiguring skin disease caused by Mycobacterium leprae.

Lepton A fundamental fermion that does not participate in strong interactions. The electrically-charged leptons are the electron, the muon, the tau, and their antiparticles. Electrically-neutral leptons are called neutrinos.

Leq Equivalent sound pressure level - the steady sound level that, over a specified period of time, would produce the same energy equivalence as the fluctuating sound level actually occurring.

Leq(1hr) The Leq noise level for a specific one-hour period.

Leq(8hr) The continuous noise level during any one hour period between 10pm and 6am.

Leq(9hr) The Leq noise level for the period 10pm to 7am.

Leq(15hr) The Leq noise level for the period 7am to 10pm.

Lethal dose 50 (LD50) Refers to the dose or number of organisms that will kill 50% of an experimental group of hosts within a specified time period.

Leukemia A progressive, malignant disease of blood-forming organs, marked by distorted proliferation and development of leukocytes and their precursors in the blood and bone marrow. Certain leukemias are caused by viruses.

Leukocidin A microbial toxin that can damage or kill leukocytes.

Leukocyte Any colourless white blood cell. Can be classified into granular and agranular lymphocytes.

Lewis acid Lewis acid is an agent capable of accepting a pair of electrons to form a coordinate bond.

Lewis base Lewis base is an agent capable of donating a pair of electrons to form a coordinate bond.

LHC The Large Hadron Collider at the CERN laboratory in Geneva, Switzerland. LHC will collide protons into protons at a center-of-mass energy of about 14 TeV. When completed in the year 2005, it will be the most powerful particle accelerator in the world. It is hoped that it will unlock many of the secrets of particle physics.

Lichen An organism composed of a fungus and either green algae or cyanobacteria in a symbiotic association.

Liebig's law of the minimum Living organisms and populations will grow until lack of a resource begins to limit further growth.

Ligand Ligand is an ion or molecule (NH_3, H_2O, NO, CO) that donates a pair of electron to a metal atom or ion in forming a coordination complex.

Ligand field theory Ligand field theory is a description of the structure of crystals containing a transition metal ion surrounded by nonmetallic ions (ligands). It is based on construction of molecular orbitals involving the d-orbitals of the central metal ion and combinations of atomic orbitals of the ligands.

Light Anything that can travel from one place to another through empty space and can influence matter, but is not affected by gravity.

Light water reactor (LWR) A common nuclear reactor cooled and usually moderated by ordinary water.

Light year Light year (ly) is a unit of distance used in astronomy, defined as the distance light travels in one year in a vacuum

(ly = $9.46052973 \times 10^{15}$ km).

Lignins Lignins are macromolecular constituents of wood related to lignans, composed of phenolic propylbenzene skeletal units, linked at various sites and apparently randomly.

Limited assembler Assembler capable of making only certain products; faster, more efficiently and less liable to abuse, than a general purpose assembler.

Linacs An abbreviation for linear accelerator, that is, an accelerator that has no bends in it.

Linear Aside from its geometric meaning, linear describes systems in which an output is directly proportional to an input. In particular, a linear elastic system is one in which the internal displacements are (at equilibrium) directly proportional to applied forces.

Lines of force Lines drawn to make an electric field strength map, with each line originating on a positive charge and ending on a negative charge; each line represents a path on which a charge would experience a constant force and lines closer together mean a stronger electric field.

Lipids Lipids are a loosely defined term for substances of biological origin that are soluble in nonpolar solvents. They consist of saponifia-ble lipids, such as glycerides (fats and oils) and phospholipids, as well as nonsaponifiable lipids, princi-pally steroids.

Lipopolysaccharide A molecule containing both lipid and polysaccharide, which is important in the outer membrane of the gram-negative cell wall.

Lipoprotein particle These are protein based carriers of triglycerides (fats) and cholesterol in the blood circulation. The low-density lipoprotein particle LDL is also known as 'bad cholesterol' as it is the major carrier of blood plasma cholesterol and high levels of LDL particles are associated to increased risk of heart disease.

Liposome A spherical particle formed by a lipid bilayer enclosing an aqueous solution. It may be used to administer chemotherapeutic agents or in diagnostic testing.

Liquids A phase of matter composed of molecules that have interactions stronger than those found in a gas but not strong enough to keep the molecules near the equilibrium positions of a solid, resulting in the characteristic definite volume but indefinite shape of a liquid.

Listeriosis A sporadic disease of animals and humans, particularly those who are immunocompromised or pregnant, caused by the bacterium Listeria monocytogenes.

Lithosphere Lithosphere is the outer layer of the solid earth, extending from the base of the mantle to the surface of the crust.

Lithotroph An organism that uses reduced inorganic compounds as its electron source.

Litre Litre (l, L) is a synonym for cubic decimeter (L = dm^3).

Lnn noise descriptors Because noise varies with time, a single noise value cannot adequately define the noise ambient. For this reason, the acoustic environment is described using a number of noise level descriptors.

Locus In genetics the place on a chromosome which is occupied by a gene. Plural: loci.

London dispersion force An attractive force caused by quantum-mechanical electron correlation. For example, a neutral spherical molecule (such as a single argon atom) has no charge and produces no external electric field, yet a pair of molecules has a distribution of electron configurations weighted toward those with lesser electron-electron repulsions; this creates a small net attraction.

Lone pair Two valence electrons of an atom that share an orbital but do not participate in a bond.

Longitudinal waves The wave in which the particles of the medium oscillate along the direction along the direction of propagation of wave is called the longitudinal wave. Sound waves are longitudinal waves.

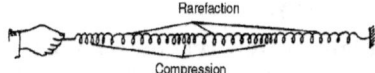

Figure Longitudinal waves

Lophotrichous A cell with a cluster of flagella at one or both ends.

Lorentz transformation The transformation between frames in relative motion.

Loudness A rise of 10 dB in sound level corresponds approximately to a doubling of subjective loudness. That is, a sound of 85 dB is twice as loud as a sound of 75 dB which is twice as loud as a sound of 65 dB and so on. That is, the sound of 85 dB is 400% times the loudness of a sound of 65 dB.

Low oxygen diffusion environment An aquatic environment in which

Lymph node

microorganisms are surrounded by deep water layers that limit oxygen diffusion to the cell surface. In contrast, microor-ganisms in thin water films have good oxygen transfer from air to the cell surface.

Low-enriched uranium Uranium enriched to less than 20% U-235. (That in power reactors is usually 3.5 - 5.0% U-235.)

Low-frequency noise Containing major components within the low frequency range (20Hz - 250Hz) of the frequency spectrum.

Low-level waste (LLW) is mildly radioactive material usually disposed of by incineration and burial.

LPG (Liquid Petroleum Gas) A mixture of short hydrocarbons with most of the volume being propane and butane. LPG is considered an alternative fuel that burns cleaner than gasoline.

LPS-binding protein A special plasma protein that binds bacterial lipopolysaccharides and then attaches to receptors on monocytes, macrophages, and other cells. This triggers the release of IL-1 and other cytokines that stimulate the development of fever and additional endotoxin effects.

Lumen Lumen (lm) is the SI derived unit of luminous flux. The lumen is the luminous flux emitted in a solid angle of one steradian by a point source having a uniform intensity of one candela (1 lm = 1 cd·sr).

Luminosity The total amount of energy radiated into space each second from the surface of a star.

Luminous An object or objects that produce visible light; for example, the sun, stars, light bulbs, and burning materials are all luminous.

Luminous flux Luminous flux (Φ) is the intensity of light from a source multiplied by the solid angle. The SI unit is lumen.

Lux Lux (lx) is the SI derived unit of illuminance. The lux is the illuminance produced by a luminous flux of one lumen uniformly distributed over a surface of one square metre (lx = lm·m^{-2}).

Lyman limit A specific wavelength (91.2nm) that corresponds to the energy needed to ionize a hydrogen atom (13.6eV). Galactic space is opaque at wavelengths shorter than the Lyman limit. Subsequently, light from cosmic objects at wave-lengths less than the Lyman limit is exceedingly difficult to detect.

Lyman series Lyman series is the series of lines in the spectrum of the hydrogen atom which corresponds to transitions between the ground state (principal quantum number $n = 1$) and successive excited states.

Lyme disease A tick-borne disease caused by the spirochete Borrella burgdorferi.

Lymph node A small secondary lymphoid organ that contains lymphocytes, macrophages, and dendritic cells.
It serves as a site for:
1. filtration and removal of foreign antigens and

2. the activation and proliferation of lymphocytes.

Lymphocyte A nonphagocytic, mono-nuclear leukocyte that is an immunologically competent cell, or its precursor. Lymphocytes are present in the blood, lymph, and lymphoid tissues. See B cell and T cell.

Lymphogranuloma venereum A sexually transmitted disease caused by *Chlamydia trachomatis* serotypes L1-L3, which affect the lymph organs in the genital area.

Lymphokine A biologically active glycoprotein secreted by activated lymphocytes, especially sensitized T cells. It acts as an intercellular mediator of the immune response and transmits growth, differentiation, and behavioral signals.

Lysis The rupture or physical disintegration of a cell.

Lysogens Bacteria that are carrying a viral prophage and have the potential of producing bacteriophages under the proper conditions.

Lysogeny The state in which a phage genome remains within the bacterial host cell after infection and reproduces along with it rather than taking control of the host and destroying it.

Lysosome A spherical membranous eucaryotic organelle that contains hydrolytic enzymes and is responsible for the intracellular digestion of substances.

Lytic cycle A virus life cycle that results in the lysis of the host cell.

M cell Specialized cell of the intestinal mucosa and other sites, such as the urogenital tract, that delivers the antigen from the apical face of the cell to lymphocytes clustered within the pocket in its basolateral face.

M phase Period of the eucaryotic cell cycle during which the nucleus and cytoplasm divide.

Machine-phase chemistry The chemistry of systems in which all potentially reactive moieties follow controlled trajectories.

Macrolide antibiotic An antibiotic containing a macrolide ring, a large lactone ring with multiple keto and hydroxyl groups, linked to one or more sugars.

Macromolecule Macromolecule is a molecule of high relative molecular mass, the structure of which essentially comprises the multiple repetition of units derived, actually or conceptually, from molecules of low relative molecular mass.

Macromolecule vaccine A vaccine made of specific, purified macromolecules derived from pathogenic microorganisms.

Macromolecules Large molecules in biological systems namely proteins, nucleic acids, and polysaccharides.

Macro-nutrients Also called caloric nutrients including proteins, carbohydrates, and fats. Some definitions include water and alcohol. The term is used by gardeners and in agriculture referring to common minerals needed for proper plant growth.

Macrophage The name for a large mononuclear phagocytic cell, present in blood, lymph, and other tissues. Macrophages are derived from monocytes. They phagocytose and destroy pathogens; some macrophages also activate B cells and T cells.

Macroscopic Used in science to describe large scale processes like the temperature, volume, pressure, and energy of a system characterizing the behaviour of a very large number of molecules. The macroscopic values tend to be predictable and represent the average behaviour of a system. They give no detailed information about the behaviour of individual molecules or units of a system.

Maduromycosis A subcutaneous fungal infection caused by *Madurella mycetoma*; also termed as eumycotic mycetoma.

Madurose The sugar derivative 3-O-methyl-D-galactose, which is characteristic of several actinomycete genera that are collectively called maduro-mycetes.

Magnetic dipole An object, such as a current loop, an atom, or a bar magnet, that experiences torques due to magnetic forces; the strength of magnetic dipoles is measured by comparison with a standard dipole consisting of a square loop of wire of a given size and carrying a given amount of current.

Magnetic domain Tiny physical regions in permanent magnets, approximately 0.01 to 1 mm, that have magnetically aligned atoms, giving the domain an overall polarity.

Magnetic field A region of space in which magnetic forces may be detected or may affect the motion of an electrically charged particle. As with gravity, magnetism has a long-range effect and magnetic fields are associated with many astronomical objects.

Magnetic field lines Imaginary lines that indicate the strength and direction of a magnetic field. The orientation of the line and an arrow show the direction of the field. The lines are drawn closer together where the field is stronger. Charged particles move freely along Magnetic field lines, but are inhibited by the magnetic force from moving across field lines.

Magnetic poles The ends, or sides, of a magnet about which the force of magnetic attraction seems to be concentrated.

Magnetic quantum number From quantum mechanics model of the atom, one of four descriptions of the energy state of an electron wave; this quantum number describes the energy of an electron orbital as the orbital is oriented in space by an external magnetic field, a kind of energy sub-sublevel.

Magnetic reversal The flipping of polarity of the earth's magnetic field as the north magnetic pole and the south magnetic pole exchange positions.

Magnetosomes Magnetite particles in magnetotactic bacteria that are tiny magnets and allow the bacteria to orient themselves in magnetic fields.

Magnification The factor by which an image's linear size is increased (or decreased). *Cf.* angular magnification.

Magnitude The size of a measurement of a vector; scalar quantities that consist of a number and unit only, no direction, for example.

Maintenance energy The energy a cell requires simply to maintain itself or remain alive and functioning properly. It does not include the energy needed for either growth or reproduction.

Major histocompatibility complex (MHC) A large set of cell surface molecules in each individual, encoded by a family of genes, that serves as a unique biochemical marker of individual identity. It can trigger T-cell responses that may lead to rejection of transplanted tissues and organs. MHC molecules are also involved in the regulation of the immune response and the interactions between immune cells.

Malaria A serious infectious illness caused by the parasitic protozoan Plasmodium. Malaria is characterized by bouts of high chills and fever that occur at regular intervals.

Malformation A fault in the primary development of an organ or tissue, and therefore present at birth.

Malignant Describes tumors and tumor cells that are invasive and/or able to undergo metasis; a malignant tumor is a cancer.

Malt Grain soaked in water to soften it, induce germination, and activate its enzymes. The malt is then used in brewing and distilling.

Mammalian Pertaining to the group of vertebrates that have:

internal development of the embryo;

mammary glands that can produce milk;

live-born young, a body covering of hair or fur;

a four-chambered heart;

a well developed cerebral cortex;

the ability to maintain a constant body temperature; and

a permanent set of teeth.

MAP (microtubule-associated protein) Any protein that binds to microtubules and modifies their properties. Many different kinds have been found, including structural proteins, such as MAP^{-2}, and motor proteins, such as dynein.

MAP kinase (mitogen-activated protein kinase) A protein kinase that performs a crucial step in relaying signals from the plasma membrane to the nucleus. Turned on by a wide range of proliferation- or differentiation-inducing signals.

Marburg viral hemorrhagic fever An acute infection caused by a virus that produces varying degrees of hemorrhage, shock, and sometimes death.

Marker A gene or DNA sequence with a known physical location on a chromosome and is associated with a certain trait or characteristic. It can be used as a point of reference when looking for other genes.

Marsupial A mammal whose distinguishing features include the birth of young at an early foetal stage of development, and generally, a pouch (marsupium) in which further development of the foetus occurs.

Mashing The process in which cereals are mixed with water and incubated in order to degrade their complex carbohydrates to more readily usable forms such as simple sugars.

Mass Mass (m) is the quantity of matter contained in a particle or body regardless of its location in the universe. Mass is constant, whereas weight is affected by the distance of a body from the center of the Earth. The SI unit is kilogram.

According to the Einstein equation

$$E = mc^2$$

All forms of energy possess a mass equivalent.

Mass action law The law which describes the relation between the densities of species involved in a chemical reaction.

Mass defect The difference between the sum of the masses of the individual nucleons forming a nucleus and the actual mass of that nucleus.

Mass fraction Mass fraction (w_a) is the ratio of the mass of substance A to the total mass of a mixture.

Mass number Compare with atomic number and atomic weight.

The total number of protons and neutrons in an atom or ion. In nuclide symbols the mass number is given as a leading superscript. In isotope names the mass number is the number following the element name.

Mass spectrometry Mass spectrometry is an analytical technique in which ions are separated according to the mass/charge (m/e) ratio and detected by a suitable detector.

In a mass spectrometer a sample is ionized and the positive ions produced are accelerated into a high-vacuum region containing electric and magnetic fields. These fields deflect and focus the ions onto a detector. A mass spectrum is thus obtained consisting of a series of peaks of variable intensity to which m/e values can be assigned. Different molecules can be identified by their characteristic pattern of lines.

Mast cell A bone marrow-derived cell present in a variety of tissues that resembles peripheral blood-borne basophils and contains an Fc receptor for IgE. It undergoes IgE-mediated degranulation.

Matter Mass and energy; fundamental component of the Universe

Matter antimatter annihilation A highly efficient energy-generation process in which equal amounts of matter and antimatter collide and destroy each other, thus producing a burst of energy.

Mean free path Mean free path is the average distance a gas molecule travels between collisions.

Mean growth rate constant (k) The rate of microbial population growth expressed in terms of the number of generations per unit time.

Measles A highly contagious skin disease that is endemic throughout the world. It is caused by a morbilli virus in the family Paramyxoviridae, which enters the body through the respiratory tract or through the conjunctiva.

Mechanical energy The form of energy associated with machines, objects in motion, and objects having potential energy that results from gravity.

Mechanical wave The waves, which need a material medium for their

propagation, are called mechanical waves. Mechanical waves are also called elastic waves. Sound waves, water waves are examples of mechanical waves.

Mechanochemistry In this volume, the chemistry of processes in which mechanical systems operating with atomic-scale precision either guide, drive, or are driven by chemical transformations. In general usage, the chemistry of processes in which energy is converted from mechanical to chemical form, or vice versa.

Mechanosynthesis Chemical synthesis controlled by mechanical systems operating with atomic-scale precision, enabling direct positional selection of reaction sites; synthetic applications of mechanochemistry. Suitable mechanical systems include AFM mechanisms, molecular mani-pulators, and molecular mill systems. Processes that fall outside the intended scope of this definition include reactions guided by the incorporation of reactive moieties into a shared covalent framework, or by the binding of reagents to enzymes or enzymelike catalysts.

Medical mycology The discipline that deals with the fungi that cause human disease.

Megaton An explosive force equal to one million metric tons of TNT. The energy released in the explosion of one megaton of TNT is equal to 4.2×10^{22} ergs.

Megawatt (MW) A unit of power, $= 10^6$ watts. MWe refers to electric output from a generator, MWt to thermal output from a reactor or heat source.

Meiosis The sexual process in which a diploid cell divides and forms two haploid cells.

Meissner effect Meissner effect is the complete exclusion of magnetic induction from the interior of a superconductor.

Melanoma A type of cancer that begins in the melanocytes - the skin cells that produce pigments. It can spread to other areas of the body if not detected and treated early.

Melting point Melting point is the temperature at which the solid and liquid phases of a substance are in equilibrium at a specified pressure. A pure substance under standard condition of pressure has a single reproducible melting point. The terms melting point and freezing point are often used interchangeably, depending on whether the substance is being heated or cooled.

Melting temperature (Tm) The temperature at which double-stranded DNA separates into individual strands; it is dependent on the G 1 C content of the DNA and is used to compare genetic material in microbial taxonomy.

Membrane A planar structure surrounding cells and organelles within eukaryotic cells separating aqueous compartments which carry out different metabolic processes. Cell membranes are electrical insulators but permeable to hydrophobic molecules such as steroidal hormones and small gases. All other water soluble and charged molecules depend on the presence of membrane proteins which provide transport pathways across the phospholipid bilayer.

Membrane attack complex (MAC) The complex complement components (c5b-C9) that create a pore in the plasma membrane of a target cell and leads to cell lysis. C9 probably forms most of the actual pore.

Membrane filter technique The use of a thin porous filter made from cellulose acetate or some other polymer to collect microorganisms from water, air, and food.

Membrane-disrupting exotoxin A type of exotoxin that lyses host cells by disrupting the integrity of the plasma membrane.

Memory B cell A lymphocyte capable of initiating the antibody-mediated immune response upon detection of a specific antigen molecule for which it is genetically programmed. It circulates freely in the blood and lymph and may live for years.

Mendelian inheritance A hereditary process where genetic traits are passed from parents to offspring and are explained in terms of chromosomes separating, independent assortment of genes and the homologous exchange of segments of DNA. There are three modes of Mendelian inheritance: autosomal dominant, autosomal recessive and X-linked inheritance. Named after Gregor Mendel, who first studied and recognised the existence of genes and this method of inheritance by experimenting with and breeding different varieties of peas.

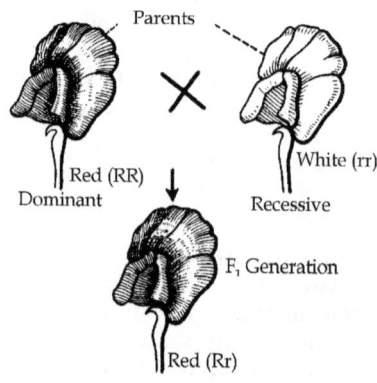

Figure Mendelian inheritance

Meningitis A condition that refers to inflammation of the brain or spinal cord meninges. The disease can be divided into bacterial (septic) meningitis and aseptic meningitis syndrome.

Meniscus Meniscus is the concave curve of a liquid surface in a graduate or narrow tube. Caused by surface tension.

Mercaptans Mercaptans are a traditional term abandoned by IUPAC, synonymous with thiols. This term is still widely used.

Meson A hadron made from an even number of quark constituents The basic structure of most mesons is one quark and one antiquark.

Mesophile A microorganism with a growth optimum around 20 to

45°C, a minimum of 15 to 20°C, and a maximum about 45°C or lower.

Messenger RNA Single-stranded RNA synthesized from a DNA template during transcription that binds to ribosomes and directs the synthesis of protein.

Metabolic channeling The localization of metabolites and enzymes in different parts of a cell.

Metabolic control engineering Modification of the controls for biosynthetic pathways without altering the pathways themselves in order to improve process efficiency.

Metabolic pathway engineering (MPE) The use of molecular techniques to improve the efficiency of pathways that synthesize specific products.

Metabolism The total of all chemical reactions in the cell; almost all are enzyme catalyzed.

Metachromatic granules Granules of polyphosphate in the cytoplasm of some bacteria that appear in different colour when stained with a blue basic dye. They are storage reservoirs for phosphate. Sometimes called volutin granules.

Metal Metals are a material in which the highest occupied energy band (conduction band) is only partially filled with electrons.

Their physical properties generally include:

They are good conductors of heat and electricity. The electrical conductivity of metals generally decreases with temperature.

They are malleable and ductile in their solid state.

They show metallic luster.

They are opaque.

They have high density.

They are solids (except mercury)

They have crystal structure in which each atom is surrounded by eight to twelve near neighbours.

Their chemical properties generally are:

They have one to four valence electrons.

They have low ionization potentials; they readily lose electrons.

They are good reducing agents.

They have hydroxides which are bases or amphoteric.

They are electropositive.

Metallic characteristics of the elements decrease and non-metallic characteristics increase with the increase of valence electrons. Also metallic characteristics increase with the number of electron shells. Therefore, there is no sharp dividing line between the metals and the non-metals.

Of the 113 elements now known, only 17 show primarily non-metallic characteristics, 7 others are metalloids, and 89 may be classed as metals.

Metal fuels Natural uranium metal as used in a gas-cooled reactor.

Metalloid Metalloid (semimetal) is any of a class of chemical elements intermediate in properties between metals and nonmetals. The classification is not clear cut, but typical. Metalloids are boron (B), silicon (Si), germanium (Ge), arsenic (As), and tellurium (Te). They are electrical semiconductors and their oxides are amphoteric.

Metastable A classical system is metastable if it is above its minimum-energy state, but requires an energy input before it can reach a lower-energy state; accordingly, a metastable system can act like a stable system, provided that energy inputs remain below some threshold. Systems with strong metastability are commonly described as stable. Quantum mechanical effects can permit metastable states to reach lower energies by tunneling, without an energy input; an associated, broader definition of metastable embraces all systems that have a long lifetime in a state above the minimum-energy state.

Metastasis The transfer of a disease like cancer from one organ to another not directly connected with it.

Methanogens Strictly anaerobic archaeons that derive energy by converting CO_2, H_2, formate, acetate, and other compounds to either methane or methane and CO_2.

Methylotroph A bacterium that uses reduced one-carbon compounds such as methane and methanol as its sole source of carbon and energy.

MeV One million electron volts.

Mho Mho is an archaic name for the SI unit siemens.

Micelle Micelle is an electrically charged colloidal particle, usually organic in nature, composed of aggregates of large molecules, e.g., in soaps and surfactants. For aqueous solutions, the hydrophilic end of the molecule is on the surface of the micelle, while the hydrophobic end points toward the center.

Michaelis constant A kinetic constant for an enzyme reaction that equals the substrate concentration required for the enzyme to operate at half maximal velocity.

Micro one millionth of a unit.

Microaerophile A microorganism that requires low levels of oxygen for growth, around 2 to 10%, but is damaged by normal atmospheric oxygen levels.

Microarray technology Profiling of gene expression by measuring binding of RNA from growing cells to an array of function-specific oligonucleotides attached to an inert surface.

Microbial dietary adjuvant A substance added to the diet to stimulate specific microbial processes and populations.

Microbial ecology The study of microorganisms in their natural environments, with a major emphasis on physical conditions, processes, and interactions that occur on the scale of individual microbial cells.

Microbial loop The mineralization of organic matter synthesized by photosynthetic phytoplankton through the activity of microorganisms such as bacteria and protozoa. This process "loops" minerals and carbon dioxide back for reuse by the primary producers and makes the organic matter unavailable to higher consumers.

Microbial mat A firm structure of layered microorganisms with complementary physiological activities that can develop on surfaces in aquatic environments.

Microbiology The study of organisms that are usually too small to be seen with the naked eye. Special techniques are required to isolate and grow them.

Microbivory The use of microorganisms as a food source by organisms that can ingest or phagocytose them.

Microenvironment The immediate environment surrounding a microbial cell or other structure, such as a root.

Microfilaments Protein filaments, about 4 to 7 nm in diameter, that are present in the cytoplasmic matrix of eucaryotic cells and play a role in cell structure and motion.

Micron Micron (μ) is an obsolete name for micrometer (μm).

Micronucleus The smaller of the two nuclei in ciliate protozoa. Micronuclei are diploid and involved only in genetic recombina-tion and the regeneration of macronuclei.

Micronutrients Nutrients such as zinc, manganese, and copper that are required in very small quantities for growth and reproduction. Also called trace elements.

Microorganism An organism that is too small to be seen clearly with the naked eye.

Microphone An electro acoustic transducer which receives an acoustic signal and delivers a corresponding electric signal.

Microscopic The description of the behaviour of individual molecules. The behaviour of an individual molecule may be very different from other identical molecules. In systems with a very large number of identical molecules, these individual deviations are negligible and contribute to the noise of a property of this system. The decay of a radioactive material is a good example of such an internal fluctuation. While the decay of isotopes can be predicted for a large clump of radioactive material, the actual time point of decay of an individual isotope cannot be predicted with accuracy and is random. However, we can assign a probability that it will decay within a certain amount of time.

Microtubules Small cylinders, about 25 nm in diameter, made of tubulin proteins and present in the cytoplasmic matrix and flagella of eucaryotic cells; they are involved in cell structure and movement.

Miliary tuberculosis An acute form of tuberculosis in which small tuberculous lesions are formed in a number of organs of the body because of dissemination of M. Tuberculosis throughout the body by the bloodstream. Also known as reactivation tuberculosis.

Millibar A measure of atmospheric pressure equivalent to 1.000 dynes per cm^2.

Millimeter of mercury Millimeter of mercury (mmhg) is a non-SI unit of pressure, equal to 133.322 Pa. The name is generally considered interchangeable with torr.

Milling Process by which minerals are extracted from ore, usually at the mine site.

Millirem A unit for measuring a person's exposure to radioactivity.

Mineralization The release of inorganic nutrients from organic matter during microbial growth and metabolism.

Minimal inhibitory concentration (MIC) The lowest concentration of a drug that will prevent the growth of a particular microorganism.

Minimal lethal concentration (MLC) The lowest concentration of a drug that will kill a particular microorganism.

Minus, or negative, strand The virus nucleic acid strand that is complementary in base sequence to the viral mRNA.

Miscible fluids Fluids that can mix in any proportion.

Missense mutation A single base substitution in DNA that changes a codon for one amino acid into a codon for another.

Mitigation Repairing or rehabilitating a damaged ecosy-stem or compensa-ting for damage by providing a substitute or replacement area.

Mitochondria Small structures in living cells which are found outside the nucleus and which contain a small number of the cell's genes. Mitochondria are often described as the 'power house of the cell'. They carry their own complement of DNA and are replicated independently so that when the cell divides, each daughter cell will receive half of the mitochondria.

Mitochondrial DNA The genetic material of the mitochondria - the organelle that generates energy for the cell. The DNA in mitochondria is different from that in the nucleus. Many scientists believe that this DNA is the remnant of a bacterium that invaded the cell in very early evolution. Mitochondrial DNA (mtDNA) is typically passed on only from the mother during sexual reproduction as it is only the nucleus of the sperm that enters the egg upon fertilisation. This means there is little change in the mtDNA from generation to generation.

Mitochondrion The eucaryotic organelle that is the site of electron transport, oxidative phosphorylation, and pathways such as the Krebs cycle; it provides most of a nonphotosynthetic cell's energy under aerobic conditions. It is constructed of an outer membrane and an inner membrane, which contains the electron transport chain.

Mitosis Nuclear division in which there is an equal qualitative and quantitative division of the chromosomal material between the two resulting nuclei; ordinary cell division.

Mitotic apparatus Collectively, the asters, spindle, centrioles, and microtubules of a dividing cell.

Mixed acid fermentation A type of fermentation carried out by members of the family Enterobacteriaceae in which ethanol and a complex mixture of organic acids are produced.

Mixed oxide fuel (MOX) Reactor fuel which consists of both uranium and plutonium oxides, usually about 5% Pu, which is the main fissile component.

Mixed perennial polyculture Growing a mixture of different perennial crop species (where the same plant persists for more than one year) together in the same plot; imitates the diversity of a natural system and is often more stable and more suitable for sustainable agriculture than monoculture of annual plants.

Mixed semidiurnal tide A tidal pattern with two successive high tides of different heights each day.

Mixing control The experimental limitation of the rate of reaction in solution by the rate of mixing of solutions of the two reactants. It can occur even when the reaction rate constant is several powers of 10 less than that for an encounter-controlled rate. Analogous (and even more important) effects of the limitation of reaction rates by the speed of mixing are encountered in heterogeneous (solid/liquid, solid/gas, liquid/gas) systems.

Mixotrophic Refers to microorganisms that combine autotrophic and hetero-trophic metabolic processes.

Mixture Matter made of unlike parts that have a variable composition and can be separated into their component parts by physical means.

Mks system The use of metric units based on the metre, kilogram, and second. Example: metres per second is the mks unit of speed, not cm/s or km/hr.

MKSA The system of physical units based on the fundamental metric units: metre kilogram, second and ampere.

Mobility The ratio of the carrier velocity to the applied electric field.

Modal action pattern (MAP) A spatiotemporal behaviour pattern that is common to members of a species; different individuals perform the pattern in a recognizably similar fashion.

Model A mental or physical representation of something that cannot be observed directly that is usually used as an aid to understanding.

Moderator A material such as light or heavy water or graphite used in a reactor to slow down fast neutrons by collision with lighter nuclei so as to expedite further fission.

Modern physics The physics developed since about 1900, which includes relativity and quantum mechanics.

Modern synthesis The combination of principles of population genetics and Darwinian evolutionary theory.

Modification A change, as in morphology, usually associated with a functional advantage.

Modified atmosphere packaging (MAP) Addition of gases such as nitrogen and carbon dioxide to packaged foods in order to inhibit the growth of spoilage organisms.

Moiety In physical organic chemistry moiety is generally used to signify part of a molecule, e.g. in an ester R^1COOR^2 the alcohol moiety is R^2O. The term should not be used for a small fragment of a molecule.

Molality Molality or molal concentration (b; formerly m) is a concentration in which the amount of solute is stated in moles and the amount of solvent in kilograms.

Molar Denoting that an extensive physical property is being expressed per amount of substance, usually per mole.

Molar mass Molar mass is the mass of one mole of a substance.

$M = m/n$

It is normally expressed in units of $gmol^{-1}$, in which case its numerical value is identical with the relative molecular mass.

Molar quantity Molar quantity is often convenient to express an extensive quantity As the actual value divided by amount of substance (number of moles). The resulting quantity is called molar volume, molar enthalpy, etc.

Molar volume Molar volume is the volume occupied by substance per unit amount of substance. The volume of the gas at 0°C and 101325 Pa is 22.4 $dm^3 mol^{-1}$.

Mold Any of a large group of fungi that cause mold or moldiness and that exist as multicellular filamentous colonies; also the deposit or growth caused by such fungi. Molds typically do not produce macroscopic fruiting bodies.

Mole The term mole is short for the name gram-molar-weight; it is not a shortened form of the word molecule. (However, the word molecule does also derive from the word molar.)

Mole fraction Mole fraction (x_a) is the ratio of the amount of substance of substance A to the total amount of substance in a mixture.

Molecular biology The science of studying the genetic composition and mechanism of living organisms at the molecular level. It historically refers to the understanding and manipulation of genes (DNA). The molecular studies of all other organic molecules like proteins, fats, and carbohydrates is called biochemistry.

Molecular chaperones Proteins that aid in the proper folding of unfolded polypeptides or partly denatured proteins and often also help transport proteins across membranes.

Molecular chronometers Nucleic acid and protein sequences that gradually change over time in a random fashion and at a steady rate, and which therefore can be used to determine phylogenetic relationships.

Molecular entity Any constitutionally or isotopically distinct atom, molecule, ion, ion pair, radical, radical ion, complex, conformer etc., identifiable as a separately distingui-shable entity.

Molecular entity is used in this glossary as a general term for singular entities, irrespective of their nature, while chemical species stands for sets or ensembles of molecular entities. Note that the name of a compound may refer to the respective molecular entity or to the chemical species, e.g. methane, may mean a single molecule of CH_4 (molecular entity) or a molar amount, specified or not (chemical species), participating in a reaction.

The degree of precision necessary to describe a molecular entity depends on the context. For example "hydrogen molecule" is an adequate definition of a certain molecular entity for some purposes, whereas for others it is necessary to distinguish the electronic state and/or vibrational state and/or nuclear spin, etc. of the hydrogen molecule.

Molecular formula Formula; chemical formula. A notation that indicates the type and number of atoms in a molecule. The molecular formula of glucose is $C_6H_{12}O_6$, which indicates that a molecule of glucose contains 6 atoms of carbon, 12 atoms of hydrogen, and 6 atoms of oxygen.

Molecular genetics The study of the biochemical structure and function of DNA.

Molecular machine A mechanical device that performs a useful function using components of nanometer scale and defined molecular structure; includes both artificial nanomachines and naturally occurring devices found in biological systems.

Molecular manipulator A device combining a proximal-probe mechanism for atomically precise positioning with a molecule binding site on the tip; can serve as the basis for building complex structures by positional synthesis.

Molecular manufacturing Manufacturing using molecular machinery, giving molecule-by molecule control of products and by-products via positional chemical synthesis.

Molecular mass The molecular mass of something is the mass of one mole of it (in CGS units), or one kilomole of it (in MKS units). The units of molecular mass are gram and kilogram, respectively. The CGS and MKS values of molecular mass are numerically equal. The molecular mass is not the mass of one molecule. Some books still call this the molecular weight.

Molecular mechanics A molecular mechanics program developed by Norman Allinger and co-workers; the MM2 model is the molecular potential energy function described by the equations, rules and parameters embodied in that program.

Molecular mechanics calculation An empirical calculational method intended to give estimates of structures and energies for conformations of molecules. The method is based on the assumption of "natural" bond lengths and angles, deviation from which leads to strain, and the existence of torsional interactions and attractive and/or repulsive van der Waals and dipolar forces between non-bonded atoms. The method is also called "(empirical) force-field calculations".

Molecular medicine A variety of pharmaceutical techniques and therapies in use today.

Molecular metal A non-metallic material whose properties resemble those of metals, usually following oxidative doping; e.g. polyacetylene following oxidative doping with iodine.

Molecular mill A mechanochemical processing system characterized by limited motions and repetitive operations without programmable flexibility.

Molecular model stick model; ball and stick model; spacefilling model A representation of a molecule. The model can be purely computational or it can be an actual physical object. Stick models show bonds, ball-and-stick models show bonds and atoms, and spacefilling models show relative atomic sizes.

Molecular nanotechnology Thorough, inexpensive control of the structure of matter based on molecule-by-molecule control of products and by-products; the products and processes of molecular manufacturing, including molecular machinery.

Molecular orbital A one-electron wavefunction describing an electron moving in the effective field provided by the nuclei and all other electrons of a molecular entity of more than one atom. Such molecular orbitals can be transformed in prescribed ways into component functions to give "localized molecular orbitals". Molecular orbitals can also be described, in terms of the number of nuclei (or "centres") encompassed, as two-centre, multi-centre, etc. molecular orbitals, and are often expressed as a linear combination of atomic orbitals. An orbital is usually depicted by sketching contours on which the wavefunction has a constant value (contour map) or by indicating schematically the

Molecule

envelope of the region of space in which there is an arbitrarily fixed high (say 96%) probability of finding the electron occupying the orbital, giving also the algebraic sign (+ or -) of the wavefunction in each part of that region.

Molecular rearrangement The term is traditionally applied to any reaction that involves a change of connectivity (sometimes including hydrogen), and violates the so-called "principle of minimum structural change". According to this over-simplified principle, chemical species do not isomerize in the course of a transformation, e.g. substitution, or the change of a functional group of a chemical species into a different functional group is not expected to involve the making or breaking of more than the minimum number of bonds required to effect that transformation. For example, any new substituents are expected to enter the precise positions previously occupied by displaced groups. The simplest type of rearrangement is an intramolecular reaction in which the product is isomeric with the reactant (one type of "intramolecular isomerization").

Molecular recognition A chemical term referring to processes in which molecules adhere in a specific way, forming a large structure; an enabling technology for nanotechnology.

Molecular surgery / molecular repair Analysis and physical correction of molecular structures in the body using medical nano-machines.

Molecular systems engineering Design, analysis and construction of systems of molecular parts working together to carry out a useful purpose.

Molecular velocity The average speed of the molecules in a gas of a given temperature.

Molecular weight Molecular mass. The average mass of a molecule, calculated by summing the atomic weights of atoms in the molecular formula. Note that the words mass and weight are often used interchangeably in chemistry.

Molecular weight The sum of all the atomic weights of a molecule.

Molecularity The number of reactant molecular entities that are involved in the "microscopic chemical event" constituting an elementary reaction. (For reactions in solution this number is always taken to exclude molecular entities that form part of the medium and which are involved solely by virtue of their solvation of solutes.) A reaction with a molecularity of one is called "unimolecular", one with a molecularity of two "bimolecular" and of three "termolecular".

Molecule A tightly knit group of two or more atoms bound together by electromagnetic forces among the atoms' electrons and nuclei. For example, water (H_2O) is two hydrogen atoms bound with one oxygen atom. Identical molecules have identical chemical properties.

Mollusca The phylum of coelomate animals whose members possess a head-foot, visceral mass, mantle, and mantle cavity. Most molluscs also possess a radula and a shell. The molluscs, Bivalves, snails, octopuses, and related animals.

Molt A process in arthropods, such as crustaceans and insects, as well as in some vertebrates, such as snakes, whereby the organism sheds its outer exoskeleton or skin periodically as it grows. Also refers to changing the pelage or feathers in a mammal or bird.

Moment of inertia The rotational analogue of mass.

Momentum Momentum is considered to be a measure of the quantity of motion in a body. The momentum of a body is defined as the product of its mass and velocity. Its SI units are kg m /s.

Monera The kingdom of life whose members are characterized by having cells that lack a membrane-bound nucleus, as well as other internal, membrane-bound organe-lles (they are prokaryotic); bacteria.

Monerans Members of the kingdom Monera, which consists of prokaryotic organisms.

Monestrous A species in which the female is receptive for only a few days once each year.

Monitored, retrievable storage Holding wastes in underground mines or secure surface facilities such as dry casks where they can be watched and repackaged, if necessary.

Monkey wrenching Environmental sabotage such as driving large spikes in trees to protect them from loggers, vandalizing construction equipment, pulling up survey stakes for unwanted developments, and destroying billboards.

Monocarpic Denoting a plant that flowers only once.

Monochromatic light Light composed of a single colour.

Monoclonal antibody An antibody of a single type that is produced by a population of genetically identical plasma cells (a clone); a monoclonal antibody is typically produced from a cell culture derived from the fusion product of a cancer cell and an antibody-producing cell (a hybridoma).

Monocot One of the two primary groups of angiosperms characterized by a single cotyledon, parallel venation of leaves, and floral parts in threes.

Monocotyledon A class of angiosperms in which the seedlings typically possess one cotyledon. Commonly abbreviated to monocot.

Monoculture agroforestry Intensive planting of a single species; an efficient wood production approach, but one that encourages pests and disease infestations and conflicts with wildlife habitat or recreation uses.

Monoculture An agricultural system in which only one crop species is cultivated.

Monocyte A mononuclear phagocytic leukocyte that circulates briefly in the blood-stream before migrating to the tissues where it becomes a macrophage.

Monocyte-macrophage system The collection of fixed phagocytic cells (including macrophages, monocytes, and specialized endothelial cells) located in the liver, spleen, lymph nodes, and bone marrow. This system is an important component of the host's general nonspecific defense against pathogens.

Monoecious Hermaphroditic; an individual that contains reproductive systems of both sexes.

Monogamous Having one mate at a time.

Monogamy The condition of having a single mate at any one time.

Monogenea The class of Platyhelminthes that has members that are called monogenetic flukes; most ectoparasites on vertebrates (usually on fishes, occasionally on turtles, frogs, copepods, squids); one life-cycle form in only one host; bear an opisthaptor. Examples: Disocotyle, Gyrodactylus, Polystoma.

Monogononta A class of rotifers containing members that possess one ovary; mastax not designed for grinding; produce mictic and amictic eggs. Example: Notommata.

Monohybrid A hybrid offspring of parents different in one specified character.

Monohybrid cross A mating between two individuals heterozygous for one particular trait.

Monokine A generic term for a cytokine produced by mononuclear phagocytes.

Monomer A molecule of simple structure, but capable of linking with others to form polymers.

Monophyletic groups Groups that contain an ancestor and all the descendants of that ancestor.

Monophyletic origin A group of organisms that evolved from a single ancestral type.

Monophyly The condition that a taxon or other group of organisms contains the most recent common ancestor of the group and all of its descendants; contrasts with polyphyly and paraphyly.

Monoplacophora The class of molluscs whose members have a single, arched shell; a broad, flat foot; and certain serially repeated structures. Neopilina.

Monosaccharide A simple sugar that cannot be decomposed into smaller sugar molecules; the most common are pentoses (such as ribose) and hexoses (such as glucose).

Monounsaturated fat Composed of fatty acid chains in which there is only a single C-C double bond; examples: canola oil and olive oil.

Mono-unsaturated Refers to molecules, such as fats, that have only one double bond in their chemical structure. Some plant oils and margarines, avocados, olives, nuts and seeds contain mostly mono-unsaturated fats.

Monoxenous Living within a single host during a parasite's life cycle.

Monozoic Tapeworms with a single proglottid, do not undergo strobila-tion to form chain of proglottids.

Monozygotic Twins that arise from a single zygote, hence, two genetically identical individuals.

Monsoon A seasonal reversal of wind patterns caused by the different heating and cooling rates of the oceans and continents.

Montane coniferous forests Coniferous forests of the mountains consisting of belts of different forest communities along an altitudinal gradient.

Moral agents Beings capable of making distinctions between right and wrong and acting accordingly. Those whom we hold responsible for their actions.

Moral standing To say that a group of organisms has moral standing is to say that their wellbeing must be given some consideration. It does not decide the question of whether they have the same moral standing as people (and thus have 'human' rights).

Moral subjects Beings that are not capable of distinguishing between right or wrong or that are not able to act on moral principles and yet are susceptible of being wronged by others. This category assumes some rights or inherent values in moral subjects that gives us duties or obligations towards them.

Morbidity Illness or disease.

Morbidity rate Measures the number of individuals who become ill as a result of a particular disease within a susceptible population during a specific time period.

Mordant A substance that helps fix dye on or in a cell.

Morphine A pain-relieving and addictive compound derived from the opium poppy (Papaver somniferum).

Morphogenesis Development of the architectural features of organisms; formation and differentiation of tissues and organs.

Morphology The science of structure includes cytology, the study of cell structure; histology, the study of tissue structure; and anatomy, the study of gross structure.

Mortality Death rate in a population; the probability of dying.

Mortality rate The ratio of the number of deaths from a given disease to the total number of cases of the disease.

Morula A stage in the embryonic development of some animals that consists of a solid ball of cells.

Mosaic An organism whose tissues are made up of two or more genetically different types.

Mosaic cleavage Embryonic development characterized by independent differentiation of each part of the embryo; determinate cleavage.

Mosaic evolution A change in a portion of an organism (e.g., a bird wing) while the basic form of the organism is retained.

Moss A group of terrestrial, nonvascular plants; the dominant plant body is the gametophyte with the sporophyte embedded in it.

Most probable number (MPN) The statistical estimation of the probable population in a liquid by diluting and determining end points for microbial growth.

Motility Ability to move.

Motivation Internal processes that arouse and direct behaviour. Today this refers more to examination of the consequences of behavior and feedback to the animal concerning the consequences of those actions.

Motor (efferent) neuron or nerve A neuron or nerve that transmits impulses from the central nervous system to an effector such as a muscle or gland.

Motor unit A motor neuron and the muscle fibers associated with it.

Mountain tundra That portion of tundra vegetation confined to alpine meadows. Low-growing grasses, sedges, and forbs with a very short growing season; permafrost is typical.

Mucigel A slimy material secreted by and covering the root cap and root hairs.

Mucilaginous Containing a mucilage, usually composed of mucopolysaccharides.

Mucin Any of a group of glycoproteins secreted by certain cells, especially those of salivary glands.

Mucociliary blanket The layer of cilia and mucus that lines certain portions of the respiratory system; it traps microorganisms up to 10 mm in diameter and then transports them by ciliary action away from the lungs.

Mucosal-associated lymphoid tissue (MALT) The defensive immune lymphoid tissue located in the intestinal mucosa.

Mucous cell A glandular cell that secretes mucus.

Mucron Apical anchoring device on an acephaline gregarine protozoan.

Mucus Viscid, slippery secretion rich in mucins produced by secretory cells such as those in mucous membranes.

Mud flat A muddy bottom that is exposed at low tide.

Muellerian mimicry Evolution by one species to resemble the coloration, body shape, or behaviour of an unrelated species that is protected from predators by a venomous stinger, bad taste, or some other adaptation.

Mulch Protective ground cover, including manure, wood chips, straw, seaweed, leaves, and other natural products, or synthetic materials, such as heavy paper or plastic, that protect the soil, save water, and prevent weed growth.

Muller's larva A free-swimming ciliated larva that resembles a modified ctenophore, characteristic of many marine polyclad turbellarians.

Muller's ratchet The steady accumulation of mutations in a population of asexual organisms over time.

Mullerian mimicry Occurs when two similar species are both distasteful to predators.

Multi-centre bond Representation of some molecular entities solely by localized two-electron two-centre bonds appears to be unsatisfactory. Instead, multi-centre bonds have to be considered in which electron pairs occupy orbitals encompassing three or more atomic centres. Examples include the three-centre bonds in diborane, the delocalized pi bonding of benzene, and bridged carbocations.

Multi-centre reaction A synonym for pericyclic reaction. The number of "centres" is the number of atoms not bonded initially, between which single bonds are breaking or new bonds are formed in the transition state. This number does not necessarily correspond to the ring size of the transition state for the pericyclic reaction. Thus, a Diels-Alder reaction is a "four-centre reaction". This terminology has largely been superseded by the more detailed one developed for the various pericyclic reactions.

Multi-drug-resistant strains of tuberculosis (MDR-TB) A multi-drug-resistant strain is defined as *Mycobacterium tuberculosis* resistant to isoniazid and rifampin, with or without resistance to other drugs.

Mumps An acute generalized disease that occurs primarily in school-age children and is caused by a paramyxovirus that is transmitted in saliva and respiratory droplets. The principal manifestation is swelling of the parotid salivary glands.

Muon (μ) The second flavour of charged leptons (in order of increasing mass), with electric charge -1.

Muon chamber The outer layers of a particle detector capable of registering tracks of charged particles. Except for the chargeless neutrinos, only muons reach this layer from the collision point.

Muscular dystrophy A group of hereditary diseases that cause progressive muscle wastage due to defects in the biochemistry of a muscle tissue. The most common type is Duchenne muscular dystrophy, which is due to a defective gene on the X chromosome. Because the condition is sex-linked, it usually only affect males. It is usually lethal by the early 20's.

Must The juices of fruits, including grapes, that can be fermented for the production of alcohol.

Mutagen A chemical or physical agent that causes mutations.

Mutation A permanent, heritable change in the genetic material.

Mutualism A type of symbiosis in which both partners gain from the association and are unable to survive without it. The mutualist and the host are metabolically dependent on each other.

Mutualist An organism associated with another in a relationship that is beneficial to both (and often obligatory).

Mycelium A mass of branching hyphae found in fungi and some bacteria.

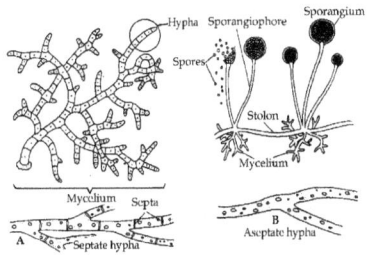

Figure Mycelium

Mycobiont The fungal partner in a lichen.

Mycolic acids Complex 60 to 90 carbon fatty acids with a hydroxyl on the b-carbon and an aliphatic chain on the a-carbon; found in the cell walls of mycobacteria.

Mycologist A person specializing in mycology; a student of mycology.

Mycology The science and study of fungi.

Mycoplasma Bacteria that are members of the class Mollicutes and order Mycoplasmatales; they lack cell walls and cannot synthesize peptidoglycan precursors; most require sterols for growth; they are the smallest organisms capable of independent reproduction.

Mycoplasmal pneumonia A type of pneumonia caused by *Mycoplasma pneumoniae*. Spread involves airborne droplets and close contact.

Mycorrhizosphere The region around a mycorrhizal fungus in which nutrients released from the fungus increase the microbial population and its activities.

Mycosis Any disease caused by a fungus.

Mycotoxicology The study of fungal toxins and their effects on various organisms.

Myeloma cell A tumor cell that is similar to the cell type found in bone marrow. Also, a malignant, neoplastic plasma cell that produces large quantities of antibodies and can be readily cultivated.

Myositis Inflammation of a striated or voluntary muscle.

Myxamoeba A free-living amoeboid cell that can aggregate with other myxamoeba to form a plasmodium or pseudo-plasmodium. Found in cellular slime molds and the myxomycetes.

Myxobacteria A group of gram-negative, aerobic soil bacteria characterized by gliding motility, a complex life cycle with the production of fruiting bodies, and the formation of myxospores.

Myxospores Special dormant spores formed by the myxobacteria.

NAD⁺ (nicotine adenine dinucleotide) Coenzyme that participates in an oxidation reaction by accepting a hydride ion (H⁻) from a donor molecule. The NADH formed is an important carrier of electrons for oxidative phosphorylation.

NADP⁺ (nicotine adenine dinucleotide phosphate) Coenzyme closely related to NAD⁺ that is used extensively in biosynthetic, rather than catabolic, pathways.

Nano A prefix meaning one billionth (1/1,000,000,000).

Nanocell surgery Modifying cellular structures by the use of medical nanomachines.

Nanocomputer A computer with parts built on a molecular scale.

Nanoelectronics Electronics on a nanometer scale, whether by current techniques or nanotechnology; includes both molecular electronics and nanoscale devices resembling today's semiconductor devices.

Nanomachine An artificial eutactic mechanical device that relies on nanometer-scale components.

Nanomechanical Pertaining to nanomachines.

Nanometer (NM) Unit of length commonly used to measure molecules and cell organelles. 1 nm = 10^{-3} μm = 10^{-9} m.

Nanoscale On a scale of nanometers, from atomic dimensions to ~100 nm.

Nanosurgery A generic term including molecular repair and cell surgery.

Nanosystem A eutactic set of nanoscale components working together to serve a set of purposes; complex nanosystems can be of macroscopic size.

Nanotechnology A technology that creates small materials at the scale of molecules by manipulating single atoms. The name nano comes from the size of molecules which is measured in nanometers - or one billionth of a meter (0.000000001 meter). The dimension of single atoms is ten fold smaller. The molecular processes of life, particularly the activity of proteins (enzymes) and the self-organizing behaviour of many biological molecules has greatly inspired nanotechnology and molecular motors could be considered the result of natures nanotechnology.

Napkin (diaper) candidiasis Typically found in infants whose diapers are not changed frequently and are therefore not kept dry. Caused by Candida species of fungi.

Narrow-spectrum drugs Chemothera-peutic agents that are effective only against a limited variety of microorganisms.

Natural abundance The average fraction of atoms of a given isotope of an element on Earth.

Natural attenuation The decrease in the level of an enviromental contaminant that results from natural chemical, physical, and biological processes.

Natural classification A classification system that arranges organisms into groups whose members share many characteristics and reflect as much as possible the biological nature of organisms.

Natural frequency The frequency of vibration of an elastic object that depends on the size, composition, and shape of the object.

Natural killer (NK) cell A non-T, non-B lymphocyte present in nonimmunized individuals that exhibits MHC-independent cytolytic activity against tumor cells.

Natural uranium Uranium with an isotopic composition as found in nature, containing 99.3% U-238, 0.7% U-235 and a trace of U-234. Can be used as fuel in heavy water-moderated reactors.

Naturally acquired active immunity The type of active immunity that develops when an individual's immunologic system comes into contact with an appropriate antigenic stimulus during the course of normal activities; it usually arises as the result of recovering from an infection and lasts a long time.

Naturally acquired passive immunity The type of temporary immunity that involves the transfer of antibodies from one individual to another.

Nature, acoustic The innate or essential quality of the noise. That which makes one noise distinguishable from another.

Nautical mile Nautical mile is a legal international unit of length temporarily maintained with the SI. It is still used in navigation (mercantile marine, aviation). It is equal to the length of an arc of one minute measured at a latitude of N45° (mile = 1852m). The international nautical mile has been taken equal to the nautical mile.

Necrotizing fasciitis A disease that results from a severe invasive group A streptococcus infection. Necrotizing fasciitis is an infection of the subcutaneous soft tissues, particularly of fibrous tissue, and is most common on the extremities. It begins with skin reddening, swelling, pain, and cellulitis, and proceeds to skin breakdown and gangrene after 3 to 5 days.

Neel temperature Neel temperature (T_N) is the critical temperature above which an antiferromagnetic substance becomes paramagnetic. The phenomenon was discovered around 1930 by L.E.F. Neel.

Negative electric charge One of the two types of electric charge; repels other negative charges and attracts positive charges.

Negative ion Atom or particle that has a surplus, or imbalance, of electrons and, thus, a negative charge.

Negative staining A staining procedure in which a dye is used to make the background dark while the specimen is unstained.

Negri bodies Masses of viruses or unassembled viral subunits found within the brain neurons of rabies-infected animals.

Neoprene Neoprene is a synthetic rubber made by polimerizing the compound 2-chlorobuta-1,2-diene. Neoprene is often used in place of natural rubber in applications requiring resistance to chemical attack.

Nessler's reagent Nessler's reagent is a solution of mercury(II) iodide (HgI_2) in potassium iodide and potassium hydroxide named after Julius Nessler (1827-1905). It is used in testing for ammonia, with which it forms a brown coloration or precipitate.

Net force The resulting force after all vector forces have been added; if a net force is zero, all the forces have canceled each other and there is not an unbalanced force.

Neurotoxin A toxin that is poisonous to or destroys nerve tissue; especially the toxins secreted by *C. tetani, Corynebacterium diphtheriae,* and *Shigella dysenteriae.*

Neurotransmitter A chemical substance released from neurons in synapses that binds to corresponding receptors on nearby cell surfaces causing a physiological stimulus in form of a membrane current or second messenger cascade activating channels, pumps, kinases, or proteases. The molecular mechanisms of activation are similar to those of hormones.

Neustonic The micro-organisms that live at the atmospheric interface of a water body.

Neutral 1. having no net electrical charge. Atoms are electrically neutral; ions are not.

2. A solution containing equal concentrations of H^+ and OH^-.

Neutralization Neutralization is the process in which an acid reacts with a base to form a salt and water.

$$H^+ + OH^- \rightleftharpoons H_2O$$

Neutrino A neutral, weakly interacting elementary particle having a very tiny mass. Stars like the Sun produce more than 200 trillion trillion trillion neutrinos every second. Neutrinos from the Sun interact so weakly with other matter that they pass straight through the Earth as if it weren't there.

Neutrino detector A device designed to detect neutrinos.

Neutron An uncharged elementary particle found in the nucleus of every atom except hydrogen. Solitary mobile neutrons travelling at various speeds originate from fission reactions. Slow (thermal) neutrons can in turn readily cause fission in nuclei of "fissile" isotopes, e.g. U-235, Pu-239, U-233; and fast neutrons can cause fission in nuclei of "fertile" isotopes such as U-238, Pu-239. Sometimes atomic nuclei simply capture neutrons.

Neutron number Neutron number (N) is a characteristic property of a specific isotope of an element, equal to the number of neutrons in the nucleus.

Neutrophil A mature white blood cell in the granulocyte lineage formed in bone marrow. It has a nucleus with three to five lobes and is very phagocytic.

Newton Newton (N) is the SI unit of force, being the force required to give a mass of one kilogram an acceleration of 1 ms^{-2} (N = kg ms^{-2}). It is named after British scientist Sir Isaac Newton (1642-1727).

Newton's first law of motion A body continues in a state of rest or of uniform motion in a straight line unless it is acted upon by an external force.

Newton's law of gravitation The gravitational force of attraction acting between any two particles is directly proportional to the product of their masses, and inversely proportional to the square of the distance between them. The force of attraction acts along the line joining the two particles. Real bodies having spherical symmetry act as point masses with their mass assumed to be concentrated at their center of mass.

Newton's second law of motion The rate of change of momentum is equal to the force applied OR the force acting on a body is directly proportional to the product of its mass and acceleration produced by the force in the body.

Newton's third law of motion To every action there is an equal and opposite reaction. The action and reaction act on two different bodies simultaneously.

Niche (nich) The function of an organism in a complex system, including place of the organism, the resources used in a given location, and the time of use.

Nicotinamide adenine dinucleotide An electron-carrying coenzyme; it is particularly important in catabolic processes and usually donates its electrons to the electron transport chain under aerobic conditions.

Nitrification The oxidation of ammonia to nitrate.

Nitrifying bacteria Chemolithotrophic, gram-negative bacteria that are members of the family Nitrobacteriaceae and convert ammonia to nitrate and nitrite to nitrate.

Nitrogen fixation The metabolic process in which atmospheric molecular nitrogen is reduced to ammonia; carried out by cyanobacteria, Rhizobium, and other nitrogen-fixing bacteria.

Nitrogen oxygen demand (NOD) The demand for oxygen in sewage treatment, caused by nitrifying microorganisms.

Nitrogen saturation point The point at which mineral nitrogen, when added to an ecosystem, can no longer be incorporated into organic matter through biological processes.

Nitrogenase The enzyme that catalyzes biological nitrogen fixation.

Noble gas Noble gas refers to any element of the group of six elements in group 18 of the periodic table. They are helium (He), neon (Ne), argon (Ar), krypton (Kr), xenon (Xe), and radon (Rn). Unlike most elements, the noble gases are monoatomic. The atoms have stable configurations of electrons. Therefore, under normal conditions they do not form compounds with other elements.

They were generally called inert gases until about 1962 when xenon tetrafluoride, XeF_4, was produced in the laboratory. This was the first report of a stable compound of a noble gas with another single element.

Nocardioforms Bacteria that resemble members of the genus Nocardia; they develop a substrate mycelium that readily breaks up into rods and coccoid elements (a quality sometimes called fugacity).

Noise Sounds made up of groups of waves of random frequency and intensity.

Nomenclature A system for naming things. For example, "organic nomenclature" is the system used to name organic compounds.

Non thermal radiation Radiation that is not produced from heat energy — for example, radiation released when a very fast-moving charged particle (such as an electron) interacts with a magnetic force field. Because the electron's velocity in this case is not related to the gas temperature, this process has nothing to do with heat.

Non uniform acceleration When the velocity of a body increases by unequal amounts in equal intervals of time, it is said to have non-uniform acceleration.

Non uniform speed When a body travels unequal distances in equal intervals of time then it is said to have non-uniform speed.

Non uniform velocity When a body covers unequal distances in equal intervals of time in a particular direction, or when it covers equal distances in equal intervals but changes its direction it is said to have non uniform velocity.

Noncyclic photophosphorylation The process in which light energy is used to make ATP when electrons are moved from water to NADP1 during photosynthesis; both photosystem I and photosystem II are involved.

Nongonococcal urethritis (NGU) Any inflammation of the urethra not caused by *Neisseria gonorrhoeae*.

Noninertial frame An accelerating frame of reference, in which Newton's first law is violated.

Non-metals Non-metals are defined as elements that are not metals. Their physical properties generally include:

They are poor conductors.

They are brittle, not ductile in their solid state.

They show no metallic luster.

They may be transparent or translucent.

They have low density.

They form molecules which consists of atoms covalently bonded; the noble gases are monoatomic.

Their chemical properties are generally:

They usually have four to eight valence electrons.

They have high electron affinities (except the noble gases)

They are good oxidizing agents (except the noble gases)

They have hydroxides which are acidic (except the noble gases)

They are electronegative.

Nonsense codon A codon that does not code for an amino acid but is a signal to terminate protein synthesis.

Nonsense mutation A mutation that converts a sense codon to a nonsense or stop codon.

Nonspecific resistance Refers to those general defense mechanisms that are inherited as part of the innate structure and function of each animal; also known as nonspecific, innate or natural immunity.

Nonthermal particle A particle that is not part of a thermal gas. These particles cannot be described by a conventional temperature.

Nonthermal radiation Radiation emitted by nonthermal electrons.

Nonuniform circular motion Circular motion in which the magnitude of the velocity vector changes.

Normal A line perpendicular to the surface of a boundary.

Normal force The force that keeps two objects from occupying the same space.

Normal microbiota The microorganisms normally associated with a particular tissue or structure.

Normalization The property of probabilities that the sum of the probabilities of all possible outcomes must equal one.

Nosocomial infection An infection that develops within a hospital and is produced by an infectious organism acquired during the stay of the patient.

Nuclear binding energy Energy needed to break an atomic nucleus into separate protons and neutrons.

Nuclear energy The form of energy from reactions involving the nucleus, the innermost part of an atom.

Nuclear envelope The complex double-membrane structure forming the outer boundary of the eucaryotic nucleus. It is covered by pores through which substances enter and leave the nucleus.

Nuclear fission Nuclear reaction of splitting a massive nucleus into more stable, less massive nuclei with an accompanying release of energy.

Nuclear force One of four fundamental forces, a strong force of attraction that operates over very short distances between subatomic particles; this force overcomes the electric repulsion of protons in a nucleus and binds the nucleus together.

Nuclear fusion Nuclear reaction of low mass nuclei fusing together to form more stable and more massive nuclei with an accompanying release of energy.

Nuclear magnetic resonance Nuclear magnetic resonance (NMR) is a type of radio-frequency spectroscopy based on the magnetic field generated by the spinning of electrically charged atomic nuclei. This nuclear magnetic field is caused to interact with a very large (1T - 5T) magnetic field of the instrument magnet. NMR techniques have been applied to studies of electron densities and chemical bonding and has become a fundamental research tool for structure determinations in organic chemistry.

Nuclear reactor Nuclear reactor is an assembly of fissionable material designed to produce a sustained and controlable chain reaction for the generation of electric power. The essential components of a nuclear reactor are: 1. The core, metal rods containing enough fissionable material to maintain a chain reaction at the necessary power level (as much as 50 t of uranium may be required).

2. A source of neutrons to initiate the reaction (such as a mixture of polonium and beryllium)

3. A moderator to reduce the energy of fast neutrons for more efficient fission (material such as graphite, beryllium, heavy water, and light water are used)

4. A coolant to remove the fission-generated heat (water, sodium, helium, and nitrogen may be used)

5. A control system such as rods of boron or cadmium that have high capture cross sections (to absorbs neutrons)

6. Adequate shielding, remote-control equipment, and appropriate instrumentation are essential for personnel safety and efficient operation.

Nuclear transformation The process by which an atomic nucleus is transformed into another type of atomic nucleus. For example, by removing an alpha particle from the nucleus, the element radium is transformed into the element radon.

Nucleic acids Nucleic acids are macromolecules, the major organic matter of the nuclei of biological cells, made up of nucleotide units, and hydrolyzable into certain pyrimidine or purine bases, D-ribose or 2-deoxy-D-ribose.

Nucleic acid hybridization The process of forming a hybrid double-stranded DNA molecule using a heated mixture of single-stranded DNAs from two different sources; if the sequences are fairly complemen-tary, stable hybrids will form.

Nucleocapsid The nucleic acid and its surrounding protein coat or capsid; the basic unit of virion structure.

Nucleoid An irregularly shaped region in the procaryotic cell that contains its genetic material.

Nucleolus The organelle, located within the eucaryotic nucleus and not bounded by a membrane, that is the location of ribosomal RNA synthesis and the assembly of ribosomal subunits.

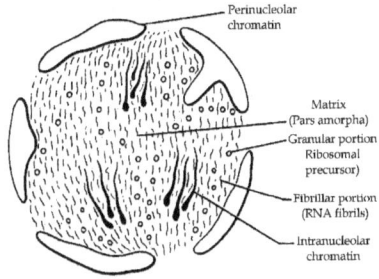

Figure Nucleolus

Nucleons Name used to refer to both the protons and neutrons in the nucleus of an atom.

Nucleoside A combination of ribose or deoxyribose with a purine or pyrimidine base.

Nucleosome A complex of histones and DNA found in eucaryotic chromatin; the DNA is wrapped around the surface of the beadlike histone complex.

Nucleotide A combination of ribose or deoxyribose with phosphate and a purine or pyrimidine base; a nucleoside plus one or more phosphates.

Nucleus Tiny, relatively massive and positively charged center of an atom containing protons and neutrons; the small, dense center of an atom numerical constant a constant without units; a number.

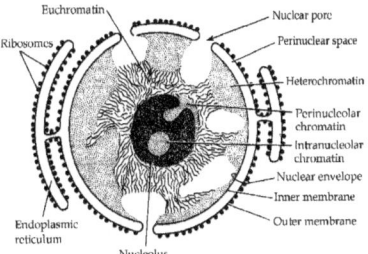

Figure Nucleus

Nuclide An atom or ion with a specified mass number and atomic number. For example, uranium-235 and carbon-14 are nuclides.

Nuclide symbol A symbol for a nuclide that contains the mass number as a leading superscript and the atomic number as a leading subscript. For ions, the ionic charge is given as a trailing superscript. For example, the nuclide symbol for the most common form of the chloride ion is $_{35}Cl^{17}$, where 35 is the mass number,

17 is the atomic number, and the charge on the ion is -1. The atomic number is sometimes omitted from nuclide symbols.

Numerical aperture The property of a microscope lens that determines how much light can enter and how great a resolution the lens can provide.

Numerical taxonomy The grouping by numerical methods of taxonomic units into taxa based on their character states.

Nutraceuticals Chemicals that have beneficial effects on our physiology if taken in appropriate amounts with food. Plants are the major source of nutraceuticals also known as phytochemicals. Plants produce those molecules for self-defense or to attract insects and animals to facilitate pollen distribution. For the latter purpose, they often are colorants while tasting bitter to ward of animals.

Nutrient A substance that supports growth and reproduction.

Nystatin A polyene antibiotic from Streptomyces noursei that is used in the treatment of Candida infections of the skin, vagina, and alimentary tract.

Obligate anaerobes Microorganisms that cannot tolerate the presence of oxygen and die when exposed to it.

Oblique Describes a force that acts at some other angle, one that is not a direct repulsion or attraction.

Octane (C_8H_{18}) Flammable liquid compounds found in petroleum and natural gas. There are 18 different octanes- they have different structural formulas but share the molecular formula C_8H_{18}. Octane is used as a fuel and as a raw material for building more complex organic molecules. It is the eighth member of the alkane series.

Odontopathogens Dental pathogens.

Oersted Oersted (Oe) is a non-SI unit of magnetic field (H), equal to 79.57747157A/m. The unit is named after the H.C. Oersted (1777-1851).

Ohm Ohm (Ω) is the SI derived unit of electric resistance. The ohm is the electric resistance between two points of a conductor when a constant difference of potential of one volt, applied between these two points, produces in this conductor a current of one ampere, this conductor not being the source of electromotive force (W = V/A). The unit is named after the German physicist Georg Simon Ohm (1789-1854).

Ohmic Describes a substance in which the flow of current between two points is proportional to the voltage difference between them.

Ohm's law The electric potential difference is directly proportional to the product of the current times the resistance.

Okazaki fragments Short stretches of polynucleotides produced during discontinuous DNA replication.

Olefins Olefins are acyclic and cyclic hydrocarbons having one or more carbon-carbon double bonds, apart from the formal ones in aromatic compounds. The class olefins subsumes alkenes and cycloalkenes and the corresponding polyenes.

Oligomer Oligomer is a substance consisting of molecules of intermediate relative molecular mass (molecular weight), the structure of which essentially comprises the multiple repetition of units derived, actually or conceptually, from molecules of low relative molecular mass. In contrast to a polymer, the properties of an oligomer can vary significantly with the removal of one or a few of its units.

Oligotrophic environment An environment containing low levels of nutrients, particularly nutrients that support microbial growth.

Oncogene A gene whose activity is associated with the conversion of normal cells to cancer cells.

One-step growth experiment An experiment used to study the reproduction of lytic phages in which one round of phage reproduction occurs and ends with the lysis of the host bacterial population.

Onsager relations Onsager relations are an important set of equations in the thermodynamics of irreversible processes. They express the symmetry between the transport coefficients describing reciprocal processes in systems with a linear dependence of flux (J_i) on driving forces (X_j).

$$J_i = \sum_{j=1}^{m} L_{ij} X_j$$

In Onsager's theory the coupling coefficients are equal, $L_{ij} = L_{ji}$. These are known as reciprocal relations. The theory was developed by the Norwegian chemist Lars Onsager (1903-1976) in 1931.

Onychomycosis A fungal infection of the nail plate producing nails that are opaque, white, thickened, friable, and brittle. Also called ringworm of the nails and tinea unguium. Caused by Trichophyton and other fungi such as C. Albicans.

Oocyst Cyst formed around a zygote of malaria and related protozoa.

Oogonia Mitotically dividing female structures that produce primary oocytes and gametes.

Oomycetes A collective name for members of the division Oomycota; also known as the water molds.

Ooplasmic transplantation Adding some of the cytoplasm of an ovum from a donor to the ovum of another woman so that the recipient will receive healthy mitochondria. As the mitochondria contain some 30 or so genes the child resulting from the fertilised treated ovum would strictly have 3 genetic parents. By May 2001 some 30 children were reported to have been born by this IVF variant.

Opacity The degree to which light is prevented from passing through an object or a substance. Opacity is the opposite of transparency. As an object's opacity increases, the amount of light passing through it decreases. Glass, for example, is transparent and most clouds are opaque.

Open circuit A circuit that does not function because it has a gap in it.

Open reading frame (ORF) A reading frame sequence not interrupted by a stop codon; it is usually determined by nucleic acid sequencing studies.

Operational definition A definition that states what operations should be carried out to measure the thing being defined.

Operator The segment of DNA to which the repressor protein binds; it controls the expression of the genes adjacent to it.

Operon The sequence of bases in DNA that contains one or more structural genes together with the operator controlling their expression.

Ophthalmia neonatorum A gonorrheal eye infection in a newborn, which may lead to blindness. Also called conjunctivitis of the newborn.

Opportunistic microorganism or pathogen A microorganism that is usually free-living or a part of the host's normal microbiota, but which may become pathogenic under certain circumstances, such as when the immune system is compromised.

Opsonization The action of opsonins in making bacteria and other cells more readily phagocytosed. Antibodies, complement, and fibronectin are potent opsonins.

Optical radiation Electromagnetic radiation (light) that is visible to the human eye.

Optical tweezer The use of a focused laser beam to drag and isolate a specific microorganism from a complex microbial mixture.

Orbital Orbital is the area in space about an atom or molecule in which the probability of finding an electron is greatest.

The possible atomic orbitals correspond to subshells of the atom. Thus there is one s-orbital for each shell. There are three p-orbitals and five d-orbitals. The shapes of orbitals depend on the value of l.

Orbital period The amount of time it takes a spacecraft or other object to travel once around it's orbit.

Orchitis Inflammation of the testes.

Organelle A structure within or on a cell that performs specific functions and is related to the cell in a way similar to that of an organ to the body.

Organic Organic compound. Compounds that contain carbon chemically bound to hydrogen. They often contain other elements. Organic compounds were once thought to be produced only by living things. We now know that any organic compound can be synthesized in the laboratory.

Organotrophs Organisms that use reduced organic compounds as their electron source.

Origin The only point on a graph where both the x and y variables have a value of zero at the same time.

Oscillatory motion The to and fro motion of a body about its mean position is called oscillatory motion. Oscillatory motion is also called vibratory motion. Oscillatory motion is periodic in nature.

Osmophilic microorganisms Microorganisms that grow best in or on media of high solute concentration.

Osmosis Osmosis is the flow of a solvent in a system in which two solutions of different concentration are separated by a semipermeable membrane which cannot pass solute molecules. The solvent will flow from the side of lower concentration to that of higher concentration, thus tending to equalize the concentrations. The pressure that must be applied to the more concentrated side to stop the flow is called the osmotic pressure.

Osmotic pressure Osmotic pressure (Π) is the excess pressure necessary to maintain osmotic equilibrium between a solution and the pure solvent separated by a membrane permeable only to the solvent. In an ideal dilute solution

$$\Pi = c_b RT$$

Where c_b is the amount-of-substance concentration of the solute, R is the molar gas constant, and T the temperature.

Osmotolerant Organisms that grow over a Fairly wide range of water activity or solute concentration.

Ostwald's dilution law Ostwald's dilution law is a relation for the concentration dependence of the molar conductivity Λ of an electrolyte solution, viz.

$$\frac{1}{\Lambda} = \frac{1}{K_6 \Lambda_0^2} c\Lambda + \frac{1}{\Lambda}$$

Where c is the solute concentration, K_c is the equilibrium constant for dissociation of the solute, and L_0 is the conductivity at $c\lambda = 0$. The law was first put forward by the German chemist Wilhelm Ostwald (1853-1932).

Outbreak The sudden, unexpected occurrence of a disease in a given population.

Outer membrane A special membrane located outside the peptidoglycan layer in the cell walls of gram-negative bacteria.

Output traits Traits produced in genetically modified crops that are beneficial or of direct value to the consumer. For example, enhancing the quality of food, fibre, lowering the fat content or increasing anti-oxidant levels.

Overlap Orbitals lack sharply defined surfaces, declining in amplitude exponentially in their surface regions. When two orbitals are brought together, regions of substantial amplitude overlap. The resulting system can be described as two new orbitals, one formed by joining the two original orbitals without introducing a node in the wave function, and the other formed with a node between them. The nodeless joining reduces the energy of the electrons relative to the separate orbitals, resulting in a bonding interaction; joining with a node raises the energy, producing an antibonding interaction. If both new orbitals are occupied, antibonding forces dominate, resulting in overlap repulsion. Molecular mechanics models give an approximate description of overlap (and other) forces for a certain range of atoms and geometries.

Overlap repulsion A repulsive force resulting from the nonbonding overlap of two atoms.

Overpotential Overpotential (η) is a potential that must be applied in an electrolytic cell in addition to the theoretical potential required to liberate a given substance at an electrode. The value depends on the electrode material and on the current density.

Oxidation The term oxidation originally meant a reaction in which oxygen combines chemically with another substance. More generally, oxidation is a part of a chemical reaction in which a reactant loses electrons. Simultaneous reduction of a different reactant must occur.

Oxidation-reduction (redox) reactions Reactions involving electron transfers; the reductant donates electrons to an oxidant.

Oxidative phosphorylation The synthesis of ATP from ADP using energy made available during electron transport.

Oxide fuels Enriched or natural uranium in the form of the oxide UO_2, used in many types of reactor.

Oxidizing agent or oxidant The electron acceptor in an oxidation-reduction reaction.

Oximes Oximes are organic compounds of structure $R_2C=NOH$ derived from condensation of aldehydes or ketones with hydroxylamine. Oximes from aldehydes may be called aldoximes; those from ketones may be called ketoximes.

Oxo compounds Oxo compounds are organic compounds that contain the karbonyl group, C=O. The term thus embraces aldehydes, carboxylic acids, ketones, amides, and esters.

Oxygenic photosynthesis Photosynthesis that oxidizes water to form oxygen; the form of photosynthesis characteristic of eucaryotic algae and cyanobacteria.

Ozone Ozone is an alotropic form of oxygen. It is unstable blue gas with pungent odour. It is a powerful oxidizing agent. The gas is made by passing oxygen through a silent electric discharge.

$$3O_2(g) <=> 2O_3(g)$$

P

Pacemaker enzyme The enzyme in a metabolic pathway that catalyzes the slowest or rate-limiting reaction; if its rate changes, the pathway's activity changes.

Palindromic sequence Nucleotide sequence that is identical to its complementary strand when each is read in the same chemical direction - for example, GATC.

Pandemic An increase in the occurrence of a disease within a large and geographically widespread population.

Paneth cell The granular cell located at the base of glands in the small intestine; it produces the enzyme lysozyme.

Pannus A superficial vascularization of the cornea with infiltration of granulation tissue.

Panzootic The wide dissemination of a disease in an animal population.

Parabola The mathematical curve whose graph has y proportional to x^2.

Paraffins Paraffins are obsolescent term for alkanes. Still widely used in the petrochemical industry.

Paralytic shellfish poisoning Dinoflagellates (Gonyaulax spp.) Produce a powerful neurotoxin called saxitoxin. Shellfish accumulate saxitoxin and are poisonous when consumed by animals and humans. Saxitoxin paralyzes the striated respiratory muscles by inhibiting sodium transport. Paralytic shellfish poisoning is characterized by numbness of the mouth, lips, face, and extremities.

Paramagnetism Paramagnetism is a type of magnetism characterized by a positive magnetic susceptibility, so that the material becomes weakly magnetized in the direction of an external field. The magnetization disappears when the field is removed.

Parasite An organism that lives on or within another organism (the host) and benefits from the association while harming its host. Often the parasite obtains nutrients from the host.

Parasitism A type of symbiosis in which one organism adversely affects the other (the host), but cannot live without it.

Parenteral route A route of drug administration that is nonoral (e.g., by injection).

Parfocal A microscope that retains proper focus when the objectives are changed.

Paronychia Inflammation involving the folds of tissue surrounding the nail; usually caused by Candida albicans.

Particle A subatomic object with a definite mass and charge.

Partition coefficient K The partition coefficient most often refers to the oil-water or air-water partition coefficient expressing the concentra-tion ratio of a solute in a two-phasic system. After thoroughly mixing an oil-water solution with a particular solute the concentration of the solute are measured in each phase after the system comes to rest and the oil (gas) phase is well separated from the water phase. The ratio thus is an expression of the relative solubility of a molecule in oil vs water quantifying its hydrophobicity, or its ability to be soluble in oil. The oil-water partition coefficient of molecules is a good indicator if a molecule can easily diffuse across cell membranes or not. The more soluble it is in oil, the better its permeation across membranes. However, very high oil solubility is also an indicator of small molecules to function as general anesthetics, because they tend to stick in cell membranes rather than diffuse across it, thus altering the composition and physical properties of membranes and some of its proteins. If membrane solubility affects neuronal membranes, a loss of sensation or consciousness can be the result.

Partition function A function determined by the probability distribution describing a thermally equilibrated system; many thermodynamic quantities can be expressed in terms of the partition function and its derivatives.

Pascal 1. it is a Computer Language developed from Algol.

2. It is a unit of pressure equal to one Newton per square meter.

Paschen series Paschen series are the series of lines in the spectrum of the hydrogen atom which corresponds to transitions between the state with principal quantum number $n = 3$ and successive higher states.

Passive diffusion The process in which molecules move from a region of higher concentration to one of lower concentration as a result of random thermal agitation.

Passive immunization The induction of temporary immunity by the transfer of immune products, such as antibodies or sensitized T cells, from an immune vertebrate to a nonimmune one.

Pasteur effect The decrease in the rate of sugar catabolism and change to aerobic respiration that occurs when microorganisms are switched from anaerobic to aerobic conditions.

Pasteurization The process of heating milk and other liquids to destroy microorganisms that can cause spoilage or disease.

Pathogen Any virus, bacterium, or other agent that causes disease.

Pathogenic potential The degree that a pathogen causes morbid signs and symptoms.

Pathogenicity The condition or quality of being pathogenic, or the ability to cause disease.

Pathogenicity island A large segment of DNA in some pathogens that contains the genes responsible for virulence; often it codes for the type III secretion system that allows the pathogen to secrete virulence proteins and damage host cells. A pathogen may have more than one pathogenicity island.

Pathway architecture The analysis, design, and modification of biochemical pathways to increase process efficiency.

Pauli exclusion principle Pauli exclusion principle is the statement that two electrons in an atom cannot have identical all four quantum numbers. It was first formulated in 1925 by Austrian-born Swiss physicst Wolfgang Ernst Pauli (1900-1958).

PCR (polymerase chain reaction) Technique for amplifying specific regions of DNA by multiple cycles of DNA polymerization, each followed by a brief heat treatment to separate complementary strands.

Ped A natural soil aggregate, formed partly through bacterial and fungal growth in the soil.

Pellicle A relatively rigid layer of proteinaceous elements just beneath the plasma membrane in many protozoa and algae. The plasma membrane is sometimes considered part of the pellicle.

Peltier effect Peltier effect is the absorption or generation of heat (depending on the current direction) which occurs when an electric current is passed through a junction between two materials.

Pelvic inflammatory disease (PID) A severe infection of the female reproductive organs. The disease that results when gonococci and chlamydiae infect the uterine tubes and surrounding tissue.

Penicillins A group of antibiotics containing a b-lactam ring, which are active against gram-positive bacteria.

Penton or pentamer A capsomer composed of five protomers.

Pentose phosphate pathway The pathway that oxidizes glucose 6-phosphate to ribulose 5-phosphate and then converts it to a variety of three to seven carbon sugars; it forms several important products (NADPH for biosynthesis, pentoses, and other sugars) and also can be used to degrade glucose to CO_2.

Peplomer or spike A protein or protein complex that extends from the virus envelope and often is important in virion attachment to the host cell surface.

Peptic ulcer disease A gastritis caused by Helicobacter pylori.

Peptide interbridge A short peptide chain that connects the tetrapeptide chains in some peptidoglycans.

Peptides Peptides are amides derived from two or more amino acids (the same or different) linked by peptide bonds. These bonds are formed by the reaction between adjacent carboxyl (-COOH) i amino ($-NH_2$) groups with the elimination of water.

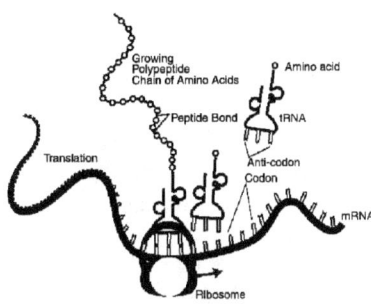

Figure Peptide

Peptidoglycan A large polymer composed of long chains of alternating N-acetylglucosamine and N-acetylmuramic acid residues. The polysaccharide chains are linked to each other through connections between tetrapeptide chains attached to the N-acetylmuramic acids. It provides much of the strength and rigidity possessed by bacterial cell walls.

Peptidyl or donor site (P site) The site on the ribosome that contains the peptidyl-tRNA at the beginning of the elongation cycle during protein synthesis.

Peptidyl transferase The enzyme that catalyzes the transpeptidation reaction in protein synthesis; in this reaction, an amino acid is added to the growing peptide chain.

Peptones Water-soluble digests or hydrolysates of proteins that are used in the preparation of culture media.

Perforin pathway The cytotoxic pathway that uses perforin protein, which polymerizes to form membrane pores that help destroy cells during cell-mediated cytotoxicity. Perforin is produced by cytotoxic T cells and NK cells and stored in granules that are released when a target cell is contacted.

Period Periods are horizontal rows in the periodic table. Each period beginning with an alkali metal (one electron in the outermost principal quantum level) and ending with a noble gas (each having eight electrons in the outermost principal quantum level, except for helium, which is limited to two).

Period of infectivity Refers to the time during which the source of an infectious disease is infectious or is disseminating the pathogen.

Periodic motion Motion that repeats itself over and over.

Periodic table Periodic table is a table of the elements, written in sequence in the order of atomic number or atomic weight and arranged in horizontal rows (periods) and vertical columns (groups) to illustrate the occurrence of similarities in the properties of the elements as a periodic function of the sequence. The original form was proposed by Dmitri Mendeleev (1834-1907) in 1869 using relative atomic masses.

Periodic wave A wave in which the particles of the medium oscillate continuously about their mean positions regularly at fixed intervals of time is called a periodic wave.

Periodontal disease A disease located around the teeth or in the periodontium-the tissue investing and supporting the teeth, including the cementum, periodontal ligament, alveolar bone, and gingiva.

Periodontitis An inflammation of the periodontium.

Periodontosis A degenerative, noninflammatory condition of the periodontium, which is characterized by destruction of tissue.

Periplasm The substance that fills the periplasmic space.

Periplasmic flagella The flagella that lie under the outer sheath and extend from both ends of the spirochete cell to overlap in the middle and form the axial filament. Also called axial fibrils and endoflagella.

Periplasmic space The space between the plasma membrane and the outer membrane in gram-negative bacteria, and between the plasma membrane and the cell wall in gram-positive bacteria.

Peritrichous A cell with flagella evenly distributed over its surface.

Permeability The ability to transmit fluids through openings, small passageways, or gaps.

Permease A membrane-bound carrier protein or a system of two or more proteins that transports a substance across the membrane.

Peroxides Peroxides are compounds of structure ROOR in which R may be any organic group. In inorganic chemistry, salts of the anion O^{-2}. They are strong oxidizing agents.

Pertussis An acute, highly contagious infection of the respiratory tract, most frequently affecting young children, usually caused by Bordetella pertussis or B. Parapertussis. Consists of peculiar paroxysms of coughing, ending in a prolonged crowing or whooping respiration; hence the name whooping cough.

Petri dish A shallow dish consisting of two round, overlapping halves that is used to grow microorganisms on solid culture medium; the top is larger than the bottom of the dish to prevent contamination of the culture.

Petroleum ether Petroleum ether is the petroleum fraction consisting of C_5 and C_6 hydrocarbons and boiling in the range 35°C to 60°C; commonly used as a laboratory solvent.

pH pH is a convenient measure of the acid-base character of a solution, usually defined by

$$pH = -\log c(H^+)$$

Where $c(H^+)$ is the concentration of hydrogen ions in moles per liter. The more precise definition is in terms of activity rather than concentration.

Phenols

A solution of pH 0 to 7 is acid, pH of 7 is neutral, pH over 7 to 14 is alkaline.

Phage A virus which infects bacteria.

Phagocyte General term for a professional phagocytic cell - that is, a cell such as a macrophage or neutrophil that is specialized to take up particles and micro-organisms by phagocytosis.

Phagocytic vacuole A membrane-delimited vacuole produced by cells carrying out phagocytosis. It is formed by the invagination of the plasma membrane and contains solid material.

Phagocytosis The endocytotic process in which a cell encloses large particles in a membrane-delimited phagocytic vacuole or phagosome and engulfs them.

Phagolysosome The vacuole that results from the fusion of a phagosome with a lysosome.

Phagovar A specific phage type.

Pharming The process of farming genetically engineered plants or animals to be used as living pharmaceutical factories. The practice has used cows, sheep, pigs, goats, rabbits and mice to produced large amounts of human proteins in their milk. Plants are being used to produce vaccines and diagnostic reagents.

Pharyngitis Inflammation of the pharynx, often due to a S. Pyogenes infection.

Phase Phase is a portion of a physical system that is homogeneous throughout, has definable boundaries, and can be separated physically from other phases.

Phase change The action of a substance changing from one state of matter to another; a phase change always absorbs or releases internal potential energy that is not associated with a temperature change.

Phase diagram Phase diagram is a graphical representation of the equilibrium relationships between phases of a chemical compound, mixture of compounds, or solution.

Phase-contrast microscope A microscope that converts slight differences in refractive index and cell density into easily observed differences in light intensity.

Phases of matter The different physical forms that matter can take as a result of different molecular arrangements, resulting in characteristics of the common phases of a solid, liquid, or gas.

Phenetic system A classification system that groups organisms together based on the similarity of their observable charactistics.

Phenol coefficient test A test to measure the effectiveness of disinfectants by comparing their activity against test bacteria with that of phenol.

Phenols Phenols are compounds having one or more hydroxy groups attached to benzene or other arene ring.

Phenomics Phenomics is the study of an overall organism and how the characteristics or traits of an organism that we can see fits with the information we know about its genes and proteins.

Phenotype The characteristic of a species or individual of a species that is inherited from generation to generation. Each phenotype is the result of a genotype, i.e., the genetic information stored in DNA. Most phenotypes are morphological, i.e., they describe a particular structure, size, texture, or colour of an organism or part of an organism. Examples are the shape and arrangement of leaves of plants, or the legs, wings, and body segmentation of insects. These morphological phenotypes are the bases of most taxonomic classifica-tion of an organism, i.e., the organization of the evolutionary relationship among all life on Earth thought to originate from a single ancestral cell type. Phenotypes can also be functional characteristics and can best be thought of as hereditary diseases or metabolic processes.

Phenylketonuria (PKU) A rare recessive inherited disorder affecting about 1 in 10,000 births. Affected individuals inherit the abnormal gene from each parent and are unaffected at birth; but, with the introduction of feeding, a substance in the blood builds up and causes brain damage, so that the untreated children become severely handi-capped. Every baby in the UK has a blood test for phenylalanine at about 6 days of age and if the diagnosis is confirmed a special diet is started.

Phonon A quantum of acoustic energy, analogous to the quantum of electromagnetic radiation, the photon. Thermal excitations in a crystal or in an elastic continuum can be described as a population of phonons. In highly inhomogeneous solids, a description in terms of phonons breaks down and localized vibrational modes become important.

Phosphatase An enzyme that catalyzes the hydrolytic removal of phosphate from molecules.

Phosphate group transfer potential A measure of the ability of a phosphorylated molecule such as ATP to transfer its phosphate to water and other acceptors. It is the negative of the $dgo\_$ for the hydrolytic removal of phosphate.

Phospholipid Main lipid component of cell membranes. Phospholipids are a heterogeneous type of molecule composed of glycerol, phosphate, two fatty acid residues, and 'headgroups' with different chemical properties. The organization of phospholipids in cell membranes is known as phospholipid bilayer where the fatty acid residues face the center of the membrane and the headgroups forming the surface of the membrane. As such, bilayers separate water filled compartments and provide an electrically insulating barrier between these two compartments. This barrier is overcome by the placement of membrane proteins penetrating the fatty acid core of the membrane and forming channels and transport pathways for metabolites. The latter are usually water soluble and/or charged and would not diffuse across cell membranes without the help of these transport proteins.

Photoautotroph See photolithotrophic autotrophs.

Photoelectric effect Photoelectric effect is the complete absorption of a photon by a solid with the emission of an electron.

Photolithotrophic autotrophs Organisms that use light energy, an inorganic electron source (e.g., H_2O, H_2, H_2S), and CO_2 as a carbon source.

Photon Photon is an elementary particle of zero mass and spin 1/2. The photon is involved in electromagnetic interactions and is the quantum of electromagnetic radiation. The photon may also be regarded as a unit of energy equal to

$$E = h\nu$$

Where h is Planck constant and ν is the frequency of the radiation.

Photoorganotrophic heterotrophs Microorganisms that use light energy and organic electron donors, and also employ simple organic molecules rather than CO_2 as their carbon source.

Photoreactivation The process in which blue light is used by a photoreactivating enzyme to repair thymine dimers in DNA by splitting them apart.

Photosphere The visible surface of the Sun. It consists of a zone in which the gaseous layers change from being completely opaque to radiation to being transparent. It is the layer from which the light we actually see (with the human eye) is emitted.

Photosynthesis The trapping of light energy and its conversion to chemical energy, which is then used to reduce CO_2 and incorporate it into organic form.

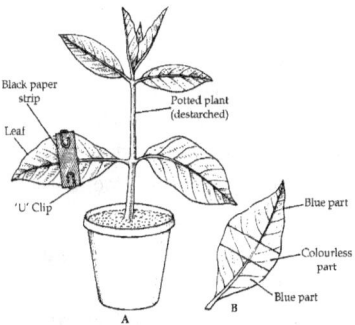

Figure Photosynthesis Experiment

Photosystem I The photosystem in eucaryotic cells that absorbs longer wavelength light, usually greater than about 680 nm, and transfers the energy to chlorophyll P700 during photosynthesis; it is involved in both cyclic photophosphorylation and noncyclic photophosphorylation.

Photosystem II The photosystem in eucaryotic cells that absorbs shorter wavelength light, usually less than 680 nm, and transfers the energy to chlorophyll P680 during photosynthesis; it participates in noncyclic photophosphorylation.

Phototrophs Organisms that use light as their energy source.

Phycobiliproteins Photosynthetic pigments that are composed of proteins with attached tetrapyrroles; they are often found in cyanobacteria and red algae.

Phycobilisomes Special particles on the membranes of cyanobacteria that contain photosynthetic pigments and electron transport chains.

Phycobiont The algal or cyanobacterial partner in a lichen.

Phycocyanin A blue phycobiliprotein pigment used to trap light energy during photosynthesis.

Phycoerythrin A red photosynthetic phycobiliprotein pigment used to trap light energy.

Phycology The study of algae; algology.

Phyllosphere The surface of plant leaves.

Phylogenetic A classification system based on evolutionary relationships rather than the general similarity of contemporary characteristics.

Phylogenetic tree A graph made of nodes and branches, much like a tree in shape, that shows phylogenetic relationships between groups of organisms and sometimes also indicates the evolutionary development of groups.

Physical change A change of the state of a substance but not the identity of the substance pitch the frequency of a sound wave.

Physics The study of properties of the Universe via measuring experiments.

Phytoplankton A community of floating photosynthetic organisms, largely composed of algae and cyanobacteria.

Phytoremediation The use of plants and their associated microorganisms to remove, contain, or degrade environmental contaminants.

Piedra A fungal disease of the hair in which white or black nodules of fungi form on the shafts.

Pinocytosis The endocytotic process in which a cell encloses a small amount of the surrounding liquid and its solutes in tiny pinocytotic vesicles or pinosomes.

Pion The least massive type of meson, pions can have electric charges of +1, -1, or 0.

Pitched Pertaining to inoculation of a nutrient medium with yeast, for example, in beer brewing.

Pk Pk is the negative logarithm (base 10) of an equilibrium constant K.

Plague An acute febrile, infectious disease, caused by the bacillus Yersinia pestis, which has a high mortality rate; the two major types are bubonic plague and pneumonic plague.

Planck constant Planck constant (h) is a constant that when multipled by the frequency of radiation gives the quantity of energy contained in one quantum.

$$E = h\nu$$

Equal to $6.6260755(40) \times 10^{-34}$ Js. It is named after Max Planck (1858-1947).

Planck curve The graphical representation of the mathematical relationship between the frequency (or wavelength) and intensity of radiation emitted from an object by virtue of its heat energy.

Planck time The first 10^{-43} seconds of the Universe when time as humans recognize it did not exist because gravity, which defines spacetime, had not yet split from the other forces; instead, a time system that allowed more than one object to occupy the same space was in operation.

Planck's constant Proportionality constant in the relationship between the energy of vibrating molecules and their frequency of vibration; a value of 6.63×10^{-34} joule-sec.

Plankton Free-floating, mostly microscopic microorganisms that can be found in almost all waters; a collective name.

Plaque 1. A clear area in a lawn of bacteria or a localized area of cell destruction in a layer of animal cells that results from the lysis of the bacteria by bacteriophages or the destruction of the animal cells by animal viruses.

2. The term also refers to dental plaque, a film of food debris, polysaccharides, and dead cells that cover the teeth. It provides a medium for the growth of bacteria, leading to a microbial plaque ecosystem that can produce dental decay.

Plasma Plasma consists of a gas heated to sufficiently high temperatures that the atoms ionize. The properties of the gas are controlled by electromagnetic forces among constituent ions and electrons, which results in a different type of behaviour. Plasma is often considered the fourth state of matter. Most of the matter in the Universe is in the plasma state.

Plasma cell A mature, differentiated B lymphocyte chiefly occupied with antibody synthesis and secretion; a plasma cell lives for only 5 to 7 days.

Plasma membrane The selectively permeable membrane surrounding the cell's cytoplasm; also called the cell membrane, plasmalemma, or cytoplasmic membrane.

Plasmid A double-stranded DNA molecule that can exist and replicate independently of the chromosome or may be integrated with it. A plasmid is stably inherited, but is not required for the host cell's growth and reproduction.

Plasmid fingerprinting A technique used to identify microbial isolates as belonging to the same strain because they contain the same number of plasmids with the identical molecular weights and similar phenotypes.

Plasmodial A member of the division Myxomycota that exists as a thin, streaming, multinucleate mass of protoplasm, which creeps along in an amoeboid fashion.

Plasmodium A stage in the life cycle of myxomycetes (plasmodial slime molds); a multinucleate mass of protoplasm surrounded by a membrane. Also, a parasite of the genus Plasmodium.

Plasmolysis The process in which water osmotically leaves a cell, which causes the cytoplasm to shrivel up and pull the plasma membrane away from the cell wall.

Plastic strain An adjustment to stress in which materials become molded or bent out of shape under stress and do not return to their original shape after the stress is released.

Plastid A cytoplasmic organelle of algae and higher plants that contains pigments such as chlorophyll, stores food reserves, and often carries out processes such as photosynthesis.

Pleomorphic Refers to bacteria that are variable in shape and lack a single, characteristic form.

Pluralism The belief that there are multiple opinions about an issue, each of which contains part of the truth but none contain the whole truth.

Pluripotent The ability to be able to produce any cell in the body. Usually used when referring to embryonic stem cells.

Plus strand or positive strand The virus nucleic-acid strand that is equivalent in base sequence to the viral mRNA.

Plutonium A transuranic element, formed in a nuclear reactor by neutron capture. It has several isotopes, some of which are fissile and some of which undergo spontaneous fission, releasing neutrons. Weapons-grade plutonium is produced in special reactors to give >90% Pu-239, reactor-grade plutonium contains about 30% non-fissile isotopes. About one third of the energy in a light water reactor comes from the fission of Pu-239, and this is the main isotope of value recovered from reprocessing spent fuel.

Pneumocystis pneumonia, Pneumocystis carinii pneumonia (PCP) A type of pneumonia caused by the protist *Pneumocystis carinii*.

Point mutation A mutation that affects only a single base pair in a specific location.

Poisson's ratio A bar of an isotropic, elastic material ordinarily shrinks laterally when it is stretched longitudinally. The lateral contracting strain divided by the applied tensile strain is Poisson's ratio, which varies from material to material.

Polar flagellum A flagellum located at one end of an elongated cell.

Polarity When applied to solvents, this rather ill-defined term covers their overall solvation capability

Polyatomic ion

(solvation power) for solutes (i.e. in chemical equilibria: reactants and products; in reaction rates: reactants and activated complex; in light absorptions: ions or molecules in the ground and excited state), which in turn depends on the action of all possible, nonspecific and specific, intermolecular interactions between solute ions or molecules and solvent molecules, excluding such interactions leading to definite chemical alterations of the ions or molecules of the solute. Occasionally, the term solvent polarity is restricted to nonspecific solute/solvent interactions only (i.e. to van der Waals forces).

Polarized A description for a membrane that has a potential difference due to an unequal distribution of ions across the membrane.

Polarized light Light radiations in which the vibrations of all light waves present are confined to planes parallel to each other.

Polaroid A film that transmits only polarized light.

Polaroplast Organelle, apparently a vacuole, near the polar filament of a microsporidean.

Polian vesicles Vesicles opening into ring canal in most asteroids and holothuroids.

Poliomyelitis An acute, contagious viral disease that attacks the central nervous system, injuring or destroying the nerve cells that control the muscles and sometimes causing paralysis; also called polio or infantile paralysis.

Pollen grain The structure into which a haploid microspore develops; contains a halpoid tube nucleus and two haploid sperm nuclei at maturity.

Pollen The collective term for pollen grains, the male gametophytes.

Pollen tube A tube that develops from the pollen grain and carries the sperm to the ovule.

Pollex The thumb.

Pollination The transfer of pollen to a receptive surface; the stigma in angiosperms or the pollination droplet in most gymnosperms.

Pollinator An organism that effects pollination.

Pollution charges Fees assessed per unit of pollution based on the "polluter pays" principle.

Poloidal radius The radius of the actual loop structure. For a dough-nut, it is measured from the center to the edge of the pastry.

Polyandrous Having more than one male mate. Polyandry is advantageous when food is plentiful but, because of predation or other factors, the chances of successfully rearing young are low.

Polyandry Condition of having more than one male mate at one time.

Polyatomic ion A polyatomic ion is a charged particle that contains more than two covalently bound atoms. See Polyatomic Ions for more.

Polyatomic molecule A polyatomic molecule is an uncharged particle that contains more than two atoms.

Poly-b-hydroxybutyrate A linear polymer of b-hydroxybutyrate used as a reserve of carbon and energy by many bacteria.

Polycarpic Denoting a plant that flowers more than once during its lifetime.

Polycentric complex Cities with several urban cores surrounding a once dominant central core.

Polychaeta The class of annelids whose members are mostly marine and are characterized by a head with eyes and tentacles and a body with parapodia. Parapodia bear numerous setae. Examples: Nereis, Arenicola.

Polychlorinated biphenyls (PCBs) A group of nonbiodegradable pollutants.

Polychromatic light Light composed of several colours.

Polycyclic A cyclic structure contains rings of bonds; a structure having many such rings is termed polycyclic. In the polycyclic structures of interest in this volume, a large fraction of the atoms are members of multiple small rings, resulting in considerable rigidity.

Polyembryony Development of a single zygote into more than one offspring.

Polygamy Condition of having more than one mate at a time.

Polygenes Genes at multiple loci that influence a trait in a quantitative fashion.

Polygenic Multiple genetic influences controlling a single trait, causes the trait to display continuous variation.

Polygenic trait Traits that are influenced by many genes and that are usually continuously distributed within a population.

Polygynous Having more than one female mate. Polygyny tends to occur in species whose young are relatively independent at birth or hatching.

Polygyny Condition of having more than one female mate at one time.

Polygyny threshold The point at which a female will benefit more by joining an already mated male possessing a good territory rather than an unmated male on a poor territory.

Polykinetid Rows or fields of kinetids in ciliates linked by fibrous networks.

Polymer Polymer is a substance composed of molecules of high relative molecular mass the structure of which essentially comprises the multiple repetition of units derived, actually or conceptually, from molecules of low relative molecular mass (monomers). In most cases the number of monomers is quite large and often is not precisely known. A single molecule of a polymer is called a macromolecule.

Polymerase chain reaction (PCR) An *in vitro* technique used to synthesize large quantities of specific nucleotide sequences from small amounts of DNA. It employs oligonucleotide primers complementary to specific sequences in the target gene and special heat-stable DNA polymerases.

Polymerization The process of forming a polymer or polymeric compound.

Polymorph Polymorphism; polymorphic. Compare with isotope and allotrope. Solid substances that occur in several distinct forms. Polymorphs have different chemical and physical properties. Allotropes are polymorphs of elements.

Polymorphic A locus that contains two or more alleles within a population.

Polymorphism The presence in a species of more than one structural type of individual.

Polymorphonuclear leukocyte (PMN) A leukocyte that has a variety of nuclear forms.

Polynomial A scientific name for an organism composed of more than two words.

Polynucleotide A nucleotide of many mononucleotides combined.

Polynucleotide chains Attachment of one nucleotide to another in a linear fashion.

Polyp Individual of the phylum Cnidaria, generally adapted for attachment to the substratum at the aboral end, often form colonies.

Polypeptide A molecule consisting of many joined amino acids, not as complex as a protein.

Polypeptides Polypeptides are peptides containing ten or more amino acid residues. The properties of a polypeptide are determined by the type and sequence of its constituent amino acids.

Polyphasic taxonomy An approach in which taxonomic schemes are developed using a wide range of phenotypic and genotypic information.

Polyphyletic group An assemblage of organisms that includes multiple evolutionary lineages. Polyphyletic assemblages usually reflect insufficient knowledge regarding the phylogeny of a group of organisms.

Polyphyly The condition that a taxon or other group of organisms does not contain the most recent common ancestor of all members of the group, implying that it has multiple evolutionary origins; such groups are not valid as formal taxa and are recognized as such only through error. Contrasts with monophyly and paraphyly.

Polyphyodont Having several sets of teeth in succession.

Polypide An individual or zooid in a colony, specifically in ectoprocts, which has a lophophore, digestive tract, muscles, and nerve centers.

Polyplacophora The class of molluscs whose members are elongate, dorsoventrally flattened, and have a shell consisting of eight dorsal plates.

Polyploid An organism possessing more than two full homologous sets of chromosomes.

Polyploidy Refers to the number of chromosomes in a cell. Most cells are normally diploid, i.e. have two sets of chromosomes. When the number is increased the cell shows polyploidy.

Polypod larva Caterpillar type of larva found in Lepidoptera and some Hymenoptera. It has thoracic appendages and abdominal locomotory processes (prolegs). Also called cruciform.

Polyribosome A complex of several ribosomes with a messenger RNA; each ribosome is translating the same message.

Polysaccharides Polysaccharides are compounds consisting of a large number of monosaccharides linked together by glycosidic bonds. Some important examples are starch, glycogen, and cellulose.

Polysome Two or more ribosomes connected by a molecule of messenger RNA.

Polytene chromosomes Chromosomes in the somatic cells of some insects in which the chromatin replicates repeatedly without undergoing mitosis.

Polyunsaturated fat A fat having several to many double bonds between carbon atoms.

Polyzoic A tapeworm forming a strobila of several to many proglottids; also, a colony of many zooids.

Pome A fleshy fruit derived from a compound inferior ovary; the fleshy edible part is the ripened tissue surrounding the ovary (derived from receptacle and perianth tissue); the ovary matures into the core and contains the seed. For example: apple or pear.

Pongid Of or relating to the primate family Pongidae, comprising the anthropoid apes (gorillas, chimpanzees, gibbons, orangutans).

Pons A portion of the brain stem above the medulla oblongata and below the midbrain.

Pontiac fever A bacterial disease caused by *Legionella pneumophila* that resembles an allergic disease more than an infection. First described from Pontiac, Michigan. See Legionnaires' disease.

Population A group of organisms of the same species inhabiting a specific geographical locality.

Population crash A sudden population decline caused by predation, waste accumulation, or resource depletion; also called a dieback.

Population explosion Growth of a population at exponential rates to a size that exceeds environmental carrying capacity; usually followed by a population crash.

Population genetics The study of events occurring in gene pools.

Population hurdle The need for investment in infrastructure and social services in a rapidly growing population that prevents the capital investment necessary for real economic development.

Population momentum A potential for increased population growth as young members reach reproductive age.

Populational gradualism The observation that new genetic variants become established in a population by increasing their frequencies across generations incrementally, initially from one or a few individuals and eventually characterizing a majority of the population.

Pore cell The tube-like cell of sponges that forms a pore.

Pore space Space between soil particles.

Porifera The animal phylum whose members are sessile and either asymmetrical or radially symmetrical. Body organized around a system of water canals and chambers. Cells are not organized into tissues or organs. Sponges.

Porin proteins Proteins that form channels across the outer membrane of gram-negative bacterial cell walls. Small molecules are trans-ported through these channels.

Porocyte Type of cell found in asconoid sponges through which water enters the spongocoel.

Porose area Sunken areas on the basis capituli of certain mites and ticks.

Porosity The relative amount of pore space versus soil particulate space in soil.

Portal system System of large veins beginning and ending with a bed of capillaries; for example, hepatic portal and renal portal system in vertebrates.

Positional cloning Isolation of a gene through knowledge of its specific location on a particular chromosome.

Positional synthesis Control of chemical reactions by precisely positioning the reactive molecules, the basic principle of assemblers.

Positive electric charge One of the two types of electric charge; repels other positive charges and attracts negative charges.

Positive ion Atom or particle that has a net positive charge due to an electron or electrons being torn away.

Positive rays Rays coming through holes in a cathode on the side opposite the anode in a discharge tube Positively charged ions.

Positron Positron is the antiparticle of the electron. It has the same mass and spin as an electron, and an equal but opposite charge.

Postanal tail A tail that extends posterior to the anus; one of the four unique characteristics of chordates.

Posterior Situated at or toward the rear of the body; situated toward the back; in human anatomy the upright posture makes posterior and dorsal identical.

Posterior station Development of a protozoan in the hindgut or posterior midgut of its insect host, such as in the section Stercoraria of the Trypanosomatidae.

Postharvest physiology The study of the storage and perishability of fruits following harvest.

Postherpetic neuralgia The severe pain after a herpes infection.

Post-kala-azar dermal leishmanoid Disfiguring dermal condition developing about one to two years after inadequate treatment of kala-azar.

Postmaterialist values A philosophy that emphasizes quality of life over acquisition of material goods.

Postmating isolation Isolation that occurs when fertilization is prevented even though mating has occurred.

Posttranscriptional modification The processing of the initial RNA transcript, heterogeneous nuclear RNA, to form mRNA.

Potable Refers to water suitable for drinking.

Potential difference The work done per unit charge as a charge is moved between two points in an electric field.

Potential energy The energy of an object owing to its position in a force field or its internal condition, as opposed to kinetic energy, which depends on its motion. Examples of objects with potential energy include a diver on a diving board and a coiled spring.

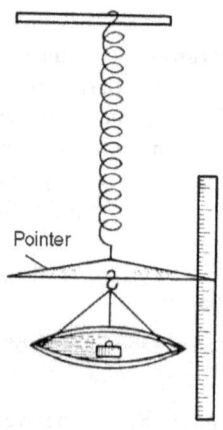

Figure Potential Energy

Potential well In a potential energy surface, the region surrounding a local energy minimum. Typically taken to include at least those points in configuration space such that a path of steadily declining energy can be found that leads to the minimum in question, and such that no similar path can be found to any other minimum. If the PES were a landscape, this would be the region around the minimum that could be filled with water without any flowing down and away toward another minimum.

Potential-energy profile A curve describing the variation of the potential energy of the system of atoms that make up the reactants and products of a reaction as a function of one geometric coordinate, and corresponding to the "energetically easiest passage" from reactants to products (i.e. along the line produ-ced by joining the paths of steepest descent from the transition state to the reactants and to the products). For an elementary reaction the relevant geometric coordinate is the reaction coordinate; for a stepwise reaction it is the succession of reaction coordinates for the successive individual reaction steps. (The reaction coordinate is sometimes approximated by a quasi-chemical index of reaction progress, such as "degree of atom transfer" or bond order of some specified bond.)

Potocytosis Endocytosis of certain small molecules and ions bound to specific receptors limited to small areas on the cell surface. The areas of the receptors are invaginated and pinch off to form tiny vesicles.

Pour plate A petri dish of solid culture medium with isolated microbial colonies growing both on its surface and within the medium, which has been prepared by mixing microorganisms with cooled, still liquid medium and then allowing the medium to harden.

Power The term power has quite a few different meanings. For Biotechnology Online, we are referring to an organization or individual's ability to act effectively according to their intentions, needs, or values.

Prairie An area of land dominated by grasses with occasional shrubby plants and small trees occurring where the grass cover is broken and with herbaceous perennials during certain seasons.

Praniza Parasitic larva of the isopod suborder Gnathiidea. It parasitizes fishes and feeds on blood.

Preadaptation Occurs when a structure or a process present in members of a species proves useful in promoting reproductive success when an individual encounters new environmental situations.

Prebiotic Prebiotic refers to the state of matter before life existed, but was conducive to the formation of life. The prebiotic 'soup' is the mixture of organic molecules in bodies of water that are thought to have spontaneous, self-assembly property for the first formation of an organic complex with self-replicating qualities.

Prebiotic synthesis The chemical synthesis that occurred before the emergence of life.

Precambrian The geological era beginning with the formation of the earth, about 4700 million years ago and extending until about 590 million years ago. During this time the origin of life, the origin of eukaryotes, and multicellular life-forms appeared.

Precession The motion that results from the application of a torque that tends to displace the axis of rotation of a rotating object.

Precious corals Gorgonians that secrete a red or pink skeleton consisting of fused calcareous spicules.

Precipitation Moisture falling from the atmosphere in the form of rain, sleet, snow, or hail.

Precipitin The antibody responsible for a precipitation reaction.

Precise Sharply or clearly defined. Having small experimental uncertainty. A precise measurement may still be inaccurate, if there were an unrecognized determinate error in the measurement (for example, a miscalibrated instrument).

Precision The agreement between the numerical values of two or more measurements made in the same way and expressed in terms of deviation; the reproducibility of measured data.

Precocial Having developed to a high degree of independence at the time of hatching or birth.

Precocial young Young that are born or hatched at a relatively advanced state of development and are capable of a more independent existence beginning at birth or hatching. Compare to altricial.

Precycling Making environmentally sound decisions at the store and reducing waste before we buy.

Predaceous, predacious Living by killing and consuming other animals; predatory.

Predation The derivation of an organism of elements essential for its existence from organisms of other species that it consumes and destroys. The ingestion of prey by a predator for energy and nutrients.

Predator An organism that preys on other organisms for its food.

Predictive model A somewhat simplified representation of a physical process that yields information with predictive value

Pre-equilibrium (or prior equilibrium) A rapidly reversible step preceding the rate-limiting step in a stepwise reaction.

Preformation The erroneous idea that gametes contain miniaturized versions of all of the elements present in an adult.

Prehensile Adapted for grasping.

Premating isolation When behaviours or other factors prevent animals from mating.

Premunition Resistance to reinfection or superinfection, conferred by a still existing infection, that does not destroy the organisms of the infection already present.

Prenymph Nonfeeding, quiescent stage in the life cycle of a chigger mite.

Preoptic nuclei Neurons in the hypothalamus that produce various neuropeptides.

Preparedness The genetically based predisposition to learn. Depending upon the learning situation, animals of a particular species may be prepared, unprepared, or contra-prepared to learn.

Prepatent Developmental stage in an infection before agents produce evidence of their presence.

Presoma The proboscis, neck, and attached muscles and organs of an acanthocephalan.

Pressure Flow Hypothesis The theory that organic solutes move along a concentration gradient from source to sink through the phloem.

Pressure law The pressure of an ideal gas is directly proportional to the thermodynamic temperature at constant volume.

Pressure potential The water force created by a real pressure against a membrane.

Pressure The weight exerted over a unit area of surface. This is equal to 1 atmosphere (14.7 lbs per square inch) at the sea surface and 1 atmosphere plus the pressure exerted by the water column, which is 1 atmosphere per 10 m (33 ft) of depth.

Pressurised water reactor (PWR) The most common type of light water reactor (LWR), it uses water at very high pressure in a primary circuit and steam is formed in a secondary circuit.

Prevalance In epidemiology, the number of cases of a disease at a given time; that is, a static measurement. Contrast with incidence.

Prevalence rate Refers to the total number of individuals infected at any one time in a given population regardless of when the disease began.

Prevention of significant deterioration A clause of the Clean Air Act that prevents degradation of existing clean air; opposed by industry as an unnecessary barrier to development.

Prey model A type of optimal foraging model that addresses the types of organisms an individual should try to catch and eat (i.e., its diet).

Priapulida A phylum of aschelminths commonly called priapulids.

Pribnow box A special base sequence in the promoter that is recognized by the RNA polymerase and is the site of initial polymerase binding.

Price elasticity A situation in which supply and demand of a commodity respond to price.

Primary (frank) pathogen Any organism that causes a disease in the host by direct interaction with or infection of the host.

Primary A transformer winding that carries current and normally induces a current in one or more secondary windings.

Primary amoebic meningoencephalitis An infection of the meninges of the brain by the free living amoebae Naegleria or Acanthamoeba.

Primary bilateral symmetry Usually applied to a radially symmetrical organism descended from a bilateral ancestor and developing from a bilaterally symmetrical larva.

Primary cell An electrochemical cell in which the reacting materials must be replaced after a given amount of energy has been supplied to the external circuit.

Primary cell wall The cellulosic wall of all plant cells laid down at the time of mitosis and cytokinesis.

Primary coil Part of a transformer; a coil of wire that is connected to a source of alternating current.

Primary colours Colours in terms of which all other colours may be described or from which all other colours may be evolved by mixtures.

Primary consumer An organism that consumes a producer organism as a food source; a herbivore.

Primary endosperm nucleus The product of the fusion of a sperm and two polar nuclei in the embryo sac of angiosperms; double fertilization.

Primary germ layers Blocks or layers of embryonic cells that give rise to tissues and organs of animals.

Primary growth Growth originating in the apical meristems of shoots and roots resulting in an increase in length of the axis.

Primary immune response The initial immune response following antigen exposure.

Primary metabolites Microbial metabolites produced during the growth phase of an organism.

Primary pigments The complements of the primary colours.

Primary pit fields Regions within the primary cell wall in which plasmodesmata traverse the cell wall.

Primary pollutants Chemicals released directly into the air in a harmful form.

Primary producer An autotrophic organism; able to build its own complex organic molecules from simple inorganic substances in the environment.

Primary production The conversion of the inorganic carbon in carbon dioxide into organic carbon by autotrophs.

Primary productivity Synthesis of organic materials (biomass) by green plants using the energy captured in photosynthesis.

Primary radial symmetry Usually applied to a radially symmetrical organism that did not have a bilateral ancestor or larva, in contrast to a secondarily radial organism.

Primary standards Regulations of the 1970 Clean Air Act; intended to protect human health.

Primary succession Plant successional events occurring in a pristine or newly forming habitat.

Primary tissue Any tissue derived from the apical meristem, either shoot or root.

Primary treatment A process that removes solids from sewage before it is discharged or treated further.

Primary wall The wall layer of a plant cell deposited during cell

Principle of segregation

expansion, generally thin and elastic.

Primate Any mammal of the order Primates, which includes the tarsiers, lemurs, marmosets, monkeys, apes, and humans.

Priming pheromone A chemical signal that alters the physiology of another organism, eventually causing a change in its behaviour. Contrast with releasing pheromone.

Primite Anterior member of a pair of gregarines in syzygy.

Primitive change One of the conceptually simpler molecular changes into which an elementary reaction can be notionally dissected. Such changes include bond rupture, bond formation, internal rotation, change of bond length or bond angle, bond migration, redistribution of charge, etc.

The concept of primitive changes is helpful in the detailed verbal description of elementary reactions, but a primitive change does not represent a process that is by itself necessarily observable as a component of an elementary reaction.

Primitive Primordial; ancient; little evolved; said of characteristics closely approximating those possessed by early ancestral types.

Primitive streak A medial thickening along the dorsal margin of an amniote embryo that forms during the migration of endodermal and mesodermal cells into the interior of the embryo.

Primordial germ cells The precursors of reproductive cells within the embryo. They are detectable in an embryo after four weeks of development and will develop into either sperm or eggs.

Principal axis 1. A line drawn through the center of curvature and the vertex of a curved mirror.
2. A line drawn through the center of curvature and the optical center of a lens.

Principal focus A point at which rays parallel to the principal axis converge or from which they diverge after reflection or refraction

Principle of competitive exclusion A result of natural selection whereby two similar species in a community occupy different ecological niches, thereby reducing competition for food.

Principle of independent assortment One of Mendel's observations on the behaviour of hereditary units during gamete formation. A modern interpretation of this principle is that genes carried in one chromosome are distributed to gametes without regard to the distribution of genes in nonhomologous chromosomes.

Principle of parity For every process in nature there is a mirror-image process which is indistinguishable from the original process.

Principle of segregation One of Mendel's observations on the behaviour of hereditary units during gamete formation. A modern interpretation of the principle of segregation is that genes exist in pairs, and during gamete formation, members of a pair of genes are distributed into separate gametes.

Principle quantum number From quantum mechanics model of the atom, one of four descriptions of the energy state of an electron wave; this quantum number describes the main energy level of an electron in terms of its most probable distance from the nucleus.

Prion An infectious particle that is the cause of slow diseases like scrapie in sheep and goats; it has a protein component, but no nucleic acid has yet been detected.

Pristine Denoting a natural and undisturbed state.

Probability The likelihood that something will happen, expressed as a number between zero and one.

Probability distribution A curve that specifies the probabilities of various random values of a variable; areas under the curve correspond to probabilities.

Probe (prŏob) A short, labeled nucleic acid segment complementary in base sequence to part of another nucleic acid, which is used to identify or isolate the particular nucleic acid from a mixture through its ability to bind specifically with the target nucleic acid.

Probiotic 1. The oral administration of either living microorganisms or substances to promote the health and growth of an animal or human. 2. A living organism that may provide health benefits beyond its nutritional value when it is ingested.

Proboscis A snout or trunk. Also, tubular sucking or feeding organ with the mouth at the end as in planarians, leeches, and insects. Also, the sensory and defensive organ at the anterior end of certain invertebrates.

Procaryotes Bacteria and cyanobacteria that lack the structural complexity and defined nucleus found in eucaryotes.

Procaryotic cells Cells that lack a true, membrane-enclosed nucleus; bacteria are procaryotic and have their genetic material located in a nucleoid.

Procaryotic species A collection of strains that share many stable properties and differ significantly from other groups of strains.

Procercoid Cestode metacestode developing from a coracidium in some orders. It usually has a posterior cercomer.

Procuticle Thicker layer beneath the epicuticle of arthropods that lends mass and strength to the cuticle. It contains chitin, sclerotin, and also inorganic salts in Crustacea. The layers within the procuticle vary in structure and composition.

Prodromal stage The period during the course of a disease in which there is the appearance of signs and symptoms, but they are not yet distinctive and characteristic enough to make an accurate diagnosis.

Product development control The term is used for reactions under kinetic control where the selectivity parallels the relative (thermodynamic) stabilities of the products. Product development control is usually associated with a transition state occurring late on the reaction coordinate.

Product-determining step The step of a stepwise reaction, in which the product distribution is determined. The product-determining step may be identical to, or occur later than, the rate-controlling step on the reaction coordinate.

Production In ecology, the energy accumulated by an organism that becomes incorporated into new biomass.

Production frontier The maximum output of two competing commodities at different levels of production.

Productivity The amount of plant product resulting from a combination of water, nutrients and environmental factors.

Profile A graph that shows changes in temperature, salinity, or any other parameter with depth

Profundal zone The deepest portion of a lake.

Progametangia Swollen hyphae of fungi that fuse at the point of contact and eventually form gametangia.

Progametangium The cell that gives rise to a gametangium and a proximal suspensor during the early stages of sexual reproduction in zygomycetous fungi.

Progesterone Hormone secreted by the corpus luteum and the placenta; prepares the uterus for the fertilized egg and maintains the capacity of the uterus to hold the embryo and fetus.

Proglottid One set of reproductive organs in a tapeworm strobila; usually corresponds to a segment. One of the linearly arranged segmentlike sections that make up the strobila of a tapeworm.

Progymnosperm An extinct group of plants, the Progymnospermophyta, which included woody plants bearing large plannated braching systems; the prototypes of the gymnospems (e.g., Archaeopteris).

Prohaptor Collective adhesive and feeding organs at the anterior end of a monogenetic trematode.

Prohormone A precursor of a hormone, especially a peptide hormone.

Projectile An object thrown into space either horizontally or at an acute angle and under the action of gravity is called a projectile. The path followed by a projectile is called its trajectory. The horizontal distance traveled by a projectile is called its range. The time taken by a projectile from the moment it is thrown until it touches the ground is called its time of flight.

Prokaryote Organism in which the chromosomes are not contained within membrane-bound nuclei.

Prokaryotic Procaryotic, Not having a membrane-bound nucleus or nuclei. Prokaryotic cells characterize the bacteria and cyanobacteria.

Prokaryotic cell A type of cell lacking a nucleus and membrane-bound organelles; found in the Kingdom Monera.

Prolegs Unjointed abdominal appendage in the larva of Lepidoptera and some other insects.

Proliferative kidney disease A protozoan disease caused by an unclassified myxozoan in salmonids throughout the world.

Promastigote Form of Trypanosomatidae with the free flagellum and the kinetoplast anterior to the nucleus, as in Leptomonas.

Promethean environmentalism A form of technological optimism that predicts that human ingenuity and enterprise will find cures for all our problems.

Promiscuity A mating system in which there is no prolonged association between the sexes and multiple mating by at least one sex.

Promoter The region on DNA at the start of a gene that the RNA polymerase binds to before beginning transcription.

Pronatalist pressures Influences that encourage people to have children.

Pronephros Most anterior of three pairs of embryonic renal organs of vertebrates, functional only in adult hagfishes and larval fishes and amphibians, and vestigial in mammalian embryos. Adj., pronephric.

Proof 1. A measure of ethanol concentration of an alcoholic beverage; proof is double the concentration by volume; for example, 50 percent by volume is 100 proof.

2. A term from logic and mathematics describing an argument from premise to conclusion using strictly logical principles. In mathematics, theorems or propositions are established by logical arguments from a set of axioms, the process of establishing a theorem being called a proof.

The colloquial meaning of 'proof' causes many problems in physics discussions and is best avoided. Since mathematics is such an important part of physics, the mathematician's meaning of proof should be the only one we use. Also, we often ask students in upper level courses to do proofs of certain theorems of mathematical physics, and we are not asking for experimental demonstration.

Prop roots Adventitious roots arising on a stem above the ground and imparting some mechanical support to plants. The angled roots may provide for absorption of water and nutrients.

Propagate To travel through a material or space.

Propagated epidemic An epidemic that is characterized by a relatively slow and prolonged rise and then a gradual decline in the number of individuals infected. It usually results from the introduction of an infected individual into a susceptible population, and the pathogen is transmitted from person to person.

Propagation The act of propagating The action of traveling through a material or space.

Propane A colourless, odorless, flammable gas, found in petroleum and natural gas. It is used as a fuel and as a raw material for building more complex organic molecules. Propane is the third member of the alkane series.

Property A measurable aspect of matter, e.g., mass and inertia.

Prophase The stage of mitosis during which the chromosomes become visible under a light microscope. The first stage of mitosis during which the chromosomes are condensed but not yet attached to a mitotic spindle.

Proplastids Membrane-bound particles that develop some internal structure; may subsequently develop into chloroplasts, chromoplasts, or leucoplasts.

Propodeum First abdominal segment of hymenopterans, fused to the thorax.

Propodosoma Portion of the podosoma that bears the first and second pairs of legs of a tick or mite.

Propolar cells Anterior tier of cells in the calotte of a dicyemid mesozoan.

Proportionality constant A constant applied to a proportionality statement that transforms the statement into an equation.

Proprioceptor Sensory receptor located deep within the tissues, especially muscles, tendons, and joints, that is responsive to changes in muscle stretch, body position, and movement.

Prosimian Any member of a group of arboreal primates including lemurs, tarsiers, and lorises, but excluding monkeys, apes, and humans.

Prosoma Anterior part of an invertebrate in which primitive segmentation is not visible; fused head and thorax of arthropod; cephalothorax.

Prosopyle Connections between the incurrent and radial canals in some sponges.

Prostaglandins A family of fatty-acid hormones, originally discovered in semen, known to have powerful effects on smooth muscle, nerves, circulation, and reproductive organs.

Prostate The prostate gland is "before" the bladder.

Prostate gland Gland located around the male urethra below the urinary bladder that adds its secretions to seminal fluid during ejaculation.

Prostheca An extension of a bacterial cell, including the plasma membrane and cell wall, that is narrower than the mature cell.

Prosthetic group Nonprotein groups that are attached to an enzyme or other protein and necessary for its function.

Prostomium Anterior closure of a metameric animal, anterior to the mouth.

Protandric hermaphroditism A pattern of sexuality in which a single individual functions as male and then female in sequence.

Protandrous Condition of hermaphroditic animals and plants in which male organs and their products appear before the corresponding female organs and products, thus preventing self-fertilization.

Protandry The condition in a monoecious organism in which male gonads mature before female gametes; prevents self-fertilization.

Protease An enzyme that digests proteins; includes proteinases and peptidases.

Proteasome A large, cylindrical protein complex that degrades ubiquitin-labeled proteins to peptides in an ATP-dependent process.

Protective coloration Coloration that benefits the individual by providing concealment from predators.

Protein A macromolecule of carbon, hydrogen, oxygen, and nitrogen and sometimes sulfur and phosphorus; composed of chains of amino acids joined by peptide bonds; present in all cells.

Protein engineering The rational design of proteins by constructing specific amino acid sequences through molecular techniques, with the objective of modifying protein characteristics.

Protein splicing The post-translational process in which part of a precursor polypeptide is removed before the mature polypeptide folds into its final shape; it is carried out by self-splicing proteins that remove inteins and join the remaining exteins.

Protein synthesis The assemblage of protein as determined by the nucleotide sequence of a messenger RNA and the assistance of transfer RNA aligning amino acids in the proper arrangement.

Protelean parasite Organism parasitic during its larval or juvenile stages and free living as an adult, usually changing form with each stage.

Proteobacteria A large group of bacteria, primarily gram-negative, that 16S rRNA sequence comparisons show to be phylogenetically related; proteobacteria contain the purple photosynthetic bacteria and their relatives and are composed of the a, b, g, d, and e subgroups.

Proterosoma Combination of the gnathosoma and propodosoma of the body of a tick or mite.

Prothallial cell Sterile cells present in the pollen grain of gymnosperms, believed to represent the last remnant of the vegetative male gametophyte thallus.

Prothoracic gland An invertebrate endocrine gland located in the prothorax region directly behind the head, which secretes ecdysone, a steroid hormone that promotes molting.

Prothorax The first of the three thoracic segments of an insect; usually contains the first pair of walking appendages.

Prothrombin A constituent of blood plasma that is changed to thrombin by a catalytic sequence that includes thromboplastin, calcium, and plasma globulins; involved in blood clotting.

Protist A member of the kingdom Protista, generally considered to include the protozoa and eukaryotic algae.

Protista The kingdom whose members are characterized by being eukaryotic and unicellular or colonial.

Protochordates Chordates that lack a backbone.

Protocoel The anterior coelomic compartment in some deuterostomes, corresponds to the axocoel in echinoderms.

Protocooperation A mutually beneficial interaction between organisms in which the interaction is not physiologically necessary to the survival of either.

Protoderm The dermal or outer tissue of an apical meristem that gives rise to the epidermis.

Protogynous Hermaphroditism in which the female gonads mature before the male gonads.

Protogyny A sequentially hermaphro-ditic species in which individuals change from females to males.

Protolysis This term has been used synonymously with proton (hydron)-transfer reaction. Because of its misleading similarity to hydrolysis, photolysis, etc., its use is discouraged.

Protomerite Anterior half of a cephaline gregarine protozoan.

Proton (p) The most common hadron, a baryon with electric charge +1 equal and opposite to that of the electron. Protons have a basic structure of two up quarks and one down quark (bound together by gluons). The nucleus of a hydrogen atom is a proton. A nucleus with electric charge Z contains Z protons; therefore the number of protons is what distinguishes the different chemical elements.

Proton affinity The negative of the enthalpy change in the gas phase reaction (real or hypothetical) between a proton (more appropriately hydron) and the chemical species concerned, usually an electrically neutral species to give the conjugate acid of that species.

Proton donor Acid. Because a free H^+ ion is technically a bare proton, acids are sometimes referred to as "proton donors" because they release hydrogen ions in solution. The term "proton donor" is misleading, since in aqueous solution, the hydrogen ion is never a bare proton- it's covalently bound to a water molecule as an H_3O^+ ion. Further, acids don't "donate" protons; they yield them to bases with a stronger affinity for them.

Proton motive force (PMF) The force arising from a gradient of protons and a membrane potential that is thought to power ATP synthesis and other processes.

Proton proton chain A series of nuclear events occurring in the core of a star whereby hydrogen nuclei (protons) are converted into helium nuclei. This process releases energy.

Protoplast A bacterial or fungal cell with its cell wall completely removed. It is spherical in shape and osmotically sensitive.

Protoplast fusion The joining of cells that have had their walls weakened or completely removed.

Protothecosis A disease of humans and animals produced by the green alga *Prototheca moriformis*.

Prototroph A microorganism that requires the same nutrients as the majority of naturally occurring members of its species.

Protozoan or protozoon A microorganism belonging to the Protozoa subkingdom. A unicellular or acellular eucaryotic protist whose organelles have the functional role of organs and tissues in more complex forms. Protozoa vary greatly in size, morphology, nutrition, and life cycle.

Protozoology The study of protozoa.

Proviral DNA Viral DNA that has been integrated into host cell DNA. In retroviruses it is the double-stranded DNA copy of the RNA genome.

Pseudomurein A modified peptidoglycan lacking D-amino acids and containing N-acetyltalosaminuronic acid instead of N-acetylmuramic acid; found in methanogenic archaea.

Pseudoplasmodium A sausage-shaped amoeboid structure consisting of many myxamoebae and behaving as a unit; the result of myxamoebal aggregation in the cellular slime molds; also called a slug.

Psittacosis A disease due to a strain of Chlamydia psittaci, first seen in parrots and later found in other birds and domestic fowl. It is transmissible to humans.

Psychrophile A microorganism that grows well at 0°C and has an optimum growth temperature of 15°C or lower and a temperature maximum around 20°C.

Psychrotroph A microorganism that grows at 0°C, but has a growth optimum between 20 and 30°C, and a maximum of about 35°C.

Puerperal fever An acute, febrile condition following childbirth; it is characterized by infection of the uterus and/or adjacent regions and is caused by streptococci.

Pulmonary anthrax A form of anthrax involving the lungs. Also known as woolsorter's disease.

Pulsar A neutron star (burnt-out star) that emits radio waves which pulse on and off.

Pulse A wave of short duration confined to a small portion of the medium at any given time is called a pulse. A pulse is also called a wave pulse.

Pure culture A population of cells that are identical because they arise from a single cell.

Purine A basic, heterocyclic, nitrogen-containing molecule with two joined rings that occurs in nucleic acids and other cell constituents; most purines are oxy or amino derivatives of the purine skeleton. The most important purines are adenine and guanine.

Purple membrane An area of the plasma membrane of Halobacterium that contains bacteriorhodopsin and is active in photosynthetic light energy trapping.

Putrefaction The microbial decomposition of organic matter, especially the anaerobic breakdown of proteins, with the production of foul-smelling compounds such as hydrogen sulfide and amines.

Pyrenoid The differentiated region of the chloroplast that is a center of starch formation in green algae and stoneworts.

Pyrimidine A basic, heterocyclic, nitrogen-containing molecule with one ring that occurs in nucleic acids and other cell constituents; pyrimidines are oxy or amino derivatives of the pyrimidine skeleton. The most important pyrimidines are cytosine, thymine, and uracil.

P brine An infectious disease of silkworms caused by the protozoan *Nosema bombycis*.

Q fever An acute zoonotic disease caused by the rickettsia Coxiella burnetii.

Quantum mechanics Describes a system of particles in terms of a wave function defined over the configuration of particles having distinct locations is implicit in the potential energy function that determines the wave function, the observable dynamics of the motion of such particles from point to point. In describing the energies, distributions and behaviours of electrons in nanometer-scale structures, quantum mechanical methods are necessary. Electron wave functions help determine the potential energy surface of a molecular system, which in turn is the basis for classical descriptions of molecular motion. Nanomechanical systems can almost always be described in terms of classical mechanics, with occasional quantum mechanical corrections applied within the framework of a classical model.

Qualia A property of self, of experiencing the environment such as colours, tastes, or pain. The qualia refers to a part of consciousness that is different from the physical nature of the stimulus that provokes it. For example, in describing a colour - red, blue, or green - we talk about a qualia of an object. The physical existence of a colour is a quantum mechanical state that emits energy in form of electromagnetic radiation that is decoded by our sensory organs - the eye and the visual cortex in the brain as red, blue, or green. We can only assert that the radiation has a certain energy who's quanta can elicit quantum mechanical effect in the retinal cell layer of our eyes.

Qualitative analysis Qualitative analysis involves determining the nature of a pure unknown compound or the compounds present in a mixture.

Quality, acoustic An attribute, characteristic or property of the noise, its duration, its time-varying characteristics or its frequency content. Examples are the "screech" of screaming, the "rumble" of an airconditioner, the "dripping" of a tap.

Quality factor The number of oscillations required for a system's energy to fall off by a factor of 535 due to damping.

Quanta Fixed amounts; usually referring to fixed amounts of energy absorbed or emitted by matter.

Quantitative analysis Quantitative analysis is the determination of the amount of substances present in a sample.

Quantized Describes quantity such as money or electrical charge, that can only exist in certain amounts.

Quantum Quantum is the smallest quantity of energy that can be emitted (or absorbed) in the form of electromagnetic radiation. Energy of a quantum (E) is equal to

$$E = hv$$

Where h is Planck constant and v is the frequency of the radiation.

Quantum chromodynamics (QCD) The quantum theory of the strong interaction.

Quantum electrodynamics (QED) The quantum theory of the electromagnetic interaction.

Quantum mechanics The laws of physics that apply on very small scales. The essential feature is that electric charge, momentum, and angular momentum, as well as charges, come in discrete amounts called quanta.

Quantum numbers Numbers that describe energy states of an electron; in the Bohr model of the atom, the orbit quantum numbers could be any whole number 1, 2, 3, and so on out from the nucleus; in the quantum mechanics model of the atom, four quantum numbers are used to describe the energy state of an electron wave.

Quark (q) A fundamental fermion that has strong interactions. Quarks have electric charge of either +2/3 (up, charm, top) or -1/3 (down, strange, bottom) in units where the proton charge is 1.

Quasar "Quasi-stellar radio source," possibly the most mysterious class of objects in the Universe, identified by their immense production of a wide range of electromagnetic radiation despite their relatively small size.

Quasicrystal Quasicrystal is a solid having conventional crystalline properties but whose lattice does not display translational periodicity.

Quellung reaction The increase in visibility or the swelling of the capsule of a microorganism in the presence of antibodies against capsular antigens.

Quinone An enzymatic cofactor that plays an important role in photosynthesis and respiration. More specifically, it is part of the electron transport chain in mitochondria and chloroplast membranes.

Quorum sensing The process in which bacteria monitor their own population density by sensing the levels of signal molecules that are released by the microorganisms. When these signal molecules reach a threshold concentration, the population density has attained a critical level or quorum, and quorum-dependent genes are expressed.

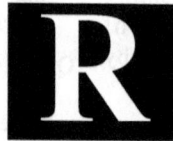

R factors or R plasmids Plasmids bearing one or more drug resistant genes.

Rabies An acute infectious disease of the central nervous system, which affects all warm-blooded animals. It is caused by an ssRNA virus belonging to the genus Lyssavirus in the family Rhabdoviridae.

Racemate Racemate is a mixture of equal quantities of the d- and l-forms of an optically active compound. A racemic mixture is not optically active.

Racking The removal of sediments from wine bottles.

Rad A measure of radiation received by a material.

Radappertization The use of gamma rays from a cobalt source for control of microorganisms in foods.

RADAR (Radio Detection and Ranging) A method of detecting, locating, or tracking an object by using beamed, reflected, and timed radio waves. RADAR also refers to the electronic equipment that uses radio waves to detect, locate, and track objects.

Radial Parallel to the radius of a circle; the in-out direction. *Cf.* tangential.

Radiant energy The form of energy that can travel through space; for example, visible light and other parts of the electromagnetic spectrum.

Radiation The transfer of heat from a region of higher temperature to a region of lower temperature by greater emission of radiant energy from the region of higher temperature.

Radiation belt A ring-shaped region around a planet in which electrically charged particles are trapped. The particles follow spiral trajectories around the direction of the magnetic field of the planet. The radiation belts surrounding Earth are known as the Van Allen belts.

Radiative process An event involving the emission or absorption of radiation. For example, a hydrogen atom that absorbs a photon of light converts the energy of that radiation into electrical potential energy.

Radioactive decay The natural spontaneous disintegration or decomposition of a nucleus.

Radioactive decay constant A specific constant for a particular isotope that is the ratio of the rate of nuclear disintegration per unit of time to the total number of radioactive nuclei.

Radioactive decay series Series of decay reactions that begins with one radioactive nucleus that decays to a second nucleus that decays to a third nucleus and so on until a stable nucleus is reached.

Radioactivity Radiation; radioactive; Spontaneous emission of particles or high-energy electromagnetic radiation from the nuclei of unstable atoms. "Radiation" refers to the emissions, and "radioactive source" refers to the source of the radiation.

Radioimmunoassay A very sensitive assay technique that uses a purified radioisotope-labelled antigen or antibody to compete for antibody or antigen with unlabelled standard and samples to determine the concentration of a substance in the samples.

Radionuclide A radioactive isotope of an element.

Radiotoxicity The adverse health effect of a radionuclide due to its radioactivity.

Radium A radioactive decay product of uranium often found in uranium ore. It has several radioactive isotopes. Radium-226 decays to radon-222.

Radon (Rn) A heavy radioactive gas given off by rocks containing radium (or thorium). Rn-222 is the main isotope.

Radon daughters Short-lived decay products of radon-222 (Po-218, Pb-214, Bi-214, Po-214).

Raman effect Raman effect is a type of scattering of electromagnetic radiation in which light suffers a change in frequency and a change in phase as it passes through a material medium. Is named according to the Indian physicist C. V. Raman (1889-1970). The intensity of Raman scattering is about one-thousandth of that in Rayleigh scattering in liquids.

Rankine cycle Rankine cycle is a thermodynamic cycle which can be used to calculate the ideal performance of a heat engine that uses a condensable vapour as the working fluid.

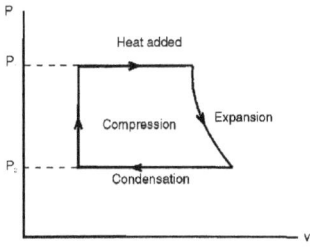

Figure Rankine cycle

Raoult's law Raoult's law is the expression for the vapour pressure p_a of component A in an ideal solution, viz.,

$$P_a = p_A^O X_a$$

Where X_a is the mole fraction of component A and p_A^O the vapour pressure of the pure substance A.

Rapeseed (Brassica napus) The seed of the rape plant which is a source of edible oil. The rape plant is a bright yellow flowering member of the Brassicaceae (mustard) family and a specific variety is known as canola. It is generally grown and cultivated for animal feed, vegetable oil and biodiesel.

Rare earth elements Rare earth elements are the elements Sc, Y, and the lanthanides. These elements got their name from the fact that chemists first isolated them in their oxide forms. These oxides somewhat resemble calcium, magnesium and aluminum oxides, sometimes called common earths.

Rarefaction A part of a longitudinal wave in which the density of the particles of the medium is less than the normal density is called a rarefaction.

Ras protein One of a large family of GTP-binding proteins that help relay signals from cell-surface receptors to the nucleus. Named for the ras gene, first identified in viruses that cause rat sarcomas.

Rayleigh scattering Rayleigh scattering is the scattering of light by particles which are much smaller than the wavelength of the light.

Reaction In chemistry, any process in which the arrangement of atoms into molecules is changed.

Reactor pressure vessel The main steel vessel containing the reactor fuel, moderator and coolant under pressure.

Reading frame The way in which nucleotides in DNA and mRNA are grouped into codons or groups of three for reading the message contained in the nucleotide sequence.

Reagin Antibody that mediates immediate hypersensitivity reactions. IgE is the major reagin in humans.

Real image A place where an object appears to be, because the rays diffusely reflected from any given point on the object have been bent so that they come back together and then spread out again from the new point.

Receptor Protein that binds a specific extracellular signaling molecule (ligand) and initiates a response in the cell. Cell-surface receptors, such as the acetylcholine receptor and the insulin receptor, are located in the plasma membrane, with their ligand-binding site exposed to the external medium. Intracellular receptors, such as steroid hormone receptors, bind ligands that diffuse into the cell across the plasma membrane.

Recessive gene or allele A gene that exercises little or no outward effect unless it is present in both of a pair of chromosomes, and therefore has been inherited from both parents, is said to be recessive.

Recessive trait The quality of a gene or allele regarding its ability to express a phenotype. A recessive allele can only express its phenotype if both copies in a diploid organisms are identical. Often, a recessive allele is matched with a dominant allele, which overrides the activity of the recessive one. In this case, the effect of the gene cannot be seen, but it can still be inherited. These are important considerations in genetic diseases that are often caused by defective copies of a gene (allele) that cause the disease only, if both copies of the gene are defective. Heterozygous individuals with a healthy allele do not suffer the disease but are carriers. Examples of recessive genetic diseases are cystic fibrosis and hypercholesterolemia.

Recombinant DNA Any DNA molecule formed by joining DNA segments from different sources. Recombinant DNAs are widely used in the cloning of genes, in the genetic modification of organisms, and in molecular biology generally.

Recombinant DNA technology The techniques used in carrying out genetic engineering; they involve the identification and isolation of a specific gene, the insertion of the gene into a vector such as a plasmid to form a recombinant molecule, and the production of large quantities of the gene and its products.

Recombinant-vector vaccine The type of vaccine that is produced by the introduction of one or more of a pathogen's genes into attenuated viruses or bacteria. The attenuated virus or bacterium serves as a vector, replicating within the vertebrate host and expressing the gene(s) of the pathogen. The pathogen's antigens induce an immune response.

Recombination The process in which a new recombinant chromosome is formed by combining genetic material from two organisms.

Recombination repair A DNA repair process that repairs damaged DNA when there is no remaining template; a piece of DNA from a sister molecule is used.

Rectilinear motion The motion of a body in a straight line is called rectilinear motion.

Red shift Lowered frequency of light from a source receding from the observation point as a result of the Doppler effect

Red tides Red tides occur frequently in coastal areas and often are associated with population blooms of dinoflagellates. Dinoflagellate pigments are responsible for the red colour of the water. Under these conditions, the dinoflagellates often produce saxitoxin, which can lead to paralytic shellfish poisoning.

Redfield ratio The carbon-nitrogen-phosphorus ratio of aquatic microorganisms. This ratio is important for predicting limiting factors for microbial growth.

Reducing agent or reductant The electron donor in an oxidation-reduction reaction.

Reductive dehalogenation The cleavage of carbon-halogen bonds by anaerobic bacteria that creates a strong electron-donating environment.

Reflected ray A line representing direction of motion of light reflected from a boundary.

Refraction The deflection of a light ray from a straight path as it passes from one medium to another.

Refractive index The ratio of the velocity of light in the first of two media to that in the second as it passes from the first to the second.

Refuge A stand of non-genetically modified crop in a GM crop designed to minimise the build up of pesticide resistance genes in the pest population by interbreeding of the two pest populations, i.e. exposed and unexposed to the pesticide concerned, thereby diluting the resistance genes.

Regenerative medicine A term applied to new medical advances in which damaged body parts or body tissue is replaced or the body is encouraged to heal itself. From our understanding of our genes and how they work to control the growth, building and repair of our body, regenerative medicine is studying how to create new tissues for transplant, transplant stem cells into the body or how to induce the body to regenerate from the body's own cells.

Regulator T cell Regulator T cells control the development of effector T cells. Two types exist: T-helper cells (CD41 cells) and T-suppressor cells. There are three subsets of T-helper cells: TH1, TH2, and TH0. TH1 cells produce IL-2, IFN-g, and TNF-b. They effect cell-mediated immunity and are responsible for delayed-type hypersensitivity reactions and macrophage activation. TH2 cells produce IL-4, IL-5, IL-6, IL-10, IL-13. They are helpers for B-cell antibody responses and humoral immunity; they also support IgE responses and eosinophilia. TH0 cells exhibit an unrestricted cytokine profile.

Regulatory mutants Mutant organisms that have lost the ability to limit synthesis of a product, which normally occurs by regulation of activity of an earlier step in the biosynthetic pathway.

Regulon A collection of genes or operons that is controlled by a common regulatory protein.

Relative atomic mass Relative atomic mass (A_r) is the ratio of the average mass per atom of the naturally occurring form of an element to 1/12 of the mass of nuclide ^{12}C. The term atomic weight is synonymous with relative atomic mass.

Relative density Relative density is the ratio of the density of a substance to the density of some reference substance. For liquids or solids it is the ratio of the density to the density of water at 4°C. This quantity was formerly called specific gravity.

Relative humidity = (m/ms) × 100 where m is the actual mass of water vapour present in certain volume of the air and ms is the mass of water vapor required to saturate the same volume of the air at the same temperature.

Relative molecular mass Relative molecular mass (M_r) is the ratio of the average mass per molecule or

Repulsive

specified entity of a substance to 1/12 of the mass of nuclide ^{12}C. Also called molecular weight. It is equal to the sum of the relative atomic masses of all the atoms that comprise a molecule. For example

$M_r(H_2SO_4) = 2 \times A_r(H) + A_r(S) + 4 \times A_r(O)$

$= 2 \times 1.0079 + 32.066 + 4 \times 15.999$

$= 2.0158 + 32.066 + 63.996$

$= 98.078$

Relativity A theory of physics that describes the dynamical behaviour of matter and energy. The consequences of relativity can be quite strange at very high velocities and very high densities. A direct result of the theory of relativity is the equation $E=mc^2$, which expresses a relationship between mass (m), energy (E), and the speed of light(c).

Rem Rem (rem) is a non-SI unit of dose equivalent employed in radioprotection.

Replica plating A technique for isolating mutants from a population by plating cells from each colony growing on a nonselective agar medium onto plates with selective media or environmental conditions, such as the lack of a nutrient or the presence of an antibiotic or a phage; the location of mutants on the original plate can be determined from growth patterns on the replica plates.

Replication The process in which an exact copy of parental DNA or RNA is made with the parental molecule serving as a template.

Replication fork The Y-shaped structure where DNA is replicated. The arms of the Y contain template strand and a newly synthesized DNA copy.

Replicative form A double-stranded form of nucleic acid that is formed from a single-stranded virus genome and used to synthesize new copies of the genome.

Replicon A unit of the genome that contains an origin for the initiation of replication and in which DNA is replicated.

Repository A permanent disposal place for radioactive wastes.

Repressible enzyme An enzyme whose level drops in the presence of a small molecule, usually an end product of its metabolic pathway.

Repressor protein A protein coded for by a regulator gene that can bind to the operator and inhibit transcription; it may be active by itself or only when the corepressor is bound to it.

Reprocessing Chemical treatment of spent reactor fuel to separate uranium and plutonium from the small quantity of fission product waste products and transuranic elements, leaving a much reduced quantity of high-level waste.

Repulsive Describes a force that tends to push the two participating objects apart. *Cf.* attractive, oblique.

Reservoir A site, alternate host, or carrier that normally harbours pathogenic organisms and serves as a source from which other individuals can be infected.

Reservoir host An organism other than a human that is infected with a pathogen that can also infect humans.

Residual interaction Interaction between objects that do not carry a charge but do contain constituents that have that charge. Although some chemical substances involve electrically-charged ions, much of chemistry is due to residual electromagnetic interactions between electrically-neutral atoms. The residual strong interaction between protons and neutrons, due to the strong charges of their quark constituents, is responsible for the binding of the nucleus.

Residuesphere The region surrounding organic matter such as a seed or plant part in which microbial growth is stimulated by increased organic matter availability.

Resistance Resistance (R) is electric potential difference divided by current when there is no electromotive force in the conductor. This definition applies to direct current. More generally, resistance is defined as the real part of impedance.

Resistivity The ratio of the applied voltage to the current.

Resolution The ability of a microscope to separate or distinguish between small objects that are close together.

Resonance The tendency of a vibrating system to respond most strongly to a driving force whose frequency is close to its own natural frequency of vibration.

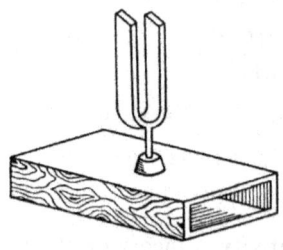

Figure Resonance Expt.

Respiration An energy-yielding process in which the energy substrate is oxidized using an exogenous or externally derived electron acceptor.

Respiratory burst The respiratory burst occurs when an activated phagocytic cell increases its oxygen consumption to support the increased metabolic activity of phagocytosis. The burst generates highly toxic oxygen products such as singlet oxygen, superoxide radical, hydrogen peroxide, hydroxyl radical, and hypochlorite.

Respiratory syncytial virus A member of the family Paramyxoviridae and genus Pneumovirus; it is a negative-sense ssRNA virus that causes respiratory infections in children.

Rest mass The rest mass of a particle is the mass defined by the energy of the isolated (free) particle at rest, divided by the speed of light squared. When particle physicists use the word "mass", they always mean the "rest mass" of the object in question.

Restoring force The force which tends to bring an oscillating body towards its mean position whenever it is displaced from the mean position is called the restoring force.

Restricted transduction A transduction process in which only a specific set of bacterial genes are carried to another bacterium by a temperate phage; the bacterial genes are acquired because of a mistake in the excision of a prophage during the lysogenic life cycle.

Restriction enzymes Enzymes produced by host cells that cleave virus DNA at specific points and thus protect the cell from virus infection; they are used in carrying out genetic engineering.

Resultant force A single force, which acts on a body to produce the same effect in it as, done by all other forces collectively, is called the resultant force.

Retardation Negative acceleration is called retardation. In retardation the velocity of a body decreases with time.

Reticulate body (RB) The form in the chlamydial life cycle whose role is growth and reproduction within the host cell.

Retrotransposon A mobile genetic elements that depends on a reverse transcription step to move and to duplicate.

Retrovirus A type of virus that contains RNA as its genetic material. Once in a host cell they perform a "backwards" conversion of RNA to DNA, which inserts itself into an infected cell's own DNA. Retroviruses can cause many diseases, including some cancers and AIDS.

Retroviruses A group of viruses with RNA genomes that carry the enzyme reverse transcriptase and form a DNA copy of their genome during their reproductive cycle.

Reverberation Apparent increase in volume caused by reflections, usually arriving within 0.1 second after the original sound.

Reverse transcriptase (RT) An RNA-dependent DNA polymerase that uses a viral RNA genome as a template to form a DNA copy; this is a reverse of the normal flow of genetic information, which proceeds from DNA to RNA.

Reversible covalent modification A mechanism of enzyme regulation in which the enzyme's activity is either increased or decreased by the reversible covalent addition of a group such as phosphate or AMP to the protein.

Revolution The orbital motion of one object around another. The Earth revolves around the Sun in one year. The moon revolves around the Earth in approximately 28 days.

Reye's syndrome An acute, potentially fatal disease of childhood that is characterized by severe edema of the brain and increased intracranial pressure, vomiting, hypoglycemia, and liver dysfunction. The cause is unknown but is almost always associated with a previous viral infection.

Reynolds number Reynolds number (*Re*) is a dimensionless quantity used in fluid mechanics, defined by

$Re = \rho\, vl/\eta$

Where ρ is density, v is velocity, l is length, and η is viscosity.

Rheology Rheology is the study of the deformation and flow of materials. It has important bearing on the behaviour of viscous liquids in plastic molding.

Rheumatic fever An autoimmune disease characterized by inflammatory lesions involving the heart valves, joints, subcutaneous tissues, and central nervous system. The disease is associated with hemolytic streptococci in the body. It is called rheumatic fever because two common symptoms are fever and pain in the joints similar to that of rheumatism.

Rhizosphere A region around the plant root where materials released from the root increase the microbial population and its activities.

Rho factor The protein that helps RNA polymerase dissociate from the terminator after it has stopped transcription.

Rhoptry Saclike, electron dense structure in the anterior portion of a zoite of a member of the phylum Apicomplexa; perhaps involved in the penetration of host cells.

Ribonucleic acids Ribonucleic acids (RNA) is naturally occurring polyribonucleotides that is concerned with protein synthesis. Four types are recognized: messenger RNA (mRNA), ribosomal RNA (rRNA), transfer RNA (tRNA), and viral RNA.

Ribosomal RNA The RNA present in ribosomes; ribosomes contain several sizes of single-stranded rRNA that contribute to ribosome structure and are also directly involved in the mechanism of protein synthesis.

Ribosome The organelle where protein synthesis occurs; the message encoded in mRNA is translated here.

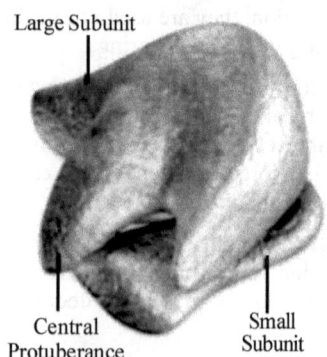

Figure Ribosomes

Ribotyping Ribotyping is the use of E. Coli rRNA to probe chromosomal DNA in Southern blots for typing bacterial strains. This method is based on the fact that rRNA genes are scattered throughout the chromosome of most bacteria and therefore polymorphic restriction endonuclease patterns result when chromosomes are digested and probed with rRNA.

Ribulose-1,5-bisphosphate carboxylase The enzyme that catalyzes the incorporation of CO_2 in the Calvin cycle.

Ringworm The common name for a fungal infection of the skin, even though it is not caused by a worm and is not always ring-shaped in appearance.

Rise period or burst The period during the one-step growth experiment when host cells lyse and release phage particles.

Risk Used as a term for a danger that arises unpredictably, such as being struck by a car.

RNA (ribonucleic acid) The most common form of nucleic acid used for storage of chemical energy, processing genetic information from genes (DNA) via messenger RNA (mRNA) into proteins. RNA is one of the most ancient form of molecular structures with enzymatic activity. As a matter of fact, protein biosynthesis is entirely controlled by RNA molecules including mRNA, transfer RNA (tRNA) for translating the DNA code into amino acid code, and ribosomal RNA (rRNA) that provide the enzymatic linkage (chemical bond formation) of amino acids into proteins. The use of RNA probably precedes the use of proteins and most modern genomes (except for some viruses) are made of DNA instead of RNA but can only be read by proteins. DNA is the more chemically stable of the two forms of nucleic acids.

RNA editing The process in which the base sequence of the RNA transcript is changed by addition of bases to the RNA molecule or by chemical transformation of one base to another. This subverts the genetic information carried in the genes.

RNA polymerase The enzyme that catalyzes the synthesis of mRNA under the direction of a DNA template.

Rocky Mountain spotted fever A disease caused by Rickettsia rickettsii.

Rolling-circle mechanism A mode of DNA replication in which the replication fork moves around a circular DNA molecule, displacing a strand to give a tail that is also copied to produce a new double-stranded DNA.

Root nodule Gall-like structures on roots that contain endosymbiotic nitrogen-fixing bacteria.

Roseola infantum A skin eruption that produces a rose-coloured rash in infants. Caused by the human herpesvirus 6. The disease is short-lived and characterized by a high fever of 3 to 4 days' duration.

Rotation The spin of an object around its central axis. Earth rotates about its axis every 24 hours. A spinning top rotates about its center shaft.

Rotational kinematics The study of objects moving with uniform angular acceleration in circles.

Rubella A moderately contagious skin disease that occurs primarily in children 5 to 9 years of age that is caused by the rubella virus, which is acquired by droplet inhalation into the respiratory system; German measles.

Rumen The expanded upper portion or first compartment of the stomach of ruminants.

Ruminant An herbivorous animal that has a stomach divided into four compartments and chews a cud consisting of regurgitated, partially digested food.

Run The straight line movement of a bacterium.

S

S phase Period of a eucaryotic cell cycle in which DNA is synthesized.

STP Standard temperature and pressure is the standard conditions used as a basis for calculations involving quantities that vary with temperature and pressure. These conditions are used when comparing the properties of gases.

Saccharomyces Genus of yeasts that reproduce asexually by budding or sexually by conjugation. Economically important in brewing and baking, they are also widely used in genetic engineering and as simple model organisms in the study of eucaryotic cell biology.

Safety Freedom from danger.

Salinity Salinity (S) is a parameter used in oceanography to describe the concentration of dissolved salts in seawater. The salinity of normal seawater is 35 parts salt per 1000 parts water.

Salmonellosis An infection with certain species of the genus Salmonella, usually caused by ingestion of food containing salmonellae or their products. Also known as Salmonella gastroenteritis or Salmonella food poisoning.

Salt Salt is an ionic compound formed by the reaction of an acid and a base. The reaction of sodium hidroxide to hydrochloric acid give sodium chloride

$$NaOH + HCl \rightleftharpoons NaCl + H_2O$$

Salt bridge Salt bridge is a permeable material soaked in a salt solution that allows ions to be transferred from one container to another. The salt solution remains unchanged during this transfer.

Sanitization Reduction of the microbial population on an inanimate object to levels judged safe by public health standards; usually, the object is cleaned.

Saprophyte An organism that takes up nonliving organic nutrients in dissolved form and usually grows on decomposing organic matter.

Saprozoic nutrition Having the type of nutrition in which organic nutrients are taken up in dissolved form; normally refers to animals or animal-like organisms.

Sarcoma Cancer of connective tissue.

Sarcomere Repeating unit of a myofibril in a muscle cell, composed of an array of overlapping thick and thin filaments between two adjacent Z discs.

Sarcoplasmic reticulum Network of internal membranes in the cytoplasm of a muscle cell that contains high concentrations of sequestered Ca^{2+} that is released into the cytosol during muscle excitation.

Satellite DNA Regions of highly repetitive DNA from an eucaryotic chromosome, usually identifiable by its unusual nucleotide composition. Satellite DNA is not transcribed and has no known function.

Saturated air Air in which equilibrium exists between evapo-ration and condensation; the relative humidity is 100 percent.

Saturated solution Saturated solution is a solution that holds the maximum possible amount of dissolved material. When saturated, the rate of dissolving solid and that of recrystallisation solid are the same, and a condition of equilibrium is reached. The amount of material in solution varies with the temperature; cold solutions can hold less dissolved solid material than hot solutions. Gases are more soluble in cold liquids than in hot liquids.

Saturation velocity Maximum velocity which can be obtained in a specific semiconductor.

Scaffolding proteins Special proteins that are used to aid procapsid construction during the assembly of a bacteriophage capsid and are removed after the completion of the procapsid.

Scalar A quantity that has no direction in space, only an amount. *Cf.* vector.

Scalar quantity A physical quantity, which is described completely by its magnitude, is called a scalar quantity.

Scale A platelike organic structure found on the surface of some cells (chrysophytes).

Scanning electron microscope (SEM) An electron microscope that scans a beam of electrons over the surface of a specimen and forms an image of the surface from the electrons that are emitted by it.

Scanning probe microscope A microscope used to study surface features by moving a sharp probe over the object's surface (e.g., the scanning tunneling microscope).

Scanning tunneling microscope A type of scanning probe microscope used to image a surface by moving a fine probe over it at a constant height, which is maintained by keeping a constant electron flow between the tip and surface.

Scarlet fever A disease that results from infection with a strain of Streptococcus pyogenes that carries a lysogenic phage with the gene for erythrogenic toxin. The toxin causes shedding of the skin. This is a communicable disease spread by respiratory droplets.

Schiff base Schiff base is a class of compounds derived by chemical reaction of aldehydes or ketones with aromatic amines, for example

$RNH_2 + R'CHO \rightleftharpoons RN:CHR' + H_2O$

Schizogony Multiple asexual fission.

Schrödinger equation Schrödinger equation is the basic equation of wave mechanics which, for systems not dependent on time, takes the form:

$$\nabla^2 \psi + \frac{8\pi^2 m}{h^2}(E-V)\psi = 0$$

Where Ψ is the wavefunction, V is the potential energy expressed as a function of the spatial coordinates, E its total energy, ∇^2 is the Laplacian operator, h is Planck's constant, and m is the mass.

Scientific law A relationship between quantities, usually described by an equation in the physical sciences; is more important and describes a wider range of phenomena than a scientific principle.

Scientific principle A relationship between quantities concerned with a specific, or narrow range of observations and behaviour.

Second Second (s) is the SI base unit of time.

The second is the duration of 9 192 631 770 periods of the radiation corresponding to the transition between the two hyperfine levels (F = 4, m_f = 0 to F = 3, m_f = 0) of the ground state of the caesium 133 atom.

Second law of motion The acceleration of an object is directly proportional to the net force acting on that object and inversely proportional to the mass of the object.

Second law of thermodynamics Physical and chemical processes proceed in such a way that the entropy of the universe increases to the maximum possible.

Second's pendulum A simple pendulum whose time period on the surface of earth is 2 seconds is called the second's pendulum.

Secondary coil Part of a transformer, a coil of wire in which the voltage of the original alternating current in the primary coil is stepped up or down by way of electroma-gnetic induction.

Secondary metabolites Products of metabolism that are synthesized after growth has been completed.

Secondary treatment The biological degradation of dissolved organic matter in the process of sewage treatment; the organic material is either mineralized or changed to settleable solids.

Secretory IgA The primary immunoglobulin of the secretory immune system. See IgA.

Secretory vacuole In protists and some animals, these organelles usually contain specific enzymes that perform various functions such as excystation. Their contents are released to the cell exterior during exocytosis.

Segmented genome A virus genome that is divided into several parts or fragments, each probably coding for the synthesis of a single polypeptide; segmented genomes are very common among the RNA viruses.

Selectins A family of cell adhesion molecules that are displayed on activated endothelial cells; examples include P-selectin and E-selectin. Selectins mediate leukocyte binding to the vascular endothelium.

Selective breeding A process in which new or improved strains of plants or animals are developed, mainly through controlled mating or crossing and selection of progeny for desired traits.

Selective media Culture media that favour the growth of specific microorganisms; this may be accomplished by inhibiting the growth of undesired microorganisms.

Selective toxicity The ability of a chemotherapeutic agent to kill or inhibit a microbial pathogen while damaging the host as little as possible.

Selenides Selenides are compounds having the structure RSER (R not equal to H). They are thus selenium analogues of ethers. Also used for metal salts of H_2Se.

Self-assembly The spontaneous formation of a complex structure from its component molecules without the aid of special enzymes or factors.

Semiconductor Semiconductor is a material in which the highest occupied energy band is completely filled with electrons at $T = 0$ K, and the energy gap to the next highest band ranges from 0 to 4 or 5 ev. With increasing temperature electrons are excited into the conduction band, leading to an increase in the electrical conductivity.

Separative Work Unit (SWU) This is a complex unit which is a function of the amount of uranium processed and the degree to which it is enriched, i.e. the extent of increase in the concentration of the U-235 isotope relative to the remainder. The unit is strictly Kilogram Separative Work Unit, and it measures the quantity of separative work (indicative of energy used in enrichment) when feed and product quantities are expressed in kilograms.

E.g., to produce one kilogram of uranium enriched to 3.5% U-235 requires 4.3 SWU if the plant is operated at a tails assay 0.30%, or 4.8 SWU if the tails assay is 0.25% (thereby requiring only 7.0 kg instead of 7.8 kg of natural U feed).

About 100-120,000 SWU is required to enrich the annual fuel loading for a typical 1000 MWe light water reactor. Enrichment costs are related to electrical energy used. The gaseous diffusion process consumes some 2400 kWh per SWU, while gas centrifuge plants require only about 60 kWh/SWU.

Sepsis Systemic response to infection. This systemic response is manifested by two or more of the following conditions as a result of infection: temperature .38 or .36°C; heart rate .90 beats per min;

respiratory rate .20 breaths per min, or pco2 .32 mm Hg; leukocyte count .12,000 cells per ml3 or .10% immature (band) forms. Sepsis also has been defined as the presence of pathogens or their toxins in blood and other tissues.

Septate Divided by a septum or cross wall; also with more or less regular occurring cross walls.

Septic shock Sepsis associated with severe hypotension despite adequate fluid resuscitation, along with the presence of perfusion abnormalities that may include, but are not limited to, lactic acidosis, oliguria, or an acute alteration in mental status. Gram-positive bacteria, fungi, and endotoxin-containing gram-negative bacteria can initiate the pathogenic cascade of sepsis leading to septic shock.

Septic tank A tank used to process small quantities of domestic sewage. Solid material settles out and is partially degraded by anaerobic bacteria as sewage slowly flows through the tank. The outflow is further treated or dispersed in aerobic soil.

Septicemia A disease associated with the presence in the blood of pathogens or bacterial toxins.

Septum A partition or cross-wall that occurs between two cells in a bacterial or fungal filament, or which partitions off fungal structures such as spores. Septa also divide parent cells into two daughter cells during bacterial binary fission.

Sequence The linear arrangement of building blocks in biological macromolecules like DNA, RNA, protein and polysaccharides. DNA and RNA macromolecules are linear polymers of nucleotides. Proteins are linear polymers of amino acids. Polysaccharides are linear and branched polymers of monosac-charides (sugars). While the sequence of RNA and proteins are encoded for by the nucleotide sequence in DNA (the genes and genomes), polysaccharides which play important roles in physiology are not encoded for by genetic information, but rather by the spatial and temporal activity of enzymes that synthesize these poly-saccharides.

Serine/threonine kinase Protein kinase that phosphorylates serines or threonines on its target protein.

Serology The branch of immunology that is concerned with in vitro reactions involving one or more serum constituents.

Serotyping A technique or serological procedure that is used to differentiate between strains of microorganisms that have differences in the antigenic composition of a structure or product.

Serum The clear, fluid portion of blood lacking both blood cells and fibrinogen. It is the fluid remaining after coagulation of plasma, the noncellular liquid faction of blood.

Serum resistance The type of resistance that occurs with bacteria such as Neisseria gonorrhoeae because the pathogen interferes with membrane attack complex forma-tion during the complement cascade.

Settling basin A basin used during water purification to chemically precipitate out fine particles, micro-organisms, and organic material by coagulation or flocculation.

Sex pilus A thin protein appendage required for bacterial mating or conjugation. The cell with sex pili donates DNA to recipient cells.

Shear stress Produced when two plates slide past one another or by one plate sliding past another plate that is not moving.

Sheath A hollow tubelike structure surrounding a chain of cells and present in several genera of bacteria.

Shell Atomic states which are associated with one principle quantum number.

Shigellosis The diarrheal disease that arises from an infection with a member of the genus Shigella. Often called bacillary dysentery.

SHIME system A set of connected chemostat-like reactors that provide a sequence of environments similar to the human digestive system.

Shine-Dalgarno sequence A segment in the leader of procaryotic mRNA that binds to a special sequence on the 16S rRNA of the small ribosomal subunit. This helps properly orient the mRNA on the ribosome.

Shingles A reactivated form of chickenpox caused by the varicella-zoster virus.

Shock wave A high-pressure wave that travels at supersonic speeds. Shock waves are usually produced by an explosion.

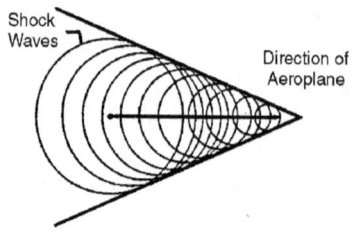

Figure Production of shock wave

Short circuit A circuit that does not function because charge is given a low-resistance "shortcut" path that it can follow, instead of the path that makes it do something useful.

Sickle cell disease A single gene disorder caused by an altered polypeptide in the globin of haemoglobin. It was the first disorder in which a mutation in a structural gene was shown to produce an altered amino acid sequence. Inheritance is autosomal recessive. In homozygotes there is severe chronic anaemia, episodes of painful infarction especially of lungs, spleen and bones, and proneness to infection. It is connected with a resistance to malaria.

Siderophore A small molecule that complexes with ferric iron and supplies it to a cell by aiding in its transport across the plasma membrane.

Siemens Siemens (S) is the SI derived unit of of electrical conductance of a conductor in which a current of one ampere is produced by an electrical potential difference of one volt ($S = A \cdot V^{-1} = \Omega^{-1}$). The unit is named after the German scientist Ernst Werner von Siemens (1816-1892).

Sievert (Sv) Unit indicating the biological damage caused by radiation. One Joule of beta or gamma radiation absorbed per kilogram of tissue has 1 Sv of biological effect; 1 J/kg of alpha radiation has 20 Sv effect and 1 J/kg of neutrons has 10 Sv effect.

Sigma bond A covalent bond in which overlap between two atomic orbitals produces a single bonding orbital in which the distribution of shared electrons has a roughly cylindrical symmetry about the axis linking the two atoms. By themselves, sigma bonds present little barrier to rotation of one substructure with respect to another, although steric effects and cyclic structures may hinder or block rotation.

Sigma factor A protein that helps the RNA polymerase core enzyme recognize the promoter at the start of a gene.

Sign An objective change in a diseased body that can be directly observed.

Significant figures Measurements are not infinitely accurate: we must estimate measurement uncertainty. The number of significant figures is all of the certain digits plus the first uncertain digit.

Rules for significant figures:

1. Disregard all initial zeros.

2. Disregard all final zeros unless they follow a decimal point.

3. All remaining digits including zeros between nonzero digits are significant.

0.0023

Have two significant figures

0.109

Have three significant figures

2.00

Have three significant figures

70

Have one significant figure

In adition and subtraction, the number of significant figures in the answer depends on the original number in the calculation that has the fewest digits to the right of the decimal point.

In multiplication and division, the number of significant figures in a calculated result is determined by the original measurement that has the fewest number of significant digits.

In a logarithm of a number, keep as many digits to the right of the decimal point as there are significant figures in the original number.

In an antilogarithm of a number, keep as many digits as there are digits to the right of the decimal point in the original number.

Silage Fermented plant material with increased palatability and nutritional value for animals, which can be stored for extended periods.

Silanes Silanes are saturated silicon hydrides, analogues of the alkanes (compounds of the general formula $si_n h_{2n+2}$).

Silent mutation A mutation that does not result in a change in the organism's proteins or phenotype even though the DNA base sequence has been changed.

Silicones Silicones are polymeric or oligomeric siloxanes, usually considered unbranched, of general formula.

Siloxanes Siloxanes are saturated silicon-oxygen hydrides with unbranched or branched chains of alternating silicon and oxygen atoms.

Simple harmonic motion The vibratory motion that occurs when there is a restoring force opposite to and proportional to a displacement.

Simple matching coefficient (SSM) An association coefficient used in numerical taxonomy; the proportion of characters that match regardless of whether or not the attribute is present.

Simple pendulum A heavy point mass, suspended by a light inextensible string from a frictionless rigid support is called a simple pendulum. A simple pendulum is a simple machine based on the effect of gravity.

Simultaneity Whether two events occur at the same time, said by special relativity to depend upon the observational reference frame.

Single radial immunodiffusion (RID) assay An immunodiffusion technique that quantitates antigens by following their diffusion through a gel containing antibodies directed against the test antigens.

Singularity The zero-dimensional "point" at the center of a black hole or other significant object at which all conceptions of space and time "break down" and become incomprehensible, defined by Hawking as a point at which spacetime curvature is infinite.

Sink A site of collection of metabolites, such as sugar; metabolic sinks may exist anywhere in the plant where organic solutes are being transported by the phloem and stored.

Sinkholes A large surface crater caused by the collapse of an underground channel or cavern; often triggered by groundwater withdrawal.

Sinus A cavity or space in tissues or in bone.

Siphon A tubular structure through which fluid flows; siphons of some molluscs allow water to enter and leave the mantle cavity.

Siphonogamy A reproductive process in seed plants in which a pollen tube carries the sperm cells to the egg located within the integumented megasporangium.

Siphonoglyph Ciliated furrow in the gullet of sea anemones.

Siphonophores Hydrozoans that exist as drifting colonies.

Siphuncle Cord of tissue running through the shell of a nautiloid, connecting all chambers with body of animal.

Sipuncula A phylum of protostomate worms whose members burrow in soft marine substrates throughout the world's oceans. Range in length from 2 mm to 75 cm. Peanut worms.

Sister chromatid One of the two identical parts of a duplicated chromosome in an eukaryotic cell. Sister chromatids consist of exact copies of a long coiled DNA molecule with associated proteins. Sister chromatids are joined at the centro-mere of a duplicated chromosome.

Sister group The relationship between a pair of species or higher taxa that are each other's closest phylogenetic relatives.

Site-specific recombination Recombination of nonhomologous genetic material with a chromosome at a specific site.

Skeletal muscle Type of muscle tissue found in muscles attached to skeletal parts.

Skin The outer integument or covering of an animal body, consisting of the dermis and the epidermis and resting on the subcutaneous tissues.

Skin-associated lymphoid tissue (SALT) The lymphoid tissue in the skin that forms a first-line defense as a part of nonspecific immunity.

SLAC The Stanford Linear Accelerator Center in Stanford, California.

Slash-and-burn agriculture The cutting down and burning of tropical vegetation to make mineral nutrients available for use by introduced agricultural crops.

Slater-type orbital An approximate atomic orbital that attempts to allow for electron-electron repulsion by scaling the nuclear charge for each orbital.

S-layer A regularly structured layer composed of protein or glycoprotein that lies on the surface of many bacteria. It may protect the bacter-ium and help give it shape and rigidity.

Sleeping sickness African trypanosomiasis and mosquito-borne, virusinduced encephalitis.

Slime ball Mass of mucus-covered cercariae of dicrocoeliid flukes, released from land snails. Also a term of derogation applied to really disgusting persons.

Slime layer A layer of diffuse, unorganized, easily removed material lying outside the bacterial cell wall.

Slime mold Members of the Myxomycetes, characterized by a creeping, plasmodial stage.

Slime The viscous extracellular glycoproteins or glycolipids produced by staphylococci and Pseudomonas aeruginosa bacteria that allows them to adhere to smooth surfaces such as prosthetic medical devices and catheters. More generally, the term often refers to an easily removed, diffuse, unorganized layer of extracellular material that surrounds a bacterial cell.

Slow sand filter A bed of sand through which water slowly flows; the gelatinous microbial layer on the sand grain surface removes water-borne microorganisms, particularly Giardia, by adhesion to the gel. This type of filter is used in some water purification plants.

Slow virus disease A progressive, pathological process caused by a transmissible agent that remains clinically silent during a prolonged incubation period of months to years after which progressive clinical disease becomes apparent.

Sludge A general term for the precipitated solid matter produced during water and sewage treatment; solid particles composed of organic matter and microorganisms that are involved in aerobic sewage treatment.

Sludge Semisolid mixture of organic and inorganic materials that settles out of wastewater at a sewage treatment plant.

Slums Legal but inadequate multifamily tenements or rooming houses; some are custom built for rent to poor people, others are converted from some other use.

Small intestine The part of the digestive system consisting of the duodenum, jejunum, and ileum.

Smallpox Once a highly contagious, often fatal disease caused by a poxvirus. Its most noticeable symptom was the appearance of blisters and pustules on the skin. Vaccination has eradicated smallpox throughout the world.

Smog Smog is a mixture of smoke and fog. The term is used to describe city fogs in which there is a large proportion of particulate matter and also a high concentration of sulphur and nitrogen gases.

Smolt A young salmon just before it migrates downstream and out to sea.

Smooth ER The portion of endoplasmic reticulum that lacks ribosomes.

Smooth muscle Type of muscle tissue found in the walls of the hollow organs; visceral muscle.

Snapping division A distinctive type of binary fission resulting in an angular or a palisade arrangement of cells, which is characteristic of the genera Arthrobacter and Corynebacterium.

Social deprivation Withholding or removal of contact with any form of stimulation from conspecifics.

Social ecology A socialist/humanist philosophy based on the communi-tarian anarchism of the Russian geographer Peter Kropotkin. It shares much with deep ecology except that it is more humanist in its outlook.

Social justice Equitable access to resources and the benefits derived from them; a system that recognizes inalienable rights and adheres to what is fair, honest, and moral.

Social organization The species-typical pattern of relationships among all members of a group. This would include spatial distribution patterns, interindividual relation-ships involving dominance hierarchies or territoriality, mating systems, parenting, and dispersal.

Society A group of individuals belonging to the same species and organized in a cooperative manner. Usually assumed to extend beyond sexual behaviour and parental care of offspring.

Sociobiology A study that involves the application of the principles of evolution to the study of the social behaviour and social systems of animals.

Sociopolitical The awareness by society of how the political process can be influenced by well-informed individuals.

Sodium-potassium ATPase pump The active transport mechanism that functions to concentrate sodium ions on the outside of a plasma membrane and potassium ions on the inside of the membrane.

Soft corals Colonial anthozoans with no hard skeleton.

Softwood General term for the wood (secondary xylem) of conifers.

Soil A complex mixture of weathered mineral materials from rocks, partially decomposed organic molecules, and a host of living organisms.

Soil horizons Horizontal layers that reveal a soil's history, characteristics, and usefulness.

Soil profile A vertical section of soil showing the zones of particle sizes from surface down to bedrock.

Sol Sols are dispersions of small solid particles in a liquid. The particles may be macromolecules or may be clusters of small molecules. Lyophobic sols are those in which there is no affinity between the dispersed phase and the liquid (e.g. Silver chloride dispersed in water). Lyophobic sols are inherently unstable, in time the particles aggregate, and form a precipitate. Lyiophilic sols, on the other hand, are more like true solutions in which the solute molecules are large and have an affinity for the solvent. Association colloids are systems in which the dispersed phase consists of clusters of molecules that have lyophobic and lyophilic parts.

Solar atmosphere The atmosphere of the Sun. An atmosphere is generally the outermost gaseous layers of a planet, natural satellite, or star. Only bodies with a strong gravitational pull can retain an atmosphere. Atmosphere is used to describe the outer layer of the Sun because it is relatively transparent at visible wavelengths. Parts of the solar atmosphere include the photosphere, chromosphere, and the corona.

Solar limb The apparent edge of the Sun as it is seen in the sky.

Solar spectrum The band of colours produced when sunlight is dispersed by a prism.

Solenia Channels through the coenen-chyme connecting the polyps in an alcyonarian colony.

Solenocyte Special type of flame bulb in which the bulb bears a flagellum instead of a tuft of flagella.

Solenoid A cylindrical coil of wire that becomes electromagnetic when a current runs through it.

Solenophage Blood-feeding arthropod that introduces its mouthparts directly into a blood vessel to feed.

Soleus The sole of the foot.

Solid state detector A device used to detect the passage of charged subatomic particles by their crystal-distorting or ionizing effects on a nonconducting or nonconducting solid.

Solidification The change of phase from a liquid to a solid.

Solids A phase of matter with molecules that remain close to fixed equilibrium positions due to strong interactions between the molecules, resulting in the characteristic definite shape and definite volume of a solid.

Solstice As the orientation of the Earth (relative to the sun) varies through the year, the sun appears to move across the sky a little higher in the sky or a little lower. During the winter, the sun is lower; in the summer, higher. During the northern hemisphere summer, the southern hemisphere sees the sun lower in the sky and experiences winter. During the northern hemisphere winter, the southern hemisphere sees the sun higher in the sky and experiences summer. The word solstice came to Middle English from the Latin solstitium (via Old French) combining sol- (sun) and -stitium (a stoppage), meaning "the sun stands still." This is the time of the year when the Sun stops drifting north or south and begins moving in the opposite direction. The solstice, thus marks the half-way point for the long days of summer and the short days for winter. The northern hemi-sphere's summer solstice (when the Earth's north pole is tilted its maximum amount towards the Sun) is the southern hemisphere's winter solstice. And vica versa (when the south pole is tilted its maximum amount towards the Sun).

Solubility product constant Solubility product constant (K_{sp}) (or the solubility product) is the product of the molar concentrations of the constituent ions, each raised to the power of its stoichiometric coefficient in the equilibrium equation. For instance, if a compound $a_a b_b$ is in equilibrium with its solution

$$A_a b_b(s) \rightleftharpoons aa^+ + bb$$

The solubility product is given by

$$K_{sp}(a_a b_b) = [A^+]^{a} [B^-]^{b}$$

Solubility Solubility is the maximum amount of solute that dissolves in a given quantity of solvent at a specific temperature. Generally, for a solid in a liquid, solubility increases with temperature; for a gas, solubility decreases. Common measures of solubility include the mass of solute per unit mass of solution, mole fraction of solute, molality, molarity, and others.

Solute Any material dissolved in a solution.

Solute potential The water potential component caused by the presence of solutes in water.

Solvation Any stabilizing interaction of a solute (or solute moiety) and the solvent or a similar interaction of solvent with groups of an insoluble material (i.e., the ionic groups of an ion-exchange resin). Such interactions generally involve electrostatic forces and van der Waals forces, as well as chemically more specific effects such as hydrogen bond formation.

Solvatochromism The change in position and sometimes intensity of an electronic absorption or emission band, accompanying a change in the polarity of the medium. Negative (positive) solvatochromism corres-ponds to a hypsochromic (batho-chromic) shift with increasing solvent polarity.

Solvent parameter Quantitative measures of the capability of solvents for interaction with solutes. Such parameters have been based on numerous different physico-chemical quantities, e.g. rate constants, solvatochromic shifts in ultraviolet/visible spectra, solvent-induced shifts in infrared frequencies, etc. Some solvent parameters are purely empirical in nature, i.e. they are based directly on some experimental measurement. It may be possible to interpret such a parameter as measuring some particular aspect of solvent-solute interaction or it may be regarded simply as a measure of solvent polarity. Other solvent parameters are based on analysing experimental results. Such a parameter is considered to quantify some particular aspect of solvent capability for interaction with solutes.

Solvent The liquid matrix in which a solute is dissolved.

Solvolysis Generally, reaction with a solvent, or with a lyonium ion or lyate ion, involving the rupture of one or more bonds in the reacting solute. More specifically the term is used for substitution, elimination and fragmentation reactions in which a solvent species is the nucleophile ("alcoholysis" if the solvent is an alcohol, etc.).

Soma The whole of an organism except the germ cells (germ plasm).

Somaclonal variant A plant showing a mutation that developed asexually during the tissue culture of a single callus.

Somatic cell Ordinary body cell; pertaining to or characteristic of a body cell. Any cell other than a germ cell or germ-cell precursor.

Somatic Either pertaining to body cells (as opposed to gametes) or to the body wall (as opposed to the viscera).

Somatic mutation A mutation that occurs in cells of leaves, stems, or roots; a mutation occurring in any cells that are not involved in gamete formation.

Somatocoel Posterior coelomic compartment of echinoderms; left somatocoel gives rise to oral coelom, and right somatocoel becomes aboral coelom.

Somatoplasm The living matter that makes up the mass of the body as distinguished from germ plasm, which makes up the reproductive cells. The protoplasm of body cells.

Somite One of the blocklike masses of mesoderm arranged segmentally (metamerically) in a longitudinal series beside the neural tube of the embryo; metamere.

Sonar A system that uses sound at sonic or ultrasonic frequencies to detect and locate objects.

Sonic boom Sound waves that pile up into a shock wave when a source is traveling at or faster than the speed of sound.

Sonication Irradiation with (often ultra) sound waves, e.g. to increase the rate of a reaction or to prepare vesicles in mixtures of surfactants and water.

Sonometer A device, consisting of two or more wires or strings stretched over a sounding board, used for testing the frequency of strings and for showing how they vibrate.

Sorocarp The fruiting structure of the Acrasiomycetes.

Sorting Differential survival and reproduction among varying individuals; often confused with natural selection which is one possible cause of sorting.

Sorus A cluster of sporangia found on a fern leaf.

SOS repair A complex, inducible repair process that is used to repair DNA when extensive damage has occurred.

Sound absorption The ability of a material to absorb sound energy through its conversion into thermal energy.

Sound intensity The rate at which sound energy flows through a unit area.

Sound level meter An instrument consisting of a microphone, amplifier and indicating device, having a declared performance and designed to measure sound pressure levels.

Sound power level Ten times the logarithm to the base 10 of the ratio of the sound power of the source to the reference sound power.

Sound pressure level The level of noise, usually expressed in decibels, as measured by a standard sound level meter with a microphone.

Sound The series of disturbances in matter to which the human ear is sensitive Also similar disturbances in matter above and below the normal range of human hearing.

Sound window The use of frequencies for communication that are transmitted through the environment with little loss of strength (attenuation).

Source The location or object from which a pathogen is immediately transmitted to the host, either directly or through an intermediate agent.

South Atlantic anomaly The region over the South Atlantic Ocean where the lower Van Allen belt of energetic, electrically charged particles is particularly close to the Earth's surface. The excess energy in the particles presents a problem for satellites in orbit around the Earth.

Southern blotting technique The procedure used to isolate and identify DNA fragments from a complex mixture. The isolated, denatured fragments are transferred from an agarose electrophoretic gel to a nitrocellulose filter and identified by hybridization with probes.

Southern pine forest United States coniferous forest ecosystem characterized by a warm, moist climate.

Sp, sp^2, sp^3 An isolated carbon atom has four valence orbitals: three mutually perpendicular p orbitals, each with a single nodal plane, and one spherically symmetric s orbital. A carbon atom in a typical molecule can be regarded as bonding with four orbitals consisting of weighted sums of these s and p orbitals. One common pattern has four equivalent orbitals, each formed by combining the three p orbitals with the s orbital; this is sp^3 hybridization. An sp^3 carbon atom forms four sigma bonds, usually in a roughly tetrahedral arrangement. Another common pattern has three equivalent orbitals formed by combining two p orbitals with the s orbital; this is termed sp^2 hybridization. An sp^2 carbon atom forms three roughly coplanar sigma bonds, usually separated by ~120, and one pi bond. If a single p orbital is combined with the s orbital, the result is sp hybridization, forming two sigma bonds and two pi bonds. Atoms of other kinds can hybridize in an analogous manner.

Space Three-dimensional realm dependent on the presence of matter in which the Universe partially exists.

Space charge The negative charge in the space between the cathode and plate of a vacuum tube.

Spacetime The four-dimensional coordinate system in which physical events are located.

Spacetime, Euclidean This description of spacetime treats only the geometry of flat surfaces such as a tabletop. The surface of a globe, for example, is not a two-dimensional Euclidean surface; it is a three-dimensional Euclidean surface.

Sparganum Cestode plerocercoid of unknown identity.

Spark chamber A device used to detect the passage of charged subatomic particles by the light flashes they trigger.

Spawning The release of gametes or eggs into the water.

Special relativity Kinematic theory that explains the relations between light and matter.

Specialists Species that occupy a narrow range of habitats and eat a narrow range of foods. Contrast with generalists.

Specialized niche A species occupying a niche with a narrow range of tolerance.

Speciation The process by which two or more species are formed from a single ancestral stock.

Species diversity The number and relative abundance of species present in a community.

Species Species of higher organisms are groups of interbreeding or potentially interbreeding natural populations that are reproductively isolated. Bacterial species are collections of strains that have many stable properties in common and differ significantly from other groups of strains.

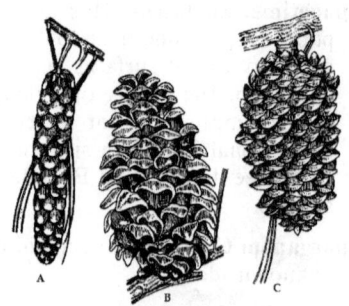

Figure Different species of pine

Species recovery plan A plan for restoration of an endangered species through protection, habitat management, captive breeding, disease control, or other techniques that increase populations and encourage survival.

Species-typical behaviour Actions and displays that are broadly characteristic of a species.

Specific catalysis The acceleration of a reaction by a unique catalyst, rather than by a family of related substances. The term is most commonly used in connection with specific hydrogen-ion or hydroxide-ion (lyonium ion or lyate ion) catalysis.

Specific gravity Specific gravity is ratio of the density of a material to that density of a water. Since one must specify the temperature of both the sample and the water to have a precisely defined quantity, the use of this term is now discouraged.

Specific heat Each substance has its own specific heat, which is defined as the amount of energy (or heat) needed to increase the temperature of one gram of a substance one degree Celsius.

Specific In physics and chemistry the word specific in the name of a quantity usually means divided by an extensive measure that is, divided by a quantity representing an amount of material. Specific volume means volume divided by mass, which is the reciprocal of the density. Specific heat capacity is the heat capacity divided by the mass.

Specific quantity Specific quantity is often convenient to express an extensive quantity. As the actual value divided by mass. The resulting quantity is called specific volume, specific enthalpy, etc.

Spectral line A line in a spectrum due to the emission or absorption of electromagnetic radiation at a discrete wavelength. Spectral lines result from discrete changes in the energy of an atom or molecule. Different atoms or molecules can be identified by the unique sequence of spectral lines associated with them.

Spectrograph An instrument that spreads light or other electromagnetic radiation into its component wavelengths (spectrum), recording the results photographically or electronically.

Spectrometer An instrument for measuring the intensity of radiation as a function of wavelength. See Spectrograph.

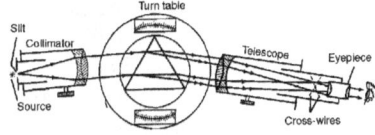

Figure Spectrometer

Spectroscope Optical instrument used for the study of spectra.

Spectrum Electromagnetic radiation arranged in order of wavelength. A rainbow is a natural spectrum of visible light from the Sun. Spectra are often punctuated with emission or absorption lines, which can be examined to reveal the composition and motion of the radiating source.

Specular reflection Reflection from a smooth surface, in which the light ray leaves at the same angle at which it came in.

Speed of light (c) The speed at which light (photons) travels through empty space is roughly 3×10^8 meters per second or 300 million meters per second.

Speed The absolute value of or, in more then one dimension, the magnitude of the velocity, i.e. the velocity stripped of any information about its direction Spring constant. The constant of proportionality between force and elongation of a spring or other object under strain.

Spent fuel Fuel assemblies removed from a reactor after several years use.

Sperm competition A situation in which one male's sperm fertilize a disproportionate number of eggs when a female copulates with more than one male.

Sperm nuclei Each pollen grain produces two sperm nuclei, which effect double fertilization in angiosperms.

Spermaceti organ a large organ in the forehead of sperm whales that is filled with a fine-quality liquid or waxy spermaceti oil.

Spermagonium A structure that produces spermatia in the rust fungi.

Spermalege Organ that receives the sperm in the female cimicid bug during copulation.

Spermatheca A sac in the female reproductive organs for the reception and storage of sperm.

Spermatid A growth stage of a male reproductive cell arising by division of a secondary spermatocyte; gives rise to a spermatozoon.

Spermatium Minute, nonmotile male gametes that occur in the rust fungi.

Spermatocyte A growth stage of a male reproductive cell; gives rise to a spermatid.

Spermatodactyl Modification in some Acari of chelicera, which functions in transfer of sperm from male's gonopore to copulatory receptacles between third and fourth coxae of female.

Spermatogenesis Formation and maturation of spermatozoa.

Spermatogonium Precursor of mature male reproductive cell; gives rise directly to a spermatocyte.

Spermatophore Formed "container" or packet of sperm that is placed in or on the body of a female, in contrast to the sperm in copulation which are conducted directly from male reproductive structures into the female's body.

Sphenoid The sphenoid bone.

Sphenophyta The vascular plant division commonly termed the horsetails to which the genus Equisetum belongs.

Spherical aberration The failure of parallel rays to meet at a single point on a spherical surface after reflection or refraction.

Spheroplast A relatively spherical cell formed by the weakening or partial removal of the rigid cell wall component. Spheroplasts are usually osmotically sensitive.

Sphincter A ringlike band of muscle fibers that constricts a passage or closes a natural orifice.

Spice A pungent, aromatic plant product derived from plants native to tropical regions and used to flavour foods.

Spicule One of the minute calcareous or siliceous skeletal bodies found in sponges, radiolarians, soft corals, and sea cucumbers.

Spike An inflorescence in which the main axis is elongated and the flowers are sessile.

Spikelet A small group of grass flowers; a unit of the inflorescence in grasses.

Spin density The unpaired electron density at a position of interest, usually at carbon, in a radical. It is often measured experimentally by electron paramagnetic resonance spectroscopy through hyperfine coupling constants of the atom or an attached hydrogen.

Spin label A stable paramagnetic group that is attached to a part of a molecular entity whose microscopic environment is of interest and may be revealed by the electron spin resonance (ESR) spectrum of the spin label.

When a simple paramagnetic molecular entity is used in this way without covalent attachment to the molecular entity of interest it is frequently referred to as a "spin probe".

Spin quantum number From quantum mechanics model of the atom, one of four descriptions of the energy state of an electron wave; this quantum number describes the spin orientation of an electron relative to an external magnetic field.

Spin trapping In certain reactions in solution a transient radical will interact with a diamagnetic reagent to form a more persistent radical. The product radical accumulates to a concentration where detection and, frequently, identification are possible by EPR/ESR spectroscopy. The key reaction is usually one of attachment; the diamagnetic reagent is said to be a "spin trap", and the persistent product radical is then the "spin adduct". The procedure is referred to as spin trapping, and is used for monitoring reactions involving the intermediacy of reactive radicals at concentrations too low for direct observation. Typical spin traps are C-nitroso compounds and nitrones, to which reactive radicals will rapidly add to form nitryl radicals. A quantitative development, in which essentially all reactive radicals generated in a particular system are intercepted, has been referred to as "spin counting". Spin trapping has also been adapted to the interception of radicals generated in both gaseous and solid phases. In these cases the spin adduct is in practice transferred to a liquid solution for observation in order to facilitate interpretation of the EPR/ESR spectra of the radicals obtained.

Spindle fibers The protein fibers formed during prophase of nuclear division; chromosomes attach to these fibers at the centromere.

Spindle The aggregation of microtubules that is involved in the movement and separation of chromosomes during mitosis and meiosis.

Spine A sharp projection from the body or main part of a bone.

Spin-orbit effect An effect that causes atomic energy levels to be split because electrons have intrinsic angular momentum (spin) in addition to their extrinsic orbital angular momentum.

Spinthariscope A device used to detect subatomic particles by the light flashes they produce on a zinc sulfide screen.

Spiracle An opening for ventilation. The opening(s) of the tracheal system of an arthropod or an opening posterior to the eye of a shark, skate, or ray.

Spiral cleavage. A type of embryonic cleavage in which cleavage planes are diagonal to the polar axis and unequal cells are produced by the alternate clockwise and counterclockwise cleavage around the axis of polarity; determinate cleavage.

Spiral valve A spiral portion in the intestine of cartilaginous fishes.

Spirillum A spirally coiled bacterium.

Spirochete A flexible, spiral-shaped bacterium with periplasmic flagella.

Spleen A secondary lymphoid organ where old erythrocytes are destroyed and blood-borne antigens are trapped and presented to lymphocytes.

Split or interrupted gene A structural gene with DNA sequences that code for the final RNA product (expressed sequences or exons) separated by regions coding for RNA absent from the mature RNA (intervening sequences or introns).

Spondylosis Degeneration of a vertebra.

Sponges Invertebrates that consist of a complex aggregation of cells, including collar cells, and have a skeleton of fibers and/or spicules.

Spongiform encephalopathies Degenerative central nervous system diseases in which the brain has a spongy appearance; they appear due to prions.

Spongin Fibrous, collagenous material making up the skeletal network of horny sponges.

Spongioblast Cell in a sponge that secretes spongin, a protein.

Spongocoel Central cavity in sponges.

Spongocyte A cell in sponges that secretes spongin.

Spongy parenchyma A tissue composed of loosely packed, irregular parenchymatous cells containing chloroplasts; commonly found in leaves.

Spontaneous generation The hypothesis that living organisms can arise from nonliving matter.

Spontaneous ovulators Species in which females release eggs whether they have copulated or not.

Spontaneous recovery A process in which a conditioned response has been extinguished and then is followed by some time interval (generally one minute up to one day or more depending upon the species and experimental conditions), after which the animal may immediately exhibit a nearly normal correct response rate upon reintroduction to the test situation.

Sporadic disease A disease that occurs occasionally and at random intervals in a population.

Sporadin Mature trophozoite of a gregarine protozoan.

Sporangiospore A spore that develops within a sporangium.

Sporangium A saclike structure or cell, the contents of which are converted into an indefinite number of spores. It is borne on a special hypha called a sporangiophore.

Spore A differentiated, specialized form that can be used for dissemination, for survival of adverse conditions because of its heat and dessication resistance, and/or for reproduction. Spores are usually unicellular and may develop into vegetative organisms or gametes. They may be produced asexually or sexually and are of many types.

Sporoblast Cell mass that will differentiate into a sporocyst within an oocyst.

Sporocyst 1. Stage of development of a sporozoan protozoan, usually with an enclosing membrane, the oocyst.

2. An asexual stage of development in some digenean trematodes that arises from a miracidium and gives rise to rediae.

Sporocyst residuum Cytoplasmic material "left over" within a sporocyst after sporozoite formation; seen as an amorphous mass.

Sporogony Multiple fission that produces sporozoites after zygote formation. Occurs in the class Sporozoea.

Sporont Undifferentiated cell mass within an unsporulated oocyst.

Sporophyll A leaf that bears sporangia.

Sporophyte The diploid, spore-producing plant in the alternation of generations; undergoes meiosis to produce the haploid spores.

Sporoplasm Amebalike portion of a microsporan or myxosporan cyst that is infective to the next host.

Sporozoite A stage in the life history of many sporozoan protozoa; released from oocysts.

Spout The water vapour and seawater that is observed when whales surface and exhale.

Spread plate A petri dish of solid culture medium with isolated microbial colonies growing on its surface, which has been prepared by spreading a dilute microbial suspension evenly over the agar surface.

Spring overturn Springtime lake phenomenon that occurs when the surface ice melts and the surface water temperature warms to its greatest density at 4C and then sinks, creating a convection current that displaces nutrient-rich bottom waters.

Spring tides The tides with a large tidal range; they occur around the times of full or new moon. Compare neap tides.

Sputum The mucous secretion from the lungs, bronchi, and trachea that is ejected (expectorated) through the mouth.

Squalene A liquid acyclic triterpene hydrocarbon found especially in the liver oil of sharks.

Squama Prominent lobe in the anal angle of a dipteran wing.

Squamous epithelium Simple epithelium of flat, nucleated cells.

Squamous Flat or scalelike.

Squatter towns Shantytowns that occupy land without owner's permission; some are highly organized movements in defiance of authorities; others grow gradually.

Stability In ecological terms, a dynamic equilibrium among the physical and biological factors in an ecosystem or a community; relative homeostasis.

Stabilizing selection Natural selection that results in the decline of both extremes in a phenotypic range; results in a narrowing of the pheno-typic range.

Stable Does not decay. A particle is stable if there exist no processes in which a particle disappears and in its place different particles appear.

Stable equilibrium One in which a force always acts to bring the object back to a certain point.

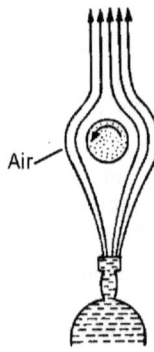

Figure Stable equilibrium

Stable runoff The fraction of water available year-round; usually more important than total runoff when determining human uses.

Stalk A nonliving bacterial appendage produced by the cell and extending from it.

Stalk-and-rush Predators that approach prey as closely as possible, then close with a sudden burst of speed. Contrast with coursers.

Stamen The floral organ that produces pollen; consisting of an anther and filament.

Staminate A unisexual flower having stamens but no pistil.

Staminate flower A flower having stamens but no carpels.

Staminodium A sterile stamen; nonfunctional anthers and often with petaloid filaments.

Standard deviation A statistical measure of the degree of variation from the mean value among the individual measurements in a series of values.

Standard electrode potential Standard electrode potential ($E°$) are defined by measuring the potential relative to a standard hydrogen electrode using 1 mol solution at 25°C. The convention is to designate the cell so that the oxidized form is written first. For example,
Pt(s)|H_2(g)H+(aq)|Zn^{2+}(aq)|Zn(s)

The e.m.f. of this cell is -0.76V and the standard electrode potential of the Zn^{2+}|Zn half cell is - 0.76V.

Standard error of the mean (SEM) A statistical measure of variation most properly restricted to use with a group of means, though often reported as a measure of variation around the mean value in a series of individual measurements.

Standard free energy change The free energy change of a reaction at 1 atmosphere pressure when all reactants and products are present in their standard states; usually the temperature is 25°C.

Standard hydrogen electrode Standard hydrogen electrode is a system in which hydrogen ion and gaseous hydrogen are present in their standard states. The convention is to designate the cell so that the standard hydrogen electrode is written first.

$H_2(g) \rightleftharpoons 2H^+(aq) + 2e^-$

The electrode is used as a reference (of zero) for the values of other standard electrode potentials.

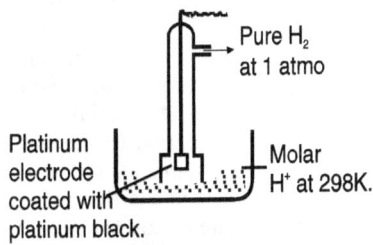

Figure Standard hydrogen electrode

Standard mean ocean water Standard mean ocean water (SMOW) is a standard sample of pure water of accurately known isotopic composition which is maintained by the International Atomic Energy Agency. It is used for precise calibration of density and isotopic composition measurements.

Standard model Physicists' name for the theory of fundamental particles and their interactions. It is widely tested and is accepted as correct by particle physicists.

Standard quantum limit The limit imposed on standard methods of measurement by the uncertainty principle within quantum mechanics.

Standard reduction potential A measure of the tendency of a reductant to lose electrons in an oxidation-reduction (redox) reaction. The more negative the reduction potential of a compound, the better electron donor it is.

Standards Standards are materials containing a known concentration of an analyte. They provide a reference to determine unknown concentrations or to calibrate analytical instruments.

The accuracy of an analytical measurement is how close a result comes to the true value. Determining the accuracy of a measurement usually requires calibration of the analytical method with a known standard. This is often done with standards of several concentrations to make a calibration or working curve.

A primary standard is a reagent that is extremely pure, stable, has no waters of hydration, and has a high molecular weight.

A secondary standard is a standard that is prepared in the laboratory for a specific analysis. It is usually standardized against a primary standard.

Standing crop total amount of plant or animal material in an area at any one time

Standing stock The total amount, or biomass, of an organism at a given time.

Standing waves Condition where two waves of equal frequency traveling in opposite directions meet and form stationary regions of maximum displacement due to constructive interference and stationary regions of zero displacement due to destructive interference.

Stapes Stirrup-shaped innermost bone of the middle ear.

Staphylococcal food poisoning A type of food poisoning caused by ingestion of improperly stored or cooked food in which *Staphylococcus aureus* has grown. The bacteria produce exotoxins that accumulate in the food.

Staphylococcal scalded skin syndrome (SSSS) A disease caused by staphylococci that produce an exfoliative toxin. The skin becomes red (erythema) and sheets of epidermis may separate from the underlying tissue.

Starch A polysaccharide composed of a thousand or more glucose molecules; the chief food storage material of most plants.

Starter culture An inoculum, consisting of a mixture of carefully selected microorganisms, used to start a commercial fermentation.

State of motion When a body changes its position with respect to a fixed point in its surroundings then it is said to be in a state of motion. The states of rest and motion are relative to the frame of reference.

State of rest When a body does not change its position with respect to a fixed point in its surrounding, then it is said to be in a state of rest. The states of rest and motion are relative to the frame of reference.

State Solution to Schrodinger equation defined by a unique set of quantum numbers.

Static electricity Electricity at rest.

Static friction A friction force between surfaces that are not slipping past each other.

Static limit The distance from a rotating black hole where no observer can possibly remain at rest (with respect to the distant stars) because of inertial frame dragging; this region is outside of the event horizon, except at the poles where it meets the horizon at a point. The region between the event horizon and the static limit is called the ergosphere.

Stationary phase The phase of microbial growth in a batch culture when population growth ceases and the growth curve levels off.

Stationary state In quantum mechanics : A state that does not evolve with time.

Statistical mechanics The study of the motion of constituent particles in a gas or other object and how they contribute to the whole.

Statistics The mathematics of the collection, organization, and interpretation of numerical data.

Statoblast Biconvex capsule containing germinative cells and produced by most freshwater ectoprocts by asexual budding. Under favourable conditions it germinates to give rise to new zooid.

Statocyst Sense organ of equilibrium; a fluid-filled cellular cyst containing one or more granules (statoliths) used to sense direction of gravity.

Statolith Small calcareous body resting on tufts of cilia in the statocyst.

Statutory law Rules passed by a state or national legislature.

STC Sound Transmission Class. This is a measure of the extent of sound reduction of noise going through a building element, presented as a rating or class. It denotes the sound attenuation properties of walls, floors and ceilings used to construct building spaces. The higher the STC the better the sound reducing performance of the construction.

Steady state The behaviour of a vibrating system after it has had plenty of time to settle into a steady response to a driving force. In the steady state, the same amount of energy is pumped into the system during each cycle as is lost to damping during the same period.

Steam-point It is the temperature of steam over pure boiling water under 1 atm pressure. The steam point is taken as the upper fixed point for temperature scales.

Stefan-Boltzmann law The radiated power p (rate of emission of electromagnetic energy) of a hot body is proportional to the radiating surface area, a, and the fourth power of the thermodynamic temperature, t. The constant of proportionality is the stefan-boltzmann constant.

Stele The central vascular cylinder of roots and stems of vascular plants.

Stem-nodulating rhizobia Rhizobia that produce nitrogen-fixing structures above the soil surface on plant stems. These most often are observed in tropical plants and produced by Azorhizobium.

Stenohaline Pertaining to aquatic organisms that have restricted tolerance to changes in environmental saltwater concentration.

Stenophagous Eating few kinds of foods.

Stepwise reaction A chemical reaction with at least one reaction intermediate and involving at least two consecutive elementary reactions.

Steradian The supplementary SI unit of solid angle defined as the solid central angle of a sphere that encloses a surface on the sphere equal to the square of the sphere's radius.

Stereocilia The short, modified cilia at the apex of a hair cell.

Stereoelectronic control Control of the nature of the products of a chemical reaction (or of its rate) by stereoelectronic factors. The term is usually applied in the framework of an orbital approximation. The variations of molecular orbital energies with relative nuclear geometry (along a reaction coordinate) are then seen as consequences of variations in basis-orbital overlaps.

Stereoelectronic Pertaining to the dependence of the properties (especially the energy) of a molecular entity in a particular electronic state (or of a transition state) on relative nuclear geometry. The electronic ground state is usually considered, but the term can apply to excited states as well. Stereoelectronic effects are ascribed to the different alignment of electronic orbitals in different arrangements of nuclear geometry.

Stereogastrula A solid type of gastrula, such as the planula of cnidarians.

Stereom Meshwork structure of endoskeletal ossicles of echinoderms.

Stereoselectivity, stereoselective Stereoselectivity is the preferential formation in a chemical reaction of one stereoisomer over another. When the stereoisomers are enantiomers, the phenomenon is called enantioselectivity and is quantitatively expressed by the enantiomer excess; when they are diastereoisomers, it is called diastereoselectivity and is quantitatively expressed by the diastereomer excess. Reactions are termed (100%) stereoselective if the discrimination is complete or partially (x%) stereoselective if one product predominates. The discrimination may also be referred to semiquantitatively as high or low stereoselectivity.

Stereospecificity, stereospecific 1. A reaction is termed stereospecific if starting materials differing only in their configuration are converted into stereoisomeric products. According to this definition, a stereospecific process is necessarily stereoselective but not all stereoselective processes are stereospecific. Stereospecificity may be total (100%) or partial. The term is also applied to situations where reaction can be performed with only one stereoisomer. For example the exclusive formation of trans-1,2-dibromocyclohexane upon bromina-tion of cyclohexene is a stereospecific process, although the analogous reaction with (E)-cyclohexene has not been performed.

2. The term has also been applied to describe a reaction of very high stereoselectivity, but this usage is unnecessary and is discouraged.

Stereotyped behaviour A pattern of behaviour repeated with little variation in performance.

Sterilization The process by which all living cells, viable spores, viruses, and viroids are either destroyed or removed from an object or habitat.

Stern-Gerlach experiment An experiment that demonstrates the features of spin (intrinsic angular momentum) as a distinct entity apart from orbital angular momentum.

Sternite Main ventral sclerite of a somite of an arthropod.

Sternum Ventral plate of an arthropod body segment; breastbone of vertebrates.

Steroid An organic substance whose molecules include four complex rings of carbon and hydrogen atoms. Examples are estrogen, cholesterol, and testosterone.

Sterol One of a class of organic compounds containing a molecular skeleton of four fused carbon rings; it includes cholesterol, sex hormones, adrenocortical hormones, and vitamin D.

Stewards Protectors, careful managers of land and nature's resources.

Stewardship A philosophy that holds that humans have a unique responsibility to manage, care for, and improve nature.

Stichosome Column of large, rectangular cells called stichocytes, supporting and secreting into the esophagus of most nematodes of the family Trichuridae.

Stieda body Plug in the inner wall of one end of a coccidian oocyst.

Stiffness The stiffness of a system with respect to a deformation is the second derivative of the energy with respect to the corresponding displacement; this measures the curvature of the potential energy surface along a particular direction. Positive stiffness is associated with stability, and a large stiffness can result in a small positional uncertainty in the presence of thermal excitation. Negative stiffnesses correspond to unstable locations on the potential energy surface. Alternative terms for stiffness include force gradient and rigidity.

Stigma A light-sensitive eyespot, which is found in some algae and photosynthetic protozoa; it is believed to be involved in phototaxis, at least in some cases.

Stimulant A psychoactive compound that excites and enhances mental alertness and physical activity; often reduces fatigue and suppresses hunger.

Stimulus Any form of energy an animal is able to detect with its receptors.

Stimulus filter The ability of the nervous system to block incoming stimuli that are unimportant for the animal.

Stipe A supporting stalk; such as those in mushrooms and brown algae.

Stipule A small appendage found in pairs at the base of leaves.

Stochastic A stochastic event is based on random behaviour. The occurrence of individual events cannot be predicted, although measuring the distribution of all observations usually follows a predictable pattern. These patterns can be described by statistical means. An example is the decay of radio active material, where a clump of matter has a measurable and thus predictable half-life time. It is impossible, however, to mark an individual atom and predict when it will decay and emit radiation. The latter process is a stochastic event.

Stock The size of a population.

Stoichiometric number Stoichiometric number (v) is the number appearing before the symbol for each compound in the equation for a chemical reaction. By convention, it is negative for reactants and positive for products.

Stoichiometry Stoichiometry is the relative proportions in which elements from compounds or in which substances react. Every chemical reaction has its characteristic proportions. For example, when methane unites with oxygen in complete combustion, 1mol of methane requires 2mol of oxygen.

$$CH_4 + 2O_2 \rightleftarrows CO_2 + 2H_2O$$

At the same time, 1mol of carbon dioxide and 2 mol of water are formed as reaction productions.

Alternatively, 16g of methane and 64g of oxygen produce 44g of carbon dioxide and 36g of water.

Stolon A rootlike extension of the body wall giving rise to buds that may develop into new zooids, thus forming a compound animal in which the zooids remain united by the stolon. Found in some colonial anthozoans, hydrozoans, ectoprocts, and ascidians.

Stoma The epidermal complex consisting of two guard cells and the pore between them.

Stomach The expansion of the alimentary canal between the esophagus and duodenum.

Stomata The pore openings underneath plant leaves that can open and close according to the metabolic needs of the plant. They are the ports for exchange of oxygen and carbon dioxide gas for photosynthesis, but also release excess water into the air. This process of water loss maintains a steady flow of water and minerals from the roots to the leaves. To minimize the water loss, many plants regulate the duration and time of day when stomatas are open.

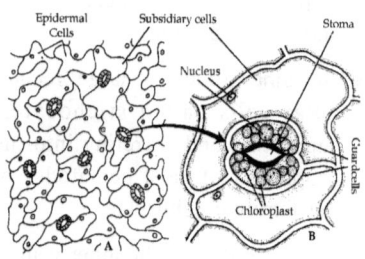

Figure Stomata

Stomates The small openings in leaves, herbaceous stems, and fruits through which gases and water vapor pass.

Stomochord Anterior evagination of the dorsal wall of the buccal cavity into the proboscis of hemi-chordates; the buccal diverticulum.

Stoneworts A group of approximately 250 species of algae that have a complex growth pattern, with nodal regions from which whorls of branches arise; they are abundant in fresh to brackish waters.

Stony corals Anthozoans, often colonial, that secrete a calcareous skeleton.

Stopped flow A technique for following the kinetics of reactions in solution (usually in the millisecond time range) in which two reactant solutions are rapidly mixed by being forced through a mixing chamber. The flow of the mixed solution along a uniform tube is then suddenly arrested. At a fixed position along the tube the solution is monitored (as a function of time following the stoppage of the flow) by some method with a rapid response (e.g. photometry).

Storage cell An electrochemical cell in which the reacting materials are regenerated by the use of a reverse current from an external source.

Strain 1. A population of organisms that descends from a single organism or pure culture isolate.

2. Strain is present in a molecular entity or transition structure if the energy is enhanced because of unfavourable bond lengths, bond angles, or dihedral angles ("torsional strain") relative to a standard.

It is quantitatively defined as the standard enthalpy of a structure relative to a strainless structure (real or hypothetical) made up from the same atoms with the same types of bonding. (The enthalpy of formation of cyclopropane is 53.6 kJ mol-1, whereas the enthalpy of formation based on three "normal" methylene groups, from acyclic models, is -62 kJ mol-1. On this basis cyclopropane is destabilized by ca. 115 kJ mol-1 of strain energy.)

Strange quark (s) The third flavour of quark, with electric charge -1/3.

Strata Layers of sedimentary rock, the oldest rocks occurring at the bottom.

Strategic minerals Materials a country cannot produce itself but that it uses for essential materials or processes.

Stratification The separation of the water column into layers, with the densest at the bottom and the least dense at the surface. A stratified water column is said to be stable. An unstable column results when the surface water becomes more dense than the water below.

Stratified In layers.

Stratosphere Stratosphere is the part of the earth's atmosphere extending from the top of the troposphere (typically 10km to 15km above the surface) to about 50km. It is characterized by an increase in temperature with increasing altitude.

Streak plate A petri dish of solid culture medium with isolated microbial colonies growing on its surface, which has been prepared by spreading a microbial mixture over the agar surface, using an inoculating loop.

Streambank erosion Washing away of soil from banks of established streams, creeks, or rivers, often as a result of the removal of trees and brush along streambanks or cattle damage to the banks.

Streptococcal pneumonia An endogenous infection of the lungs caused by *Streptococcus* *pneumoniae* that occurs in predisposed individuals.

Streptococcal sore throat One of the most common bacterial infections of humans. It is commonly referred to as "strep throat." The disease is spread by droplets of saliva or nasal secretions and is caused by *Streptococcus spp.* (particularly group A streptococci).

Streptolysin-O (SLO) A specific hemolysin produced by *Streptococcus pyogenes* that is inactivated by oxygen (hence the "O" in its name). SLO causes beta-hemolysis of blood cells on agar plates incubated anaerobically.

Streptolysin-S (SLS) A product produced by Streptococcus pyogenes that is bound to the bacterial cell but may sometimes be released. SLS causes beta hemolysis on aerobically incubated blood-agar plates and can act as a leukocidin by killing leukocytes that phagocytose the bacterial cell to which it is bound.

Streptomycin A bactericidal aminoglycoside antibiotic produced by *Streptomyces griseus*.

Stress Physical, chemical, or emotional factors that place a strain on an animal. Plants also experience physiological stress under adverse environmental conditions.

Stress shock A loose set of physical, psychological, and/or behavioural changes thought to result from the stress of excess competition and extreme closeness to other members of the same species.

Stretch receptor Sensory receptor that responds to stretch; found in muscle tissue, lungs, and other organs that undergo changes in position or size.

Stridulation The production of sound by an insect rubbing one body part against another (e.g., in male crickets).

Strike Deposition of fly eggs or larvae on a living host.

Strip-farming Planting different kinds of crops in alternating strips along land contours; when one crop is harvested, the other crop remains to protect the soil and prevent water from running straight down a hill.

Strip-mining Removing surface layers over coal seams using giant, earth-moving equipment; creates a huge open-pit from which coal is scooped by enormous surface-operated machines and transported by trucks; an alternative to deep mines.

Strobila A stage in the development of the scyphozoan jellyfish. Also, the chain of proglottids of a tapeworm.

Strobilocercoid Cysticercoid that undergoes some strobilation; found only in Schistotaenia.

Strobilus A number of sporangia- or ovule-bearing structures (sporophylls, sporangiophores, scales, etc.) Grouped together on an axis.

Stroma The matrix between the grana in chloroplasts and site of the dark reactions of photosynthesis.

Stroma thylakoid A thylakoid that does not occur in a granum; connects separate grana.

Stromatolite Dome-like microbial mat communities consisting of filamentous photosynthetic bacteria and occluded sediments (often calcareous or siliceous). They usually have a laminar structure. Many are fossilized, but some modern forms occur.

Strong force The force that binds protons and neutrons within atomic nuclei and is effective only at distances less than 10—13 centimeters.

Strong interaction The interaction responsible for binding quarks, antiquarks, and gluons to make hadrons. Residual strong interactions provide the nuclear binding force.

Strong nuclear force The force that holds nuclei together against electrical repulsion.

Strong nuclear interaction The interaction that holds the particles of the nucleus together and is independent of charge.

Structural colour A colour that results when light is reflected by a particular surface.

Structural formula A structural formula is a diagram that shows how the atoms in a molecule are bonded together. Atoms are represented by their element symbols and covalent bonds are represented by lines. The symbol for carbon is often not drawn. Most structural formulas don't show the actual shape of the molecule (they're like floor plans that show the layout but not the 3D shape of a house).

Structural gene A gene that codes for the synthesis of a polypeptide or polynucleotide with a nonregulatory function.

Structural molecule A complex molecule, such as cellulose, that provides support and protection.

Structural volume The interior of a diamondoid structure typically consists of a dense network of covalent bonds; a larger excluded volume, however, is determined by nonbonded repulsions at the surface. The structural volume corresponds to a region smaller than the excluded volume, chosen to make properties such as the strength and modulus nearly size independent by correcting for surface effects.

Structure Patterns of organization, both spatial and functional, in a community.

Structure, high-resolution The high resolution structure of a molecule refers to its atomic organization in three-dimensional space. It is either obtained from analysis of diffraction patterns of high energy radiation (X-rays, electron waves) or nuclear magnetic resonance spectra (NMR). Structural information has an important place in biological studies at the molecular level, because structures can be used to elucidate the detailed mechanism of a chemical reaction, a biological binding events such as hormone signaling or immunological defenses, or nutrient transport (absorption) across intestinal epithelial cell layers and cell membranes. The structural analysis of DNA in 1953 has helped understand the mechanism of replication of genetic information during reproduction as well as the mechanism of genetic encoding, reading (transcription), and synthesis (translation) of amino acid sequences in proteins and enzymes.

Structure-borne noise This refers to noise which is generated by vibrations induced in the ground and/or structure. These vibrations excite walls and slabs in buildings and cause them to radiate noise. This type of noise can not be attenuated by barriers or walls but requires the interposition of a resilient (neoprene, springs etc.) break between the source and the receiver.

Style Terminal segment of the antenna of a brachyceran dipteran. It is drawn into a sharp point.

Stylops Member of the insect order Strepsiptera.

Stylostome Hardened, tubelike structure secreted by a feeding chigger mite.

Subacute sclerosing panencephalitis Diffuse inflammation of the brain resulting from virus and prion infections.

Subatomic particle Any particle that is small compared to the size of the atom.

Subchelate Condition of an arthropod appendage in which the terminal podomere can fold back like a pincer against the subterminal podomere.

Subduction The downward movement of a plate into the mantle that occurs in trenches, which are also known as subduction zones.

Suberin A fatty material found in the cell walls of cork cells and the Casparian strip of the endodermis.

Subgingival plaque The plaque that forms at the dentogingival margin and extends down into the gingival tissue.

Sublimation The process by which water can move between solid and gaseous states without ever becoming liquid.

Submarine canyon A narrow, deep depression in the continental shelf formed by the erosion of rivers or glaciers before the shelf was submerged.

Submergent plant community a marine plant community restricted to subtidal environments.

Submetacentric Pertaining to a chromosome with a centromere located between the center and one end of the chromosome.

Subnivean Applied to environments beneath snow, in which snow insulates against a colder atmospheric temperature.

Subsidence A settling of the ground surface caused by the collapse of porous formations that result from withdrawal of large amounts of groundwater, oil, or other under-ground materials.

Subsoil A layer of soil beneath the topsoil that has lower organic

Substiedal body Additional plug material underlying a Stieda body.

content and higher concentrations of fine mineral particles; often contains soluble compounds and clay particles carried down by percolating water.

Substituent An atom or group of bonded atoms that can be considered to have replaced a hydrogen atom (or two hydrogen atoms in the special case of bivalent groups) in a parent mole-cular entity (real or hypothetical).

Substrate-level phosphorylation The synthesis of ATP from ADP by phosphorylation coupled with the exergonic breakdown of a high-energy organic substrate molecule.

Subsurface biosphere The region below the plant root zone where microbial populations can grow and function.

Sugar A carbohydrate with a characteristically sweet taste. Sugars are classified as monosaccharides, disaccharides, or trisaccharides.

Sulphate reduction The process of sulphate use as an oxidizing agent, which results in the accumulation of reduced forms of sulphur such as sulphide, or incorporation of sulphur into organic molecules, usually as sulphydryl groups.

Sulphonamide A chemotherapeutic agent that has the SO_2-NH_2 group and is a derivative of sulfanilamide.

Sunspot A temporary disturbed area in the solar photosphere that appears dark because it is cooler than the surrounding areas. Sunspots consist of concentrations of strong magnetic flux. They usually occur in pairs or groups of opposite polarity that move in unison across the face of the Sun as it rotates.

Superantigen Superantigens are bacterial proteins that stimulate the immune system much more extensively than do normal antigens. They stimulate T cells to proliferate nonspecifically through simultaneous interaction with class II MHC proteins on antigen-presenting cells and variable regions on the b chain of the T-cell receptor complex. Examples include streptococcal scarlet fever toxins, staphylococcal toxic shock syndrome toxin-1, and streptococcal M protein.

Superconductor Superconductor is a material that experiences a nearly total loss of electrical resistivity below a critical temperature T_c.

Super-cooled Water in the liquid phase when the temperature is below the freezing point.

Superfluid Superfluid is a fluid with near-zero viscosity and extremely high thermal conductivity. Liquid helium exhibits these properties below 2.186K (the λ point).

Superinfection A new bacterial or fungal infection of a patient that is resistant to the drug(s) being used for treatment.

Supernova The death of a star, usually a very violent process.

Superoxide Superoxide ion. A binary compound containing oxygen in the -½ oxidation state. For example, KO_2 is potassium superoxide, an ionic compound containing the superoxide ion, O_2^-.

Supersaturated Containing more than the normal saturation amount of a solute at a given temperature.

Suppressor mutation A mutation that overcomes the effect of another mutation and produces the normal phenotype.

Surface plot A three-dimensional plot mapping the intensity of radiation from a region as a distorted surface. More intense radiation is represented by higher points on the surface. Therefore, regions of intense radiation resemble mountains on the earth.

Surrogate A person or animal that functions as a substitute for another. In the case of a surrogate mother, it is where a woman or female animal carries an embryo and ultimately gives birth to a baby that was formed from the egg of another female.

Sustainable agriculture Agriculture which minimises inputs in the form of fuel and chemicals and outputs in the form of air, groundwater and soil pollutants whilst producing soils that retain fertility for future generations.

Sustainable development An approach to development that meets the needs of the present without compromising the ability of future generations to meet their own needs. It seeks to ensure that current development does not alter the environment's ability to recover from any damage sustained, and which also makes use of renewable resources.

Svedberg unit The unit used in expressing the sedimentation coefficient; the greater a particle's Svedberg value, the faster it travels in a centrifuge.

Swab A wad of absorbent material usually wound around one end of a small stick and used for applying medication or for removing material from an area; also, a dacron-tipped polystyrene applicator.

Swarm cell A flagellated cell; the term is usually applied to the motile cells of the Myxomycota.

Symbiosis The living together or close association of two dissimilar organisms, each of these organisms being known as a symbiont.

Symbiosome The final nitrogen-fixing form of Rhizobium that is active within root nodule cells.

Symptom A change during a disease that a person subjectively experiences. Sometimes the term symptom is used more broadly to include any observed signs.

Synapse The synapse is a specialized portion of a neuron or nerve cell that is used for cell to cell communi-cation with other neurons and muscle cells. The chemical synapse contains packaged neurotransmitters that can be released upon an electrical signal reaching the synapse from the dendrites and cell body of the neuron, where action potentials originate. A neuron can have multiple synapses, often with different signaling properties being excitatory or inhibitory synapses. Multiple synapses signaling to a receiving neuron or muscle can strengthen a stimulus or inhibition by activating some or all of the synapses through addition of signaling strength. In addition to chemical synapses, electrical synapses are propagating an action potential signal without a neurotransmitter, but directly by coupling membranes of adjacent cells using gap junctions. The feature of both chemical and electrical synapses allows the signal to propagate unidirectional. The signal cannot reverse. However, feedback signals between the signaling and receiving cell to strengthen or weaken the synaptic interaction, a process called synaptic plasticity.

Synchrotron A type of circular accelerator in which the particles travel in synchronized bunches at fixed radius.

Syntrophism The association in which the growth of one organism either depends on, or is improved by, the provision of one or more growth factors or nutrients by a neighbouring organism. Sometimes both organisms benefit. This type of mutualism is also known as cross-feeding or the satellite phenomenon.

Systematics The scientific study of organisms with the ultimate objective being to characterize and arrange them in an orderly manner; often considered synonymous with taxonomy.

Systematic epidemiology The field of epidemiology that focuses on the ecological and social factors that influence the development of emerging and reemerging infectious diseases.

Systeme International Fancy name for the metric system.

Systemic lupus erythematosus An autoimmune, inflammatory disease that may affect every tissue of the body.

T

Tailings Ground rock remaining after particular ore minerals are extracted.

Tails Depleted uranium, with about 0.3% U-235.

Tangential Tangent to a curve. In circular motion, used to mean tangent to the circle, perpendicular to the radial direction *Cf.* radial.

T cell or T lymphocyte A type of lymphocyte derived from bone marrow stem cells that matures into an immunologically competent cell under the influence of the thymus. T cells are involved in a variety of cell-mediated immune reactions.

T lymphocyte (T cell) Type of lymphocyte responsible for cell-mediated immunity; includes both cytotoxic T cells and helper T cells.

Tau The third flavour of charged lepton (in order of increasing mass), with electric charge -1.

Taxon A group into which related organisms are classified.

Taxonomy The science of biological classification; it consists of three parts: classification, nomenclature, and identification.

Tay sachs disease A lethal hereditary disease. The progressive accumulation of a substance called ganglioside in the brain causes paralysis, mental deterioration and blindness. Death usually occurs before the age of four.

TB skin test Tuberculin hypersensitivity test for a previous or current infection with *Mycobacterium tuberculosis*.

T-cell antigen receptor (TCR) The receptor on the T cell surface consisting of two antigen-binding peptide chains; it is associated with a large number of other glycoproteins. Binding of antigen to the TCR, usually in association with MHC, activates the T cell.

T-dependent antigen An antigen that effectively stimulates B-cell response only with the aid of T-helper cells that produce interleukin-2 and B-cell growth factor.

Teichoic acids Polymers of glycerol or ribitol joined by phosphates; they are found in the cell walls of gram-positive bacteria.

Telomere End of a chromosome, associated with a characteristic DNA sequence that is replicated in a special way. Counteracts the tendency of the chromosome otherwise to shorten with each round of replication.

Telophase Final stage of mitosis in which the two sets of separated chromosomes decondense and become enclosed by nuclear envelopes.

Telos That which makes a thing (organism) what it is.

Temperate phages Bacteriophages that can infect bacteria and establish a lysogenic relationship rather than immediately lysing their hosts.

Temperature A measure of the amount of heat energy in a substance, such as air, a star, or the human body. Because heat energy corresponds to motions and vibrations of molecules, temperature provides information about the amount of molecular motion occurring in a substance.

Template strand A strand of DNA or RNA that specifies the base sequence of a newly synthesized complementary strand of DNA or RNA.

Tensional stress The opposite of compressional stress; occurs when one part of a plate moves away from another part that does not move.

Terminator A sequence that marks the end of a gene and stops transcription.

Terminator genes Genes exploited in terminator technology.

Terminator technology A biotechnological 'technology protection system' that renders sterile the seeds which are saved the first generation after the first sowing.

Tertiary structure Complex three-dimensional form of a macromolecule, especially a protein.

Tertiary treatment The removal from sewage of inorganic nutrients, heavy metals, viruses, etc., by chemical and biological means after micro-organisms have degraded dissolved organic material during secondary sewage treatment.

Tesla Tesla (T) is the SI derived unit of magnetic flux density. The tesla is magnetic flux density of a magnetic flux of one weber per square metre ($T = Wb/m^2$). The unit is named after the Croatian scientist Nikola Tesla (1857-1943), equal to $V\ s/m^2$.

Test A loose-fitting shell of an amoeba.

Tetanolysin A hemolysin that aids in tissue destruction and is produced by *Clostridium tetani*.

Tetanospasmin The neurotoxic component of the tetanus toxin, which causes the muscle spasms of tetanus. Tetanospasmin production is under the control of a plasmid gene.

Tetanus An often fatal disease caused by the anaerobic, spore-forming bacillus *Clostridium tetani*, and characterized by muscle spasms and convulsions.

Tetracyclines A family of antibiotics with a common four ring structure, which are isolated from the genus *Streptomyces* or produced semi-synthetically; all are related to chlortetracycline or oxytetracycline.

Tetrapartite associations A mutualistic association of the same plant with three different types of microorganisms.

Thalassaemias A group of disorders in which there is reduced production of one or more of the globin chains which constitute normal haemoglobin. This imbalance of globin chains results in chronic anaemia, which is a common cause of premature death and much suffering. Inheritance of each of the many genes which may be responsible is recessive.

Thallus A type of body that is devoid of root, stem, or leaf; characteristic of some algae, many fungi, and lichens.

T-helper (TH) cell A cell that is needed for T-cell-dependent antigens to be effectively presented to B cells. It also promotes cell-mediated immune responses.

Theoretical yield Theoretical yield is the maximum quantity of a product that could be formed in a chemical reaction if all the limiting reactant reacted to form products (distinguished from actual yield).

Theory A set of principles and concepts that have survived rigorous testing and that provide a systematic account of some aspect of nature.

Thermal capacity The quantity of heat required to raise the temperature of the whole body by one degree is called its thermal capacity.

Thermal conductivity Thermal conductivity (λ) is rate of heat flow divided by area and by temperature gradient.

Thermal death time (TDT) The shortest period of time needed to kill all the organisms in a microbial population at a specified temperature and under defined conditions.

Thermal energy Careful writers make a distinction between heat and thermal energy, but the distinction is often ignored in casual speech, even among physicists. Properly, thermal energy is used to mean the total amount of energy possessed by an object, while heat indicates the amount of thermal energy transferred in or out. The term heat is used to include both meanings.

Thermal equilibrium When the two bodies in contact are at the same temperature and there is no flow of heat between them, these are said to be in thermal equilibrium. The common temperature of the bodies in thermal equilibrium is called the equilibrium temperature.

Thermal expansion The increase in the size of an object on heating is called thermal expansion.

Thermal fluctuations The thermal energy of a system has a mean value determined by the temperature and by the structure of the system. Statistical deviations about that mean are termed thermal fluctuations; these are of great importance in determining both

Thermophile

rates of chemical reactions and error rates in nanomechanical systems.

Thermal gas A collection of particles that collide with each other and exchange energy frequently, giving a distribution of particle energies that can be characterized by a single temperature.

Thermal particle A particle that is part of a thermal gas.

Thermal radiation Radiation released by virtue of an object's heat, namely, the transfer of heat energy into the radiative energy of electromagnetic waves. Examples of thermal radiation are sunlight, the orange glow of an electric range, and the light from in incandescent light bulb.

Thermal reactor A reactor in which the fission chain reaction is sustained primarily by slow neutrons, and hence requiring a moderator.

Thermoacidophiles A group of bacteria that grow best at acid phs and high temperatures; they are members of the Archaea.

Thermodynamic laws Thermodynamic laws are the foundation of the science of thermodynamics:

First law: The internal energy of an isolated system is constant; if energy is supplied to the system in the form of heat dq and work dw, then the change in energy $du = dq + dw$.

Second law: No process is possible in which the only result is the transfer of heat from a reservoir and its complete conversion to work.

Third law: The entropy of a perfect crystal approaches zero as the thermodynamic temperature approaches zero.

Thermodynamics The study of heat, work, and entropy on a level more macroscopic than statistical mechanics

Thermoelastic Both stress and temperature changes alter the dimensions of an object having a finite stiffness and a nonzero thermal expansion coefficient. Applying a stress then produces a temperature change; this can result in a heat flow which then changes the stress: these are thermoelastic effects, and result in losses of free energy.

Thermometer It is a device used for numerical measurement of temperature. The commonly used thermometer is mercury thermometer.

Thermonuclear fusion The combination of atomic nuclei at high temperatures to form more massive nuclei with the simultaneous release of energy. Thermonuclear fusion is the power source at the core of the Sun. Controlled Thermonuclear fusion reactors, when successfully implemented, could become an attractive source of power on the Earth.

Thermophile A microorganism that can grow at temperatures of 55°C or higher; the minimum is usually around 45°C.

Thermosphere Thermosphere is the layer of the earth's atmosphere extending from the top of the mesosphere to about 500 km. It is characterized by a rapid increase in temperature with increasing altitude up to about 200 km, followed by a leveling off in the 300 km - 500 km region.

Thio A prefix that means, "replace an oxygen with sulfur". For example, sulphate ion is SO_4^{2-}; thiosulphate ion is $S_2O_3^{2-}$. Cyanate ion is OCN^-; thiocyanate ion is SCN^-.

Thioester bond High-energy bond formed by a condensation reaction between an acid (acyl) group and a thiol group (- SH); seen, for example, in acetyl CoA and in many enzyme-substrate complexes.

Thiol An SH group, or a molecule containing one. Also known as a sulphydryl or mercapto group.

Third law of motion Whenever two objects interact, the force exerted on one object is equal in size and opposite in direction to the force exerted on the other object; forces always occur in matched pairs that are equal and opposite.

Three way safety bulb The three way safety bulb is used for pipeting. The attachment is placed over the mouth of the pipet. The air (A) valve is used to empty the bulb of air. The suction (S) valve is used to draw liquid into the pipet. The empty (E) valve is used to drain liquid out of a pipet.

Thrush Infection of the oral mucous membrane by the fungus Candida albicans; also known as oral candidiasis.

Thylakoid A flattened sac in the chloroplast stroma that contains photosynthetic pigments and the photosynthetic electron transport chain; light energy is trapped and used to form ATP and NAD(P)H in the thylakoid membrane.

Thymine The pyrimidine 5-methyluracil that is found in nucleosides, nucleotides, and DNA.

Thymus A primary lymphoid organ in the chest that is necessary in early life for the development of immunological functions. T-cell maturation takes place here.

Ti or Ri plasmid A plasmid obtained from Agrobacterium tumefaciens that is used to insert genes into plant cells.

Tight junction Cell-cell junction that seals adjacent epithelial cells together, preventing the passage of most dissolved molecules from one side of the epithelial sheet to the other.

Tight-receptor structures A receptor structure in which a bound ligand of a particular kind is confined on all sides by repulsive interactions. A tight-receptor structure discriminates strongly against all molecules larger than the target.

Time The fourth dimension of space-time that allows events to occur linearly as humans recognize them, presumably in the direction of increased entropy.

Time dilation Relativistic incongruence of two interpretations of time due to differently accelerated reference frames.

Time period The time taken to complete one oscillation is called the time period of an oscillation. The time period of a pendulum does not depend upon the mass of the bob and amplitude of oscillation. The time period of a pendulum is directly proportional to the square root of the length and inversely proportional to the square root of the acceleration due to gravity.

Timeline Series of events of a distinguished reality

T-independent antigen An antigen that triggers a B cell into immunoglobulin production without T-cell cooperation.

Tinea A name applied to many different kinds of superficial fungal infections of the skin, nails, and hair, the specific type (depending on characteristic appearance, etiologic agent, and site) usually designated by a modifying term.

Tinea corporis A fungal infection of the smooth parts of the skin caused by either *Trichophyton rubrum, T. mentagrophytes*, or *Microsporum canis*.

Tinea cruris A fungal infection of the groin caused by either *Epidermophyton floccosum, Trichophyton* mentagrophytes, or *T. rubrum*; also known as jock itch.

Tinea manuum A fungal infection of the hand caused by *Trichophyton rubrum, T. mentagrophytes*, or *E. floccosum*.

Tinea pedis A fungal infection of the foot caused by *Trichophyton rubrum, T. mentagrophytes*, or *E. floccosum*; also known as athlete's foot.

Tinea unguium A fungal infection of the nail bed caused by either *Trichophyton rubrum* or *T. mentagrophytes*.

Tinea versicolour A fungal infection caused by the yeast, Malassezia furfur, that forms brownish-red scales on the skin of the trunk, neck, face, and arms.

Tissue A collection of cells specialised to perform a particular function. Tissues are usually composed of several cell types. Organs, e.g. heart, are made up of such tissues.

Tissue culture A process involving the separation of cells from each other and their growth in a container of liquid nutrients.

Titer Reciprocal of the highest dilution of an antiserum that gives a positive reaction in the test being used.

Titration curve Titration curve is a graphical representation of the amount of a species present vs. Volume of solution added during a titration.

Tonne Tonne (t) is an alternative name for megagram (1000 kg).

Tonsillitis Inflammation of the tonsils, especially the palatine tonsils often due to *S. pyogenes* infection.

Top quark (t) The sixth flavour of quark, with electric charge 2/3. Its mass is much greater than any other quark or lepton.

Toroidal radius In a solar loop structure, it is the distance from the axis of the loop to the center of the "semi-circle" that the loop forms. Half of the distance from one loop footpoint to the other loop footpoint. For a doughnut, it is the distance from the center of the doughnut hole to the center of the pastry. See also Poloidal Radius.

Torque The rate of change of angular momentum; a numerical measure of a force's ability to twist on an object.

Total internal reflection Condition where all light is reflected back from a boundary between materials; occurs when light arrives at a boundary at the critical angle or beyond.

Toxaemia The condition caused by toxins in the blood of the host.

Toxic shock-like syndrome (TSLS) A disease caused by an invasive group A streptococcus infection that is characterized by a rapid drop in blood pressure, failure of many organs, and a very high fever. It probably results from the release of one or more streptococcal pyrogenic exotoxins.

Toxigenicity The capacity of an organism to produce a toxin.

Toxin A microbial product or component that can injure another cell or organism at low concen-trations. Often the term refers to a poisonous protein, but toxins may be lipids and other substances.

Toxin neutralization The inactivation of toxins by specific antibodies, called antitoxins, that react with them.

Toxoid A bacterial exotoxin that has been modified so that it is no longer toxic but will still stimulate antitoxin formation when injected into a person or animal.

Toxoplasmosis A disease of animals and humans caused by the parasitic protozoan, *Toxoplasma gondii*.

Trachoma A chronic infectious disease of the conjunctiva and cornea, producing pain, inflammation and sometimes blindness. It is caused by *Chlamydia trachomatis* serotypes A-C.

Track The record of the path of a particle traversing a detector.

Transamination The removal of amino acid's amino group by transferring it to an a-keto acid acceptor.

Transcriptase An enzyme that catalyzes transcription; in viruses with RNA genomes, this enzyme is an RNA-dependent RNA polymerase that is used to make RNA copies of the RNA genomes.

Transcription The process in which single-stranded RNA with a base sequence complementary to the template strand of DNA or RNA is synthesized.

Transduction The transfer of genes between bacteria by bacteriophages.

Transfer host A host that is not necessary for the completion of a

Transfer RNA A small RNA that binds an amino acid and delivers it to the ribosome for incorporation into a polypeptide chain during protein synthesis.

Transformation A mode of gene transfer in bacteria in which a piece of free DNA is taken up by a bacterial cell and integrated into the recipient genome.

Transgenic animal or plant An animal or plant that has gained new genetic information from the insertion of foreign DNA. It may be produced by such techniques as injecting DNA into animal eggs, electroporation of mammalian cells and plant cell protoplasts, or shooting DNA into plant cells with a gene gun.

Transition metals This group of metals is distinguished from other metals not by their physical properties, but by their electronic structure. Transition metals are elements characterized by a partially filled d subshell. The First Transition Series comprises scandium (Sc), titanium (Ti), vanadium (V), chromium (Cr), manganese (Mn), iron (Fe), cobalt (Co), nickel (Ni) and copper (Cu). The Second and Third Transition Series include the lanthanides and actinides, respectively.

The transition metals are noted for their variability in oxidation state. Thus, manganese has two electrons in its outside shell and five electrons in the next shell down, and exhibits oxidation states of +1, +2, +3, +4, +5, +6 and +7.

They are also characterized by the fact that well into the series, going from left to right, the properties of succeeding metals do not differ greatly from preceding ones.

Transition mutations Mutations that involve the substitution of a different purine base for the purine present at the site of the mutation or the substitution of a different pyrimidine for the normal pyrimidine.

Translation Protein synthesis; the process by which the genetic message carried by mRNA directs the synthesis of polypeptides with the aid of ribosomes and other cell constituents.

Transmission electron microscope A microscope in which an image is formed by passing an electron beam through a specimen and focusing the scattered electrons with magnetic lenses.

Transmittance Transmittance (τ) is ratio of the radiant or luminous flux at a given wavelength that is transmitted to that of the incident radiation. Also called transmission factor.

Transmutation Changing atoms of one element into those of another by neutron bombardment, causing neutron capture.

Transovarian passage The passage of a microorganism such as a rickettsia from generation to generation of hosts through tick eggs. (No humans or other mammals are needed as reservoirs for continued propagation of the rickettsias.)

Transpeptidation 1. The reaction that forms the peptide cross-links during peptidoglycan synthesis.

2. The reaction that forms a peptide bond during the elonga-tion cycle of protein synthesis.

Transposition The movement of a piece of DNA around the chromosome.

Transposon A DNA segment that carries the genes required for transposition and moves about the chromosome; if it contains genes other than those required for transposition, it may be called a composite transposon. Often the name is reserved only for transposable elements that also contain genes unrelated to transposition.

Transuranic element A very heavy element formed artificially by neutron capture and possibly subsequent beta decay(s). Has a higher atomic number than uranium (92). All are radioactive. Neptunium, plutonium, americium and curium are the best-known.

Transverse waves A wave in which the particles of the medium oscillate in a direction perpendicular of the direction of propagation of wave is called the transverse wave. Water waves, light waves and radio waves are examples of transverse waves.

Figure Transverse waves

Transversion mutations Mutations that result from the substitution of a purine base for the normal pyrimidine or a pyrimidine for the normal purine.

Traveler's diarrhea A type of diarrhea resulting from ingestion of certain viruses, bacteria, or protozoa normally absent from the traveler's environment. One of the major pathogens is enterotoxigenic *Escherichia coli*.

Tricarboxylic acid cycle (TCA) The cycle that oxidizes acetyl coenzyme A to CO_2 and generates NADH and $FADH_2$ for oxidation in the electron transport chain; the cycle also supplies carbon skeletons for biosynthesis.

Trichome A row or filament of bacterial cells that are in close contact with one another over a large area.

Trichomoniasis A sexually transmitted disease caused by the parasitic protozoan *Trichomonas vaginalis*.

Trickling filter A bed of rocks covered with a microbial film that aerobically degrades organic waste during secondary sewage treatment.

Trihalomethanes Halogenated one-carbon compounds formed during water disinfection; many of these compounds are potential carcinogens.

Tripartite associations A mutualistic association of the same plant with two types of microorganisms.

Triple point Triple point is the point in p,T space where the solid, liquid, and gas phases of a substance are in thermodynamic equilibrium.

Trophozoite The active, motile feeding stage of a protozoan organism; in the malarial parasite, the stage of schizogony between the ring stage and the schizont.

Tropism The movement of living organisms toward or away from a focus of heat, light, or other stimulus.

Troposphere Troposphere is the lowest part of the earth's atmosphere, extending to 110 km to 15 km above the surface. It is characterized by a decrease in temperature with increasing altitude. The exact height varies with latitude and season.

Trough The point of maximum negative displacement on a transverse wave is called a trough.

Trypanosome A protozoan of the genus Trypanosoma. Trypanosomes are parasitic flagellate protozoa that often live in the blood of humans and other vertebrates and are transmitted by insect bites.

Trypanosomiasis An infection with trypanosomes that live in the blood and lymph of the infected host.

Tubercle A small, rounded nodular lesion produced by *Mycobacterium tuberculosis*.

Tuberculoid (neural) leprosy A mild, nonprogressive form of leprosy that is associated with delayed-type hypersensitivity to antigens on the surface of *Mycobacterium leprae*. It is characterized by early nerve damage and regions of the skin that have lost sensation and are surrounded by a border of nodules.

Tuberculosis An infectious disease of humans and other animals resulting from an infection by a species of *Mycobacterium* and characterized by the formation of tubercles and tissue necrosis, primarily as a result of host hypersensitivity and inflammation. Infection is usually by inhalation, and the disease commonly affects the lungs, although it may occur in any part of the body.

Tuberculous cavity An air-filled cavity that results from a tubercle lesion caused by *M. tuberculosis*.

Tularemia A plaguelike disease of animals caused by the bacterium *Francisella tularensis* subsp. Tularensis (Jellison type A), which may be transmitted to humans.

Tumble Random turning or tumbling movements made by bacteria when they stop moving in a straight line.

Tumor A growth of tissue resulting from abnormal new cell growth and reproduction (neoplasia).

Tunneling A classical particle or system could not penetrate regions in which its energy would be negative, that is, barrier regions in which the potential energy is greater than the system energy. In the real world, however, a wave function of significant amplitude may extend into and beyond such a region. If the wave function extends into another region of positive energy, the barrier is crossed with some probability; this process is termed tunneling.

Turbidostat A continuous culture system equipped with a photocell that adjusts the flow of medium through the culture vessel so as to maintain a constant cell density or turbidity.

Turbulence Unstable and disorderly motion, as when a smooth, flowing stream becomes a churning rapid.

Two-component phosphorelay system A signal transduction regulatory system that uses the transfer of phosphoryl groups to control gene transcription and protein activity. It has two major components: a sensor kinase and a response regulator.

Type III hypersensitivity A form of immediate hypersensitivity resulting from the exposure to excessive amounts of antigens in which antibodies bind to the antigens and produce antibody-antigen complexes. These activate complement and trigger an acute inflammatory response with subsequent tissue damage. Examples: poststreptococcal glomerulonephritis, serum sickness, and farmer's lung disease.

Typhoid fever A bacterial infection transmitted by contaminated food, water, milk, or shellfish. The causative organism is *Salmonella typhi*, which is present in human feces.

Ubiquitin Small, highly conserved protein present in all eucaryotic cells that becomes covalently attached to lysines of other proteins. Attachment of a chain of ubiquitins tags a protein for intracellular proteolytic destruction in a proteasome.

Ultramicrobacteria Bacteria that can exist normally in a miniaturized form or which are capable of miniaturization under low-nutrient conditions. They may be 0.2 mm or smaller in diameter.

Ultrasonic Sound waves too high in frequency to be heard by the human ear; frequencies above 20,000Hz.

Ultraviolet (UV) radiation Radiation of fairly short wave-length, about 10 to 400 nm, and high energy.

Unbalanced forces When a number of forces act on a body and the resultant force is not zero, then the forces are said to be unbalanced.

Uncertainty principle The quantum principle, first formulated by Heisenberg, that states that it is not possible to know exactly both the position x and the momentum p of an object at the same time. The same is true with energy and time (see virtual particle).

Unified atomic mass unit Unified atomic mass unit (u or m_u) is a unit of mass used in atomic, molecular, and nuclear science, defined as the mass of one atom of ^{12}C divided by 12. Its approximate value is $U = (1.660565 \pm 0.0000086) \times 10^{-27}$ kg.

Uniform acceleration When the velocity of a body increases by equal amounts in equal intervals of time it is said to have uniform acceleration.

Uniform circular motion The motion of an object in a circular path with uniform speed is called uniform circular motion. Uniform circular motion is accelerated motion.

Uniform speed When a body travels equal distances in equal intervals of time then it is said to have uniform speed.

Uniform velocity When a body travels along a straight line in particular direction and covers equal distances in equal intervals of time it is said to have uniform velocity.

Unit cell Unit cell is the smallest fragment of the structure of a solid that by repetition can generate the entire structure.

Units The quality of a number or variable.

Universal law of gravitation Every object in the universe is attracted to every other object with a force directly proportional to the product of their masses and inversely proportional to the square of the distance between the centers of the two masses.

Universal time Abbreviated *UT*. The same as Greenwich Mean Time (GMT) in England. Eastern Standard Time (EST) is five hours earlier than Universal Time.

Universe Set of all events that have been, are, or will be observable.

Unpolarized light Light consisting of transverse waves vibrating in all conceivable random directions.

Unsaturated Describes a molecule that contains one or more double or triple carbon-carbon bonds, such as isoprene or benzene.

Unsaturated hydrocarbons Unsaturated hydrocarbons are organic compounds containing double (alkenes) or triple (alkynes) bonds in its molecules.

Unsaturated solution Unsaturated solution is a solution that contains less than the maximum possible equilibrium concentration of a solute.

Unstable equilibrium One in which any deviation of the object from its equilibrium position results in a force pushing it even farther away.

Up quark The least massive flavour of quark, with electric charge 2/3.

Uracil The pyrimidine 2,4-dioxypyrimidine, which is found in nucleosides, nucleotides, and RNA.

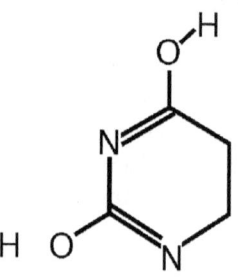

Figure Uracil

Uranium (U) A mildly radioactive element with two isotopes which are fissile and two which are fertile. Uranium is the basic fuel of nuclear energy.

Uranium hexafluoride A compound of uranium which is a gas above 56°C and is thus a suitable form in which to enrich the uranium.

Uranium oxide concentrate The mixture of uranium oxides produced after milling uranium ore from a mine. Sometimes loosely called yellowcake. It is khaki in colour and is usually represented by the empirical formula U_3O_8. Uranium is sold in this form.

UV radiation Ultraviolet radiation, an invisible, high energy component of sunlight can cause skin damage including cancer.

Vacancy Vacancy is a missing atom or ion in a crystal lattice.

Vaccine A preparation of either killed microorganisms; living, weakened microorganisms; or inactivated bacterial toxins. It is administered to induce development of the immune response and protect the individual against a pathogen or a toxin.

Vaccinomics The application of genomics and bioinformatics to vaccine development.

Valence The number of antigenic determinant sites on the surface of an antigen or the number of antigen-binding sites possessed by an antibody molecule.

Valence band Highest filled or almost filled band in a semiconductor.

Valence electrons Electrons in the outer shell of an atom.

Van Allen belts Two ring-shaped regions that girdle the Earth's equator in which electrically charged particles are trapped by the Earth's magnetic field. See South Atlantic Anomaly or radiation belts.

van der Waals' equation Van der Waals' equation is an equation of state for fluids which takes the form:

$$pV_m = RT\left(\frac{1}{V_m - b} - \frac{a}{V_m^2}\right)$$

Where p is pressure, V_m is molar volume, T is temperature, R is the molar gas constant, and a and b are characteristic parameters of the substance which describe the effect of attractive and repulsive intermolecular forces.

van der Waals' force van der Waals' force is the weak attractive force between two molecules which arises from electric dipole interactions. It can lead to the formation of stable but weakly bound dimer molecules or clusters. They are named after the Dutch physicist Johannes van der Waals (1837-1923).

Van't Hoff equation Van't Hoff equation is the equation expressing the temperature dependence of the equilibrium constant K of a chemical reaction:

$$\frac{d\ln K}{dT} = \frac{\Delta_r H^\circ}{RT^2}$$

where H° is the standard enthalpy of reaction, R the molar gas constant, and T the temperature.

Vapour The gaseous state of a substance that is normally in the liquid state.

Vapour pressure Vapour pressure is the pressure of a gas in equilibrium with a liquid at a specified temperature.

Variable region (VL and VH) The region at the N-terminal end of immunoglobulin heavy and light chains whose amino acid sequence varies between antibodies of different specificity. Variable regions form the antigen binding site.

Vasculitis Inflammation of a blood vessel.

Vector 1. In genetic engineering, another name for a cloning vector. A DNA molecule that can replicate (a replicon) and is used to transport a piece of inserted foreign DNA, such as a gene, into a recipient cell. It may be a plasmid, phage, cosmid or artificial chromosome.

2. In epidermiology, it is a living organism, usually an arthropod or other animal, that transfers an infective agent from one host to another.

Vector quantity A quantity, which needs both magnitude and direction to describe it, is called a vector quantity. Such a physical quantity should also follow the vector law of addition.

Vector-borne transmission The transmission of an infectious pathogen between hosts by means of a vector.

Vehicle An inanimate substance or medium involved in the transmission of a pathogen.

Velocity Distance traveled by a body in a particular direction per unit time is called its velocity. It can also be defined as the displacement of the body per unit time. It is a vector quantity. The SI units of velocity are m / s.

Velocity The speed of an object moving in a specific direction. A car travelling at 35 miles per hour is a measurement of speed. Observing that a car is travelling 35 miles per hour due north is a measurement of velocity.

Venereal syphilis A contagious, sexually transmitted disease caused by the spirochete Treponema pallidum.

Verrucae vulgaris The common wart; a raised, epidermal lesion with horny surface caused by an infection with a human papillomavirus.

Vibration A back and forth motion that repeats itself.

Vibrio A rod-shaped bacterial cell that is curved to form a comma or an incomplete spiral.

Viral hemagglutination The clumping or agglutination of red blood cells caused by some viruses.

Viral neutralization An antibody-mediated process in which IgA, IgM, and IgA antibodies bind to some viruses during their extracellular phase and inactivate or neutralize them.

Viremia The presence of viruses in the blood stream.

Viricide An agent that inactivates viruses so that they cannot reproduce within host cells.

Virion A complete virus particle that represents the extracellular phase

Voltage

of the virus life cycle; at the simplest, it consists of a protein capsid surrounding a single nucleic acid molecule.

Virioplankton Viruses that occur in waters; high levels are found in marine and freshwater environments.

Viroid An infectious agent of plants that is a single-stranded RNA not associated with any protein; the RNA does not code for any proteins and is not translated.

Virology The branch of microbiology that is concerned with viruses and viral diseases.

Virtual image Like a real image, but the rays don't actually cross again; they only appear to have come from the point on the image.

Virtual particle A particle that exists only for an extremely brief instant in an intermediary process. Then the Heisenberg Uncertainty Principle allows an apparent violation of the conservation of energy. However, if one sees only the initial decaying particle and the final decay products, one observes that the energy is conserved.

Virulence The degree or intensity of pathogenicity of an organism as indicated by case fatality rates and/or ability to invade host tissues and cause disease.

Virulence factor A bacterial product, usually a protein or carbohydrate, that contributes to virulence or pathogenicity.

Virulent bacteriophages Bacteriophages that lyse their host cells during the reproductive cycle.

Virus An infectious agent having a simple acellular organization with a protein coat and a single type of nucleic acid, lacking independent metabolism, and reproducing only within living host cells.

Vitamin An organic compound required by organisms in minute quantities for growth and reproduction because it cannot be synthesized by the organism; vitamins often serve as enzyme cofactors or parts of cofactors.

Vitrification The incorporation of high-level wastes into borosilicate glass, to make up about 14% of it by mass. It is designed to immobilise radionuclides in an insoluble matrix ready for disposal.

Volt Volt (V) is the SI derived unit of electric potential. One volt is the difference of potential between two points of an electical conductor when a current of 1 ampere flowing between those points dissipates a power of 1 watt. It is named after the Italian physicist Alessandro Volta (1745-1827).

Voltage drop The electric potential difference across a resistor or other part of a circuit that consumes power.

Voltage Electrical potential energy per unit charge that will be possessed by a charged particle at a certain point in space.

Voltmeter A device for measuring voltage differences.

Volume fraction Volume fraction (φ_j) is defined as

$$\phi_A = \frac{V_A}{\sum V_i}$$

Where V_j is the volume of the specified component and the V_i are the volumes of all the components of a mixture prior to mixing.

W boson A carrier particle of the weak interactions. It is involved in all electric-charge-changing weak processes.

Wart An epidermal tumor of viral Origin.

Waste; High-level waste (HLW) is highly radioactive material arising from nuclear fission. It can be recovered from reprocessing spent fuel, though some countries regard spent fuel itself as HLW. It requires very careful handling, storage and disposal.

Wastewater treatment The use of physical and biological processes to remove particulate and dissolved material from sewage and to control pathogens.

Water activity (aw) A quantitative measure of water availability in the habitat; the water activity of a solution is one-hundredth its relative humidity.

Water mold A common term for a member of the division Oomycota.

Water of crystallization Water of hydration. Water that is stoichiometrically bound in a crystal; for example, the waters in copper sulphate pentahydrate.

Watt Watt (W) is the SI derived unit of power. One watt is a power of one joule per second ($W = J/s$). It is named after the Scottish engineer James Watt (1736-1819).

Wave A vibration in some media that transfers energy from one place to another. Sound waves are vibrations passing in air. Light waves are vibrations in electromagnetic fields.

Wave mechanics Alternate name for quantum mechanics derived from the wavelike properties of subatomic particles.

Wave motion The movement of a disturbance produced in one part of a medium to another involving the transfer of energy but not the transfer of matter is called wave motion.

Wave period The time required for two successive crests or other successive parts of the wave to pass a given point.

Wave velocity The distance travelled by a wave in one second is called the wave velocity. The wave velocity of a wave depends upon the nature of the medium through which it passes.

Wavefunction The numerical measure of an electron wave, or in general of the wave corresponding to any quantum mechanical particle.

Wavelength The distance between the two nearest points on a wave, which are in the same phase, is called the wavelength of the wave. The distance between two adjacent crests or two adjacent troughs is called its wavelength.

Wave-particle duality The idea that light is both a wave and a particle.

Weak acid Weak acid is an acid that incompletely dissociated in aqueous solution.

Weak force The force that governs the change of one kind of elementary particle into another. This force is associated with radioactive processes that involve neutrons.

Weak interaction The interaction responsible for all processes in which flavour changes, hence for the instability of heavy quarks and leptons, and particles that contain them. Weak interactions that do not change flavour (or charge) have also been observed.

Weak nuclear force The force responsible for beta decay.

Weber Weber (Wb) is the SI derived unit of magnetic flux. The weber is the magnetic flux which, linking a circuit of one turn, produces in it an electromotive force of one volt as it is reduced to zero at a uniform rate in one second (Wb = V·s). The unit is named after the German scientist W.E. Weber (1804-1891).

Weight The force with which a body is attracted towards the center of the earth is called its weight. The SI unit of weight is N. The gravitational units of weight are kg-wt and g-wt. The weight of a body of mass m is given by mg. Its value will depend upon the value of g at that place. The weight of a body is measured with a spring balance.

Weightlessness The state when the apparent weight of a body becomes zero is called the state of weightlessness. All objects while falling freely under the action of gravity appear weightless.

Weil-Felix reaction A test for the diagnosis of typhus and certain other rickettsial diseases. In this test, the blood serum of a patient with suspected rickettsial disease is tested against certain strains of Proteus vulgaris (OX-2, OX-19, OX-K). The agglutination reactions, based on antigens common to both organisms, determine the presence and type of rickettsial infection.

Western blotting Technique by which proteins are separated and immobilized on a paper sheet and then analyzed, usually by means of a labeled antibody.

White blood cell (leucocyte) Nucleated blood cell lacking hemoglobin; includes lymphocytes, neutrophils, eosinophils, basophils, and monocytes.

White light Visible light that includes all colours and, therefore, all visible wavelengths.

White piedra A fungal infection caused by the yeast Trichosporon beigelii that forms light-coloured nodules on the beard and mustache.

Whole-genome shotgun sequencing An approach to genome sequencing in which the complete genome is broken into random fragments, which are then individually sequenced. Finally the fragments are placed in the proper order using sophisticated computer programs.

Whole-organism vaccine A vaccine made from complete pathogens, which can be of four types: inactivated viruses; attenuated viruses; killed microorganisms; and live, attenuated microorganisms.

Widal test A test involving agglutination of typhoid bacilli when they are mixed with serum containing typhoid antibodies from an individual having typhoid fever; used to detect the presence of Salmonella typhi and S. Paratyphi.

Wild type (WT) The wild type (WT) is a term referring to the natural genetic form of an organism. A wild type is distinguished from a mutant form. Usually, the distinction between wild type and mutant is based on a single mutation. It should be noted, that within a population of an organism, there is no such thing as a wild type. The term, however, is useful for geneticists because it allows a simple definition of a standard or control condition.

Winogradsky column A glass column with an anaerobic lower zone and an aerobic upper zone, which allows growth of microorganisms under conditions similar to those found in a nutrient-rich lake.

Wohler's synthesis Wohler's synthesis is a synthesis of urea performed by German chemist Friedrich Wohler (1800-1882) in 1828. He discovered that urea ($CO(NH_2)_2$) was formed when a solution of ammonium isocyanate (NH_4NCO) was evaporated. At the time it was believed that organic substances such as urea could be made only by living organisms, and its production form an inorganic compound was a notable discovery.

Work The amount of energy transferred into or out of a system, excluding energy transferred by heat conduction.

X chromosome One of two sex chromosomes in higher organisms that defines the gender of the adult. In almost all sexually reproducing organisms, the X-chromosome defines female characteristics.

Xenobiotics Molecules entering an organism that has no physiological function and is not found in an organism if not taken up by eating, breathing, or injury. The term xenobiotics is used to describe a foreign particle or molecule that is potentially dangerous or toxic.

Xenograft A tissue graft between animals of different species.

Xenotransplantation Animal to human organ transplants or xenografts. Their association with gene technology is because the animals will have to be genetically modified so that their organs when removed will 'look' sufficiently like human organs to the recipient's immune system that they will not be rejected.

X-linked Describes the form of inheritance of diseases for which the gene responsible is carried on the X chromosome.

X-rays X-rays are electromagnetic radiation of shorter wavelength than ultraviolet radiation (10^{-11}m to 10^{-9}m or 0.01nm to 1nm) pro-duced by bombardment of atoms by high-quantum-energy particles. X-rays can pass through many forms of matter and they are therefore used medically and industrially to examine internal structure.

X-ray spectrum X-ray spectra. A set of characteristic X-ray frequencies or wavelengths produced by a substance used as a target in an X-ray tube. Each element has a characteristic X-ray spectrum, and there is a strong correlation between atomic number and the frequencies of certain lines in the x-ray spectrum.

Y chromosome One of two sex chromosomes in higher organisms that defines the gender of the adult. In almost all sexually reproducing organisms, the Y-chromosome defines male characteristics.

Yeast A unicellular fungus that has a single nucleus and reproduces either asexually by budding or fission, or sexually through spore formation.

Yeast artificial chromosome (YAC) A stretch of DNA that contains all the elements required to propagate a chromosome in yeast and which is used to clone foreign DNA fragments in yeast cells.

Yellow fever An acute infectious disease caused by a flavivirus, which is transmitted to humans by mosquitoes. The liver is affected and the skin turns yellow in this disease.

Yellowcake Ammonium diuranate, the penultimate uranium compound in U_3O_8 production, but the form in which mine product was sold until about 1970. See also Uranium oxide concentrate.

YM shift The change in shape by dimorphic fungi when they shift from the yeast (Y) form in the animal body to the mold or mycelial form (M) in the environment.

Z

Z boson A carrier particle of the weak interactions. It is involved in all weak processes that do not change flavour.

Z disc Platelike region of a muscle sarcomere to which the plus ends of actin filaments are attached. Seen as a dark transverse line in micrographs.

Z value The increase in temperature required to reduce the decimal reduction time to one-tenth of its initial value.

Zebra fish The Zebra fish is one of many model organisms used in biomedical research to understand development of higher organisms, the functioning of nervous systems, and fundamental aspects of physiology and the cause of diseases.

Zeeman effect Zeeman effect is the splitting of the lines in a spectrum when the source of the spectrum is exposed to a magnetic field. It was discovered in 1896 by Pieter Zeeman.

Zeolite Zeolite is a natural or synthetic hydrated aluminosilicate with an open three-dimensional crystal structure, in which water molecules are held in cavities in the latice. The water can be driven off by heating and the zeolite can then absorb other molecules of suitable size. Zeolites are used for separating mixtures by selective absorption.

Zeotrope Zeotrope is a liquid mixture that shows no maximum or minimum when vapour pressure is plotted against composition at constant temperature.

Zero-order reaction Zero-order reaction is a reaction for which the rate of reaction is independent of the concentration of reactants.

Zeta potential Zeta potential (ζ) is the electric potential at the surface of a colloidal particle relative to the potential in the bulk medium at a long distance. Also called electrokinetic potential.

Zeta potential (ζ) is the potential across the interface of all solids and liquids. Specifically, the potential across the diffuse layer of ions surrounding a charged colloidal particle, which is largely responsible for colloidal stability. Also called electrokinetic potential.

Ziegler process Ziegler process is an industrial process for the manufacture of high-density polyethene using catalysts of

titanium(IV) chloride ($TiCl_4$) and aluminium alkyls (e.g. Triethylaluminium, $Al(C_2H_5)_3$). The process was introduced in 1953 by the German chemist Karl Ziegler (1898-1973). It allowed the manufacture of polythene at lower temperatures (about 60°C) and pressures (about 1 atm) than used in the original process.

Zinc finger Structural motif seen in many DNA-binding proteins, composed of a loop of polypeptide chain held in a hair-pin bend bound to a zinc atom.

Zircaloy Zirconium alloy used as a tube to contain uranium oxide fuel pellets in a reactor fuel assembly.

Zooflagellates Flagellate protozoa that do not have chlorophyll and are either holozoic, saprozoic, or symbiotic.

Zoonosis A disease of animals that can be transmitted to humans.

Zooplankton A community of floating, aquatic, minute animals and nonphotosynthetic protists.

Zoospore A motile, flagellated spore.

Zooxanthella A dinoflagellate found living symbiotically within cnidarians and other invertebrates.

Zwitterion Zwitterion is an ion that has a positive and negative charge on the same group of atoms. Zwitterions can be formed from compounds that contain both acid groups and basic groups in their molecules. It is also called ampholyte ion.

Zygomycetes A division of fungi that usually has a coenocytic mycelium with chitinous cell walls. Sexual reproduction normally involves the formation of zygospores. The group lacks motile spores.

Zygospore A thick-walled, sexual, resting spore characteristic of the zygomycetous fungi.

Zygote A zygote is a fertilized egg containing two sets of chromosomes, one form the egg and one form the sperm. The zygote is a single cell and the result of a fusion between two gametes, an egg and one sperm cell.

YOUR SPACE

www.ingramcontent.com/pod-product-compliance
Lightning Source LLC
Chambersburg PA
CBHW070742170426
43200CB00007B/623